BENEATH THE SURFACE

Intelligence Preparation of the Battlespace for Counterterrorism

Major Troy S. Thomas, U.S. Air Force
Research Fellow

JOINT MILITARY
INTELLIGENCE COLLEGE

D1715846

WASHINGTON, DC
November 2004

CONTENTS

ACKNOWLEDGMENTS

The finer qualities of this work are due to the wisdom and assistance of others. The opportunity to study was afforded by the U.S. Air Force, an institution remarkable for its commitment to the professional and intellectual development of airmen. The Defense Intelligence Agency, recognizing the value of hosting an institution for independent research in support of the Intelligence Community under the auspices of the Joint Military Intelligence College (JMIC), has since 2002 supported the Center for Strategic Intelligence Research. I benefited from these arrangements as a Research Fellow, with my research being backed by impressive organizational support and unconditional intellectual freedom as I pursued an intense examination of intelligence as it relates to counterterrorism. This research also enjoyed the financial support, and more importantly, the astute guidance, of the Institute for National Security Studies at the U.S. Air Force Academy and the Combating Terrorism Center at the U.S. Military Academy.

Collaboration with several front-line organizations allowed reality-testing of new ideas and direct exposure to the complex challenges inherent to the contemporary security landscape. Within the Directorate for Strategic Plans and Policy, Joint Chiefs of Staff, the Deputy Director for the Global War on Terror clarified the issues, shared their strategic thinking, and invited my participation in the development of a seminal counterterrorism strategy document. My own efforts were motivated and shaped by their dedication and insight. The ground-breaking and operationally focused work of professionals at the Joint Warfare Analysis Center opened the door to advanced analytical methods and cutting-edge programs for achieving effects against terrorist groups. Our cooperation in the application of systems analysis to counterterrorism will continue as ideas surfaced here are applied in the field. Collaboration with the Transformation and Experimentation Center, Joint Forces Intelligence Command, offered an opportunity to apply a systems approach to homeland defense and work with a talented group of analysts. Additional organizations that provided practical knowledge, opportunities to apply methods, or simply championed my ideas include Northern Command, the Council on Foreign Relations, the Council for Emerging National Security Affairs, the State of New Mexico Office of Homeland Security, the Joint Intelligence Task Force for Combating Terrorism, and the Joint Military Intelligence Training Center.

Wise counsel and deep expertise came from four individuals who became partners in the project. The Center for Strategic Intelligence Research is admirably led by its Director, Dr. Russell Swenson. His incisive guidance and dead-on scholarship imbues every page. An able practitioner of "soft power," Dr. Swenson successfully challenged me to overcome all obstacles. I have been learning from another of these individuals, Dr. Donald Hanle, now on the Faculty of the Joint Military Intelligence College, since he was my Flight Commander at Shaw Air Force Base a decade ago. A published expert on terrorism, his penetrating analysis and intellectual clarity remain the standard against which all others are judged. Dr. James Smith has helped me and others transform intellectual curiosity into policy-relevant scholarship for years as the Director of the Air Force's Institute for National Security Studies. Dr. Smith, with the talented support of Ms. Diana Heerdt, shepherd an impressive research program that continues to foster my own professional development. Among the many doors opened by Dr. Smith, one leading to a new partnership with the Combating Terrorism Center at West Point has been the most rewarding. Directed by Colonel Russell Howard, the Center is breaking new ground at a critical juncture by producing widely acclaimed research and publications. Colonel Howard not only championed and influenced my work, but made possible my participation in the Partnership for Peace-Combating Terrorism Working Group where I learned a great deal from a range of counterterrorism officials as well as from its co-Chairs, Colonel Howard and Dr. Rohan Gunaratna.

One must have great allies in all scholarly endeavors if only to remain sane. I thrive on the good humor, cutting intellect, selfless work, and adventurous spirit of two long-standing colleagues and friends, Majors William Casebeer and Steve Kiser. Our collaboration and travels do not always unfold as expected, but they are always rewarding and entertaining. As we move forward on several fronts, collaboration with Captain Jason Bartolomei and Lieutenant Colonel Fred Krawchuk brings much-appreciated energy and perspective. Among many others, trusted friends and world travelers Captain Thomas Coakley and Lieutenant Colonel Joseph Derdzinksi continue to offer powerful insights and grounded advice. I have also enjoyed the support and collegiality of the other Research Fellows at the JMIC, Major Steve Lambert, Major Eva Jenkins, Dr. Linda Lau, and Melanie Gutjahr. Within the Defense Intelligence Agency, I was educated by those in the forefront of counterterrorism analysis, including Dr. Mark Kauppi, Director of Counterterrorism Analysis in the Joint Military Intelligence Training Center and Cal Temple, Chief of Transnational Threats in the Joint Intelligence Task Force-Combating Terrorism.

The contributions of these individuals stand in the shadow of another. Paula Thomas shared her mind and time to ensure this project's success. Its finer qualities are truly a reflection of her worthy intellect and prized friendship.

FOREWORD

Cal Temple
Chief, Office of Intelligence Operations
Joint Intelligence Task Force-Combating Terrorism
Defense Intelligence Agency

Major Thomas' *Beneath the Surface* comes at precisely the right time in the War on Terrorism. Over the past three years the U.S. military and other instruments of national power have been able to attack and damage Usama Bin Laden's al-Qaida network. We have exploited the known, reacted to resultant opportunities, and organized a set of sustainable allies and partners to do the same.

Now for the hard part.

The remainder of the War or Terrorism—which will continue for years—requires that intelligence be on the front. The War has been, and will continue to be, an intelligence war. In such a war intelligence and operations are not separate staff components; they are instead a blend of activities that are mutually reinforcing. In this continuing war every soldier is a collector, and every collector is a soldier; operators glean intelligence directly from the field, and intelligence is always operational.

Further, the war ahead will demand new strategies for long-term success. The counterpunching phase is over. The rapid-fire operations-intelligence, counterterrorism-targeting cycle happening right now in Iraq and Afghanistan—the "find, fix, finish, exploit, then find again" process—becomes less powerful as the campaign continues. This cycle has to be underpinned by a strategic intelligence framework that ensures we are attacking a part of the enemy that matters—not just taking the near-term opportunity that inflicts little lasting damage.

The U.S. requires new strategies to collect intelligence, to manufacture new intelligence (using operations in doing so), and most importantly to organize data in new, systemic and strategic ways to make the most of what we know about this shadowy, self-healing and determined asymmetric, worldwide adversary.

In my view Major Thomas' work is one of the first coherent blueprints for the way ahead. For persons seeking to understand the complexity of terrorist violence, Chapter One provides a broad and comprehensive overview for thinking about the problem. For the counterterrorism practitioner, Chapters Two through Five are extraordinarily well-reasoned views on organizing data to maximize knowledge and potential power. Major Thomas also offers sound advice on leveraging well-organized intelligence data to derive effective courses of action and to focus operational activity for maximum effect.

We in the Department of Defense and those responsible for other U.S. instruments of national power are re-learning old lessons and refining new ones. One lesson we all learned from the 9/11 terrorist attacks is to work smarter, and more systematically. Maj. Thomas' work helps light the way toward that goal.

COMMENTARIES

Beneath the Surface: Intelligence Preparation of the Battlespace for Counterterrorism

Donald J. Hanle, Ph.D.
JMIC Faculty

Writing products related to terrorism has become a cottage industry within the Intelligence Community. Few, however, have produced a work as sweeping and as functional as has Major Troy Thomas in *Beneath the Surface*. This work represents not merely the careful and extremely useful adaptation of classic principles of Intelligence Preparation of the Battlespace (IPB) to the emerging threat of terrorism, but it offers a truly new and effective means by which intelligence professionals may approach this critical topic.

If this was all that Major Thomas had achieved in this work, it would remain an essential reference to be added to the libraries of all academicians as well as intelligence and law enforcement professionals who focus upon terrorism and its neutralization. *Beneath the Surface* represents something far more profound than merely serving as an incredibly useful analytical "tool," however. By painstakingly melding classical IPB methodologies with open systems theories, Major Thomas has achieved a means by which even the novice analyst can apprehend not merely the complexity of the terrorist threat, but its inevitable environmental, structural or sub-systemic strengths and weaknesses as well.

Beneath the Surface constitutes, therefore, a truly effective representation of the paradigm shift in warfare that has been induced by our intense focus on terrorism. Major Thomas' approach provides an entirely new means by which to think about the problem of terrorism, compelling lines of inquiry that would be extremely unlikely to emerge using previously existing methodologies. *Beneath the Surface* demands a full-spectrum examination of the threat not only from physical and social perspectives, but in terms of information and cognitive warfare. The assessment of factors ranging from geography and weather to culture and technology is essential to carrying out Major Thomas' counterterrorism IPB process. Each of these factors is then subjected to a multifaceted examination from the environmental, systemic and sub-systemic dimensions to identify centers of gravity, critical capabilities, critical requirements and, finally, critical vulnerabilities on the physical, moral and cognitive planes of war. As he demonstrates, the results can be remarkable—whether applied to a local militia group or a transnational terrorist group. *Beneath the Surface* promises to be much more than an analytical handbook; it is, in itself, a manifestation of an entirely new way of problem solving—a work that is destined to be reprinted countless times.

Lieutenant Colonel Fred Krawchuk, U.S. Army
Special Operations Command, Pacific

American strategy must look at how the U.S. government detects, deters, and defeats terrorists worldwide. The effectiveness of this strategy is, in part, based on the capacity of national and domestic agencies and the departments involved in intelligence, defense and law enforcement to think like an adaptive enemy, in anticipation of how the latter may act in a variety of situations, aided by different resources. This goal requires that departments and agencies organize themselves for maximum efficiency, information sharing, and the ability to function quickly and effectively under new operational definitions. New times make new behaviors necessary and demand the adoption of the advanced analytical methods proposed by Troy Thomas. Organizations must do what they have been reluctant to do in the past: they must reach across bureaucratic territorial divides and share resources to counter insurgencies and other emerging threats.

To develop this capacity, leaders must dedicate themselves to new, lifelong practices that are based on a value system, that involve the whole person, and that are developed and guided by seasoned instructors versed in integrated training. In addition to continuing to use the traditional "hard" skills, these leaders must learn to apply "soft" skills that require an understanding of tactics and strategies in negotiations, as well as familiarity with the fields of psychology, social and cultural anthropology, somatics, emotional intelligence, complexity theory, and systems management in a foreign-area context. As an object-lesson in how to do this, Troy's work is both informed by and reflective of an integrated understanding of the problem, and he, like few others, is able to provide a framework and the tools for moving forward.

The practices highlighted in this work will allow leaders to build the character and skills necessary to assess situations and act on them effectively, rather than helplessly succumbing to the pressure of the moment. Like the martial arts master who deftly handles multiple attacks, the counterterrorist expert, in a fast-moving and fluid environment, with "holistic" leadership development and Troy's IPB guide, can learn to adapt to any given situation in order to serve selflessly. This new attitude and behavior pattern is imperative. An integrated and comprehensive approach to counterterrorism requires a reorientation in the way the U.S. government plans, organizes, trains, and thinks about complex and unconventional threats. Troy Thomas' makes an important contribution to our achieving this imperative.

Myron Hura, Ph.D.
Senior Engineer, RAND Corporation

This study provides a well-structured and comprehensive discussion of the intelligence preparation of the battlefield process, and of the major challenges the intelligence and warfighting communities face in counterterrorist operations. It is an excellent primer on the doctrine, tactics, techniques and procedures for IPB, with a comprehensive bibliography.

The publication clearly underscores the differences between conducting IPB for traditional warfare and for counterterrorist operations, and offers suggestions on how to address those differences to ensure that the IPB process becomes effective in asymmetrical operations generally. Carefully chosen real-world examples systematically highlight each phase of the IPB process and show its relationship to intelligence, operations, and decisionmaking cycles. An in-depth understanding of these relationships is essential as we try to address counterterrorist operations in an effective manner.

In discussing the IPB process, the author provides keen insights into conducting effects-based counterterrorist operations. His discussion of how to evaluate adversary capabilities clearly illustrates the applicability of social network analysis, and emphasizes the importance of an opponent's operational code and technology choices, as well as the pertinent social dimensions of the operational environment.

LIST OF FIGURES

ACRONYMS

ACH	Analysis of Competing Hypotheses
AIAI	Al-Ittihad al-Islami
AIPB	Air Intelligence Preparation of the Battlespace
AO	Area of Operations
AOI	Area of Interest
AP	Associated Press
AT	Anti-terrorism
AUC	United Self-Defense Forces/Group of Colombia
CBRN	Chemical, Biological, Radiological, and Nuclear
CENTCOM	Central Command
CIA	Central Intelligence Agency
CJTF	Combined Joint Task Force
CNA	Computer Network Attack
COA	Course(s) of Action
COG	Center(s) of Gravity
CONPLAN	Concept Plan
CPA	Coalition Provisional Authority
CT	Counterterrorism
CTC	Counterterrorism Center
CC	Critical Capability
CR	Critical Requirement
CV	Critical Vulnerability
DARPA	Defense Advanced Research Programs Agency
DIA	Defense Intelligence Agency
DOD	Department of Defense

DPRK	Democratic Peoples Republic of Korea
DSB	Defense Science Board
EBO	Effects-based Operations
ETA	Basque Fatherland and Liberty Party
EU	European Union
EW	Electronic Warfare
EUCOM	European Command
FARC	National Liberation Army of Colombia
FAST	Functional Analysis Systems Technique
FBI	Federal Bureau of Investigations
FID	Foreign Internal Defense
FM	Field Manual
FP	Force Protection
FTO	Foreign Terrorist Organization
GIA	Armed Islamic Group
GPO	Government Printing Office
GSPC	Salafist Group for Call (Preaching) and Combat
GWOT	Global War on Terrorism
HoA	Horn of Africa
HUJI	Harakat ul-Jihadi-Islami
HUJI-B	Harakat ul-Jihad-i-Islami/ Bangladesh
HUM	Harakat ul-Mujahidin
HM	Hizb ul-Mujahidin
HPT	High Payoff Target
HUMINT	Human Intelligence
HVT	High Value Target
IC	Intelligence Community

ICRC	International Committee of the Red Cross
IGO	Intergovernmental Organizations
IHL	International Humanitarian Law
IIPB	Islamic International Peacekeeping Brigade
IMINT	Imagery Intelligence
IMU	Islamic Movement of Uzbekistan
IO	Information Operations
IPB	Intelligence Preparation of the Battlespace
IRA	Irish Republican Army
ISR	Intelligence, Surveillance and Reconnaissance
JFC	Joint Force Commander
JI	Jemaah Islamiya
JIPB	Joint Intelligence Preparation of the Battlespace
JITF-CT	Joint Intelligence Task Force-Combatting Terrorism
JFIC	Joint Forces Intelligence Center
JMIC	Joint Military Intelligence College
JWAC	Joint Warfare Analysis Center
KLF	Kashmir Liberation Front
LAW	Light Anti-tank Weapon
LTTE	Liberation Tigers of Tamil Eelam
MASINT	Measures and Signatures Intelligence
MCOO	Military Combined Obstacle Overlay
MCWP	Marine Corps Warfighting Pamphlet
MILF	Moro Islamic Liberation Front
MIO	Maritime Interdiction Operations
MOOTW	Military Operations other than War
MOUT	Military Operations on Urban Terrain

NAI	Named Area of Interest
NASIC	National Air and Space Intelligence Center
NGO	Non-governmental Organization
NORTHCOM	Northern Command
NSA	National Security Agency
OA	Operational Area
OCOKA	Observation and Fields of Fire, Concealment and Cover, Obstacles, Key Terrain, Avenues of Approach
ONA	Organizational Network Analysis
OPFOR	Opposing Force
OPLAN	Operations Plan
OPORD	Operations Order
PA	Public Affairs
PACOM	Pacific Command
PFLP	Popular Front for the Liberation of Palestine
PIR	Priority Intelligence Requirements
PIRA	Provisional Irish Republican Army
PSI	Pan Sahel Initiative
PLO	Palestinian Liberation Organization
POW	Prisoners of War
PSYOPS	Psychological Operations
PULO	Pattani United Liberation Organization
RISTA	Reconnaissance, Intelligence, Surveillance and Target Acquisition
ROK	Republic of Korea
SIGINT	Signals Intelligence
SLOC	Sea Lines of Communication
SOCOM	Special Operations Command

SOF	Special Operations Forces
SOUTHCOM	Southern Command
SNA	Social Network Analysis
TAA	Tactical Assembly Area
TCO	Transnational Criminal Organization
TTP	Tactics, Techniques and Procedures
UCP	Unified Command Plan
UN	United Nations
US	United States
USAF	United States Air Force
USA	United States Army
USMC	United States Marine Corps
USN	United States Navy
USS	United States Ship
VNSA	Violent Non-State Actor
WMD	Weapons of Mass Destruction

PREFACE

OFF THE HORN OF AFRICA

Intelligence preparation of the battlespace (IPB) in asymmetric conflict is demanding for many reasons, including the complexity of the operating environment and the elusiveness of the adversary. As the transcript below indicates, the challenges for the intelligence professional engaged in combating terrorists, who are prime examples of asymmetric opponents, are immediate and broad. These abridged remarks by Major General John F. Sattler, United States Marine Corps (USMC), Commander, Combined Joint Task Force Horn of Africa (CJTF-HoA), were made only 30 days after the CJTF was established. His expressed concerns establish a useful context for this book's exploration of how the IPB process for counterterrorism (CT) can be improved as we continue into this era of asymmetric conflict. General Sattler ascribes to intelligence a vital role in countering terrorist operations: his is a real-world view of the many collection, analysis and operational difficulties associated with confronting transnational, asymmetric opponents. He offers direct insight into the complex array of battlespace characteristics, enemy activities, coalition relationships, rules of engagement and other issues certain to challenge the intelligence professional tasked with providing "actionable" intelligence.

- -

Combined Joint Task Force Horn of Africa Briefing

10 January 2003, 1002 hours, EST

(Special briefing via telephone onboard the *USS Mount Whitney* in the Gulf of Aden. Also participating: Major Stephen Cox, public affairs officer, CJTF-HoA)

Major Cox: Good morning, ladies and gentlemen. I am Major Steve Cox, the public affairs officer for CJTF-HoA. Before we begin the question and answer session with Major General Sattler, I'd like to provide you a brief opening statement.

About 30 days ago, the headquarters for CJTF-HoA arrived on station to oversee operations in support of the global war on terrorism in the Horn of Africa region. Our mission is to detect, disrupt and defeat terrorists who pose an imminent threat to coalition partners in the region. We'll also work with host nations to deny the reemergence of terrorist cells and activities by supporting international agencies working to enhance long-term stability for the region. For this operation, we are defining the Horn of Africa region as the total airspace and land areas out to the high-water mark of Kenya, Somalia, Ethiopia, Sudan, Eritrea, Djibouti and Yemen. The CJTF headquarters has about 400 members representing all U.S. armed services, civilian personnel, and coalition force representatives, all aboard the *USS Mount Whitney,* currently operating in the Gulf of Aden. Our force also includes about 900 personnel at Camp Lemonier in Djibouti, and a small number of liaison personnel working in other parts of the region. Given organic assets and the capabilities of U.S. Central Command, CJTF-HoA has the capability and will act upon credible intelligence to attack, destroy and/or capture terrorists and support networks. Our actions in the last 30 days have set the stage for success. We visited all sovereign nations in the region, meeting heads of state in Djibouti, Yemen, Eritrea, and Ethiopia. Also, we met with coalition military leaders, and recently completed the first in a planned series of exercises and operations between CJTF-HoA and Combined Task Force 150 maritime forces.

A key to defeating terrorism lies in building trust with coalition partners. A by-product of trust is the development of actionable intelligence, which improves host-nation ability to win the battle within their borders. The global war on terrorism is not a war against any people or any religion. It is a long-term fight between the forces of freedom and those who seek to spread hatred and fear, both in the Horn of Africa region and around the world. CJTF-HoA is prepared for an extended war on terrorism. We will press the fight at every turn as long as it takes and with the help of our coalition partners, together we will win this fight.

Ladies and gentlemen, at this point, I'd like to introduce the commander, Combined Joint Task Force-Horn of Africa, Major General John F. Sattler.

Major General (Maj Gen) Sattler: Good morning, everyone. John Sattler here, and I believe I'm prepared to go ahead and answer your questions at this time.

Question (Q): General Sattler, this is Pam Hess with United Press International. Could you tell us if you all have actually done anything besides the exercise in laying the groundwork? Has there been any actionable intelligence created, and have you responded to it in any way?

Maj Gen Sattler: We've had a quite a bit of intelligence that has come in and has been shared, not only among the agencies within the Department of Defense, but also among our coalition partners and the other government agencies, [through the] inter-agency process. But to go into whether or not we have actually moved on or pressed any targets or are closing with, I really don't want to comment—or hold my comment on any possible future operations. But let's just say that we are developing the intelligence network, which is really critical in a fight against terrorism, and it's becoming more refined every day.

Q: General, this is Matt Kelley with the Associated Press. I'd like to know if there are any plans to expand the amount of personnel or materiel in your joint task force and also, what areas are of specific interest in your area of responsibility?

Figure 1. Combat Training

Soldiers from the 3rd U.S. Infantry Regiment fight off a dust storm created by a CH-53E helicopter during a combat recovery training exercise in rural Djibouti. Soldiers are currently deployed in support of the Global War on Terrorism.

Source: CJTF-HoA, URL: http://www.cjtfhoa.centcom.mil/default.asp, accessed on 14 April 2004.

Maj Gen Sattler: On the first question, when General Franks sent us out here, he made it very clear when he sent me down to Central Command, he gave me his commander's guidance that although the task force—the headquarters, the number is approximately 400, and we have close to 900 forces ashore, which are under our tactical control at all times; that as we start to develop intelligence and refine the terrorist locations, training centers, et cetera, that we have the ability to reach back, through General Franks, to come up with additional forces, if necessary.

So I'm very comfortable at this time that we have forces under our tactical control that give us the ability to respond rapidly and quickly to actionable intelligence. And if we need it or any target would exceed that capability, that's when I go back through the chain of command to General Franks and he has at his disposal obviously all the resources that are in his area of operations, plus he can go back up through his chain of command to find additional or unique forces, if necessary.

Q: The second part of the question was, what areas are of specific interest in your area of responsibility? Are you looking more specifically at places like Yemen and Somalia?

Maj Gen Sattler: Of course our mission was very broad, in that we were to track transnational terrorism across the Horn of Africa, going from Yemen across the Gulf of Aden, and then, you know, the entire Horn. We do have some areas that we're concentrating on—a couple of the border areas, some of the coastline areas, where intelligence—as we start to refine the intelligence and take the information and turn information into intelligence, where we're taking not a broad casting-of-the-net approach, but we're homing in on certain areas. You know, the porous borders with Somalia are one of the areas that we're taking a very hard look at, as well as the coastlines coming across the Gulf of Aden. So without getting any more specific than that, there are some areas that deserve watching much closer than others across the entire Horn.

Q: General, this is Mark Mazzetti with *U.S. News and World Report*. I just wanted to clarify. When you met with the heads of state of those four countries, were you given the authority to act freely at any time you gain actionable intelligence against terrorists and to operate in those countries? And do you have to ask their permission before you go? And then, finally, do you expect to get that authority in every country in your area of responsibility?

Maj Gen Sattler: The authority to actually prosecute a target in any of those sovereign countries, as we start to—oh, first of all, we're in the process of working the exchange of liaison officers, so that the countries that we are responsible for across the Horn of Africa, those who have sovereign governments, that we will take liaison officers on board that'll be on board *USS Mount Whitney* with us and will be able to have direct access back to their parent countries. But when we talked down through both the military leaders and the heads of state, and our own U.S. ambassador and country teams in each one of those countries, we talked about different types of targets and different types of action that we would do as a coalition. Now, keeping in mind that this is not a U.S. [operation] alone—this is not a unilateral effort across the Horn of Africa, it's a combined coalition and all of the countries that we have in our area of operations are, in fact, working closely with us. We have not visited Somalia, but the other countries we have talked to and we have established a relationship. And there are certain protocols we will follow, which I won't go into, but we did discuss those exact points that you just brought out.

But I would really like to stress that a lot of the information [and] intelligence-sharing—many of these countries have very capable armed forces and then very capable internal security mechanisms that they can certainly prosecute. Now, many of these terrorist targets, or many of these targets are on their own, and our role in that would be to assist them with intelligence, with information, and if they so request, possibly training and even some equipment, all over the period of time here.

Q: General, this is Jim Mannion of AFP [*l'Agence France-Presse*]. I was wondering if you could describe the scope of the Al-Qaida presence in Yemen up in the port area along Saudi Arabia; and also, whether Al-Qaida has been using Saudi territory as a haven and whether the Saudis have been cooperative in pursuing them? Thank you.

Maj Gen Sattler: [Given] the countries that we have responsibility for—obviously Yemen borders Saudi Arabia—our specific Combined Joint Task Force is not working directly with the Saudi government. Now, we've received information and intelligence across the entire inter-agency process so that we do get intelligence from other parts of the world that we're able to take and fuse with our analysts on board the ship here to help build that jigsaw puzzle that now indicates who's moving where and when. We are not just tracking Al-Qaida. Our mission is for all transnational terrorism, regardless if it's individual, if it's sponsored by an organization like Al-Qaida or even cells that we haven't heard of. So we have not honed in specifically on Al-Qaida, therefore, I can't give you a nose-count or a head-count; I just do not have that information.

Q: General, Tom Bowman with the *Baltimore Sun*. I know you said you've generated quite a bit of intelligence, and I know you can't be too specific. But I'm wondering if you can give us any general sense of the activity there. Are you seeing a greater amount of terrorist activity? More training camps, greater numbers than maybe you anticipated? Anything that surprises you? Anything in general that you can give us.

Maj Gen Sattler: You know, keeping in mind, Tom, we've just been here about 30 days right now, I would tell you that there's a lot of activity to be collected upon, that it's hard also to decipher what is just normal activity moving across borders at different points and moving across the Gulf of Aden, and what may in fact be either the smuggling of weapons, munitions, explosives, or individuals in and out of some of the countries.

So I would tell you that I would think there is a lot to collect upon, and that's where it becomes very tough, is trying to figure out what is information that has to be vetted through, and what becomes hard-core intelligence that can be used towards an action, action somewhere down the road. So there are a number of areas we're looking very, very hard at. We have not hit that point of, "Yeah, this is definitely what we thought it was," and therefore, we have not gone forward and actually conducted any attacks on any terrorist cells or training camps, et cetera.

But I would tell you that we're getting more and more information turned into intelligence every day. You know, it's not a short-term battle over here. We need to be patient because we need to be correct, absolutely correct when in fact we come forward and identify a particular location as a training site or a camp as being full or harboring terrorists.

So I would tell you there have really been no large surprises—no big surprises. But as you would know, and as anyone there can probably guess, it's going to take time to sort down through this. But the good news is that, you know, defeating the terrorists is the ultimate goal, but en route to that, while collecting the intelligence across all coalition partners and within our own interagency, the secondary goal is obviously to disrupt and keep off balance [the terrorists]. And we feel very confident that by virtue of breathing down their neck, looking at them through multiple intelligence sources, and collecting on them through multiple sources, that we are in fact disrupting—keeping them off balance until we can go to that next phase which is defeat, that is, bring [them] to justice.

Q: General, Nick Childs from the BBC. Your headquarters currently is aboard the Mount Whitney. Can you say if it is your plan to move the headquarters as well ashore? And if so, when?

Maj Gen Sattler: The *USS Mount Whitney,* which is, you know, a command and control ship, probably the most capable platform—naval platform in the world—so right now we have access and reach-back to anything and anywhere. And we can also command and control and speak with anyone that we can even, you know, remotely think that we would utilize either in operations or to go ahead and help us either do, A, analysis, or to, B, pull down intelligence from across the spectrum. So therefore, there's no hurry for us to push ashore. Right now we're off the coast of Djibouti, and we have, you know, helicopter capability on board. So I'm capable, as are others on board ship, to move into where we have our forces right now at Camp Lemonier in Djibouti. We are looking at the options to go ahead and phase ashore. That decision has not been made. There's a number of places we could do that, and obviously we're already established fairly well at Camp Lemonier in Djibouti. [Comment Removed]

Q: General, Alex Belida from Voice of America. Earlier you were discussing your relationships with the countries in your area of responsibility. I'm curious if you could discuss in perhaps more detail your relations with the government of Sudan. Do you have a liaison individual in Sudan or a Sudanese official with you? And secondly, have leaders in the region expressed concerns to you and therefore gotten you looking at activities of Islamic religious schools, *madrassahs*? Thanks.

Maj Gen Sattler: Okay, on the first question, which is a good one, we've had one trip—my number-one area tour colonel, who is our—he's our geopolitical advisor, who tripped the entire Horn. He has been in Sudan twice. And we have had another team in Sudan, working with the embassy. I have personally not gone to Sudan yet. We're still making the rounds. We've been to Yemen, we've been to Ethiopia, Eritrea, and obviously Djibouti, and we still have Kenya to pick up before we actually go ahead and attempt to go in and set up a visit into Sudan. So to answer your question, we have initial contact. We're working with the U.S. embassy there in Sudan, but we have in fact not made a formal visit yet, but that's still out there.

Figure 2. Ali Sabieh Hospital, Djibouti

Army Brigadier General Willard C. Broadwater, deputy commander CJTF-HoA speaks during a dedication ceremony at the Ali Sabieh Hospital. This project promotes economic growth to help with the mission to detect, disrupt and defeat transnational terrorism in the Horn of Africa by denying terrorists a safe haven.

Source: CJTF-HoA, URL: http://www.cjtfhoa.centcom.mil/default.asp, accessed on 14 April 2004.

On your second question, one of our goals, in addition to detecting, finding the terrorists and disrupting and then defeating, the third portion of our mission is to enhance the long-term stability of the region. We're also responsible for Central Command, to General Franks, for taking a look at civil-military operations—the building of schools, roads; enhancing the quality of life; humanitarian assistance, which, if in fact there was a drought, a famine, across any of the countries or across the entire horn, we would be looking to assist both government agencies and non-government agencies, to go in and enhance the quality of life and then shore-up, where we could and where we're asked to, stability across the region. [Comment Removed]

Q: General, Craig Gordon from *Newsday*. After the war in Afghanistan wound down, there was a great deal of concern about Al-Qaida fleeing toward Yemen, toward Somalia, places like that. I suspect that's basically why you're there. Can you give us any assessment of how much you think that actually did happen; you know, a few dozen, a few hundred—any sense of how much of that kind of movement did occur. And secondly, I was interested in your comment, if I understood it correctly, that you're not honing in on Al-Qaida; that you're looking for all transnational terrorists. Are there other groups in particular that you're looking for? I think the sense was Al-Qaida was your main focus there.

Maj Gen Sattler: To answer the first question, as the war progressed across Afghanistan, this is the exact reason, as you alluded to, why General Franks, in consult with Secretary of Defense Rumsfeld, decided to go ahead and stand up the CJTF-HoA to hone specifically on the region running from Yemen across the Gulf of Aden, and then, obviously, into the Horn of Africa. Once again, I really can't discuss, you know, any targeting—any terrorist groups that we are targeting for intelligence collection, etcetera, whether those be Al-Qaida or any other terrorist group or faction of one of the other groups that occupies or operates through that region, mainly in Somalia, as was already alluded to. So, if we find Al-Qaida, obviously, we're going to concentrate on it, collect on it, develop actionable intelligence and then prosecute, so I did not want to give, please, anyone the idea that we were taking Al-Qaida or anybody from the Al-Qaida organization lightly. But I also want to stress that this is about all terrorism, all transnational terrorism, that can either impact on us personally, that is, America, or our coalition partners.

Q: Hi, sir. This is Kathy Rhem from the American Forces Press Service. Can you describe what the camp that you have there in Djibouti is like, what are the living conditions like for the Marines and what kind of facilities are available there?

Maj Gen Sattler: The camp in Djibouti—right now, we actually have soldiers, sailors, airmen, and Marines and we have some civilians that are there working also; approximates about 900. The camp has very, very strong anti-terrorism force protection security, which we provide ourselves. The individuals living there—we are living in tents, sleeping on cots. There are environmental control units, there are environmental control units with each tent, and therefore, we do have some degree of air conditioning. There's a mess hall, chow hall, there that's also set up in tents with tables and chairs inside. It's fairly—it's very austere, but it's only there to, you know, go ahead and support the global war on terrorism. [Comment Removed]

Q: General, it's Pam Hess from UPI again. I'm interested in the vocabulary you're using. You keep using the word "prosecute." Is your mission there, after you get actionable intelligence, to participate in or support snatch-and-grab, and then putting people into the legal system? Or, are you guys bringing, say, lethal power to the question?

Maj Gen Sattler: I may be using the word "prosecute" incorrectly. A lot of times inside the military, when you prosecute a target, that just means that you go ahead and take that target—that is, it could be an artillery mission, could be an objective on a conventional attack. So I do not mean to use it as our sole goal is to, you know, ensure that we have indictments on people and that those individuals are in fact arrested and brought back to trial. That could be done, obviously, if there are terrorists or groups of terrorists that we do have an indictment out on. But that would be done mainly by civilian organizations—to go ahead and arrest.

In our particular case, it really doesn't matter. If someone arrests them to take them off the street based on intelligence information that we were able to provide, or in fact that it's a clean target and we have to go ahead and take that individual or group down, utilizing military action—I was using that term "prosecute" in both cases—I guess what I would say is one would be militarily to attack and destroy it, if in fact we couldn't go ahead and, you know, arrest them to bring them to justice.

Q: Hi, General. Bret Baier with Fox News Channel. You mentioned you are seeing things moving on the waters there—perhaps smuggling, other things. There are some reports indicating that Al-Qaida might have speedboats packed with explosives and might be trying to hit targets, either U.S. or allied, in that region on the water. Do you believe there's credible evidence [for] that? And how serious do you take that threat? Is there a higher state of alert because of that?

Maj Gen Sattler: Well, there have been, you know, two targets struck in that method in the last two years, one being the *USS Cole*, the tragedy there, and then the second one, much more recent, was the French oil tanker, the *Limburg*. So that tactic is out there for sure. We take it extremely seriously, as do our coalition partners. Each of the countries that we've worked with is very concerned about coastal security, to ensure that they have the capability to detect and, if necessary, interdict.

So a lot of our—without getting into it, a lot of our intelligence collection is focused on areas where these type of boats could, A, be stored; B, be moved to, launched from. And we also, through Combined Joint Task Force 150, the maritime component—they're constantly at sea, looking to interdict, stop and board, if necessary, you know, boats of this type, to make sure that they can't in fact come in close. We're also, especially on board our own ship—we have a tremendous anti-terrorism defense on board *USS Mount Whitney*, just to ensure that that type of attack does not happen to us. Therefore, we drill, we practice. We have alert. We have watch standers, etcetera. So we take that threat very, very seriously, and as I've indicated, it's been used twice and possibly foiled one other time. So it's out there, and we are concerned.

Figure 3. Fast Roping

A soldier with the 10th Mountain Division fast ropes out of a Marine CH-53E helicopter near Arta, Djibouti. The unit also participated in Military Operations in Urban Terrain training in order to better support CJTF-HoA in its mission to defeat transnational terrorism in East Africa.

Source: CJTF-HoA, URL: http://www.cjtfhoa.centcom.mil/default.asp, accessed on 14 April 2004.

Q: General, Tom Infield from Knight Ridder Newspapers. Just to clarify, you described the assets at Camp Lemonier, and you obviously have the Whitney. What other facilities or assets do you have as part of this task force?

Maj Gen Sattler: We have on Camp Lemonier, without getting into any great detail; we have access to some Special Operations forces that are directly under our tactical control. And I don't want to get into numbers or size. And we also have elements of the Marine Expeditionary Unit that is over here currently operating that are under our tactical control. So we are capable of massing a very credible force on very short notice to go ahead and attack a target, once in fact we would have, you know, credible intelligence that was actionable.

Q: General, I'm Carl Osgood. I write for the *Executive Intelligence Review.* I know that you have a specific area of responsibility that you're operating in, but there are also conflicts and operations going on in adjacent areas, like [the] Israeli-Palestinian issue; you have operations in the Persian Gulf, on the Arabian Sea in South Asia, and things like that. Can you say anything about the impact that all of this—things going on in these adjacent areas—have in your area of responsibility?

Maj Gen Sattler: I would say that General Franks, when he stood up the Combined Task Force, just like the one—you know, Combined Joint Task Force 180 in Afghanistan, he put Lieutenant General McNeill up there to focus on Afghanistan, not that General Franks wasn't interested or divesting himself of it, but he wanted one individual to focus solely on that to make sure that he didn't miss anything. When they decided to put the Combined Joint Task Force here in the Horn of Africa, made it very clear that's exactly what they wanted us to do, to go ahead and pull intelligence in from outside the Horn that might impact, [for example], transnational terrorism starting outside the Horn and coming into it, or if something was leaving the Horn and moving into another area, we would certainly pass all that information back up the chain. But we are really, truly focusing on those seven countries, and then the water that moves across, in conjunction with the Combined Joint Task Force 150. So the competition for resources could be out there, as in the case of any operation at any time. But right now, everything that we have asked for, everything that—every type of intelligence collection, platform that we've been looking for, we've had it made available to us, and we have not wanted for anything at this time. So, I would tell you that we are really concentrating on these seven countries and then picking up the terrorists as they move through.

Q: General, Otto Kreisher, Copley News Service. I want to follow up a little on the question earlier about your capabilities. You're used to operating off an ARG [Amphibious Readiness Group], with the helicopters, both troop carriers and gun ships. The Whitney is capable of about two helicopters. I'm interested in what your mobility is. You know, if you have to prosecute a target, where do you get your air assets, and what do you [do] about, you know, air cover—fixed-wing air cover, for what you have to do?

Maj Gen Sattler: If an operation is distant—If we are to conduct an operation, we have [such things] at our disposal, going through General Franks, it's very clear in our mission that we become the supported—the supported agency within his area of operations. And obviously, what that would mean would be that the maritime component commander, the air component commander and the land force component commander would then respond to General Franks' direction to go ahead and provide us the assets you just spoke about. Without getting into numbers, we also have—we have helicopters and other assets that are under our [...] control, that we own 24-hours a day, every day. Therefore, we have a capability to do the things you just spoke of day or night without having to reach out and ask for assistance. But if it became a larger operation, there's no doubt in my mind that, you know, we can and we would go ahead and go back through the chain of command and ask the other commanders out here to go ahead and support us for a particular operation for a particular period of time.

Q: General, it's Jim Mannion from AFP again. From the intelligence that you've gathered, is there any indication that Osama bin Laden is in your area?

Maj Gen Sattler: We have nothing at all that would indicate that Osama bin Laden is operating in any of the countries I just talked about. I have not even heard his name mentioned, as a matter of fact, over almost the entire time out here. So, the answer to that is no.

Q: General, it's Mark Mazzetti with *U.S. News* again, and I think I'm the last question. I just wanted to follow up on my earlier question about access to these countries. I guess the nature of actionable intelligence is that there's only a— there's a shrinking time window before it no longer becomes actionable. And I'm just wondering whether you feel that you're confident that you have worked out all of the bureaucracy now to allow you to act quickly in these countries without having to go through a lot of the red tape it might normally take. You know, in other words, do you feel like you can—if you had to prosecute a target today that you didn't have a lot of time, that you'd be able to do it successfully?

Maj Gen Sattler: Boy, that's a—I'm smiling because that is a great question, and that's the one that we constantly ask ourselves. If it's a very fleeting target, very time-sensitive, you're right, you need to have all those—that chain of command, the sequence of events that has to unfold to go in and prosecute that target need to be well defined so that phone numbers are known, individuals to be spoken with are known to get that clearance. I will tell you that we are comfortable that we have that now, but I will never be totally comfortable to the point that we won't keep going back and reminding—traveling back through the countries that we've already been to [, to] make second and tertiary appearances to make sure that they know that we're with them, we're coalition partners, and anything that we do will in fact be coordinated and orchestrated with them to make sure that we know exactly who has the authority and who we need to speak with, and in some cases, who on our side, with—inside the Combined Joint Task Force, within my chain of command, needs to make the call for the final clearance. So we're very concerned about that, meaning that we have taken a look at it in a number of different situations, and we're working to make sure that we have that in fact codified in both our mind and in our coalition partners' mind.

Staff: Thank you very much, sir. We appreciate your time.[1]

- -

IPB is the method for achieving the actionable intelligence expected by Major General Sattler and required by CJTF-HoA to prosecute targets with U.S. or coalition military forces. The interview correctly highlights important issues and concepts that are at the focus of this work, which seeks to be a primer, or hand-

---

[1]   Full text available from the U.S. Department of Defense, News Transcript. *Joint Task Force Horn of Africa Briefing,* 10 January 2003, 10:02 a.m. EST, URL: http://www. defenselink.mil/transcripts/2003/ t01102003_t0110hoa.html, accessed 12 April 2004.

book, for conducting IPB CT. As a precursor to concepts that will be explored in detail in the pages ahead, General Sattler clearly outlines operational objectives (deter, disrupt, defeat), breaks down combating terrorism into its elements (antiterrorism and counterterrorism), characterizes the nature of the threat (transnational, shadowy, networked), highlights the varying aspects of the battlespace (neighboring conflicts, state failure, coalition partnerships), and most importantly, drives home the central operational role of intelligence. In the end, he offers valuable boots-on-the-ground/deck testimony about the need for decision-quality intelligence. The following document develops and advocates a method whereby the Intelligence Community can handle information on asymmetric conflict in a manner that applies directly to operational requirements.

Chapter 1

COUNTERING TERRORISTS

Donkey carts laden with rocket-propelled grenades, teenage girls wrapped in nails and explosives, and civilian airliners filled with fuel and travelers. These are the weapons found in the arsenal of today's most insidious adversary—the terrorist. With few exceptions, terrorists play a prominent role in nearly every humanitarian and political crisis faced by the international community. A sample from across today's geo-political landscape reveals a Hamas suicide bomber haunting the streets of Jerusalem, Nepalese Maoists launching another round of bombings in Katmandu, and a Jemaah Islamiya (JI) militant preparing a car bomb to rival the 2002 attack in Bali. In addition to threatening U.S. interests and allies, terrorists pose a direct threat to the U.S. as evidenced in just the last decade by attacks on the World Trade Center (1993), Khobar Towers (1996), embassies in Kenya and Tanzania (1998), the USS *Cole* (2000), and the combined attacks of 11 September 2001.

As terrorists gain greater access to resources through globalized networks, they secure footholds on the terrain of illegal trade in drugs, guns and humans. The broad spectrum of objectives and asymmetric methods of these contemporary Assassins and Barbary Pirates fractures traditional warfighting concepts and challenges intelligence capabilities. Countering terrorists demands the full spectrum of national power instruments as well as a long-term perspective, particularly given the dominant ideological context of the confrontation. Within this strategic environment, the U.S. military mitigates underlying conditions that spawn terrorists and takes down organizations that commit terrorism.

Figure 4. Khobar Towers

The explosion of a fuel truck set off by terrorists at 2:55 p.m. EDT, Tuesday, 25 June 1996, outside the northern fence of the Khobar Towers complex near King Abdul Aziz Air Base, killed 19 and injured over 260 airmen.

Source: U.S. Army, URL: http:www.army.mil/fmso/ fmsopubs/issues/terror/KHOBAR7.gif, accessed 20 April 2004.

The national strategy for deterring, disrupting and defeating terrorist groups hinges on intelligence. The National Commission on Terrorism in its report to the 105th Congress, *Countering the Changing Threat of International Terrorism*, contends that

> Good intelligence is the best weapon against international terrorism. Obtaining information about the identity, goals, plans, and vulnerabilities of terrorists is extremely difficult. Yet, no other single policy effort is more important for preventing, preempting, and responding to attacks.[1]

Intelligence contributes to policy decisions, informs military strategy, shapes operational planning, enables tactical execution and assesses progress in countering terrorism. Intelligence seeks profound insight into the adversary's capabilities and intentions, and strives to do so inside the adversary's decision-cycle. As joint military forces develop and execute plans for combating terrorists, the pressures to deliver <u>actionable</u> intelligence to affect targets now, while simultaneously crafting long-range, <u>decision-quality</u> threat estimates, has never been greater. Remarking on the Global War on Terrorism (GWOT), Secretary of Defense Donald Rumsfeld asserts that the Intelligence Community (IC) has a tough and often thankless job with little margin for error. "If they fail, the world knows it."[2]

Important steps to enhance the intelligence contribution are underway on several fronts, including improving inter-agency cooperation, establishing new "fusion" organizations, expanding human intelligence (HUMINT) capabilities, and adapting innovative technologies. Military intelligence professionals work to provide tailored support to operations in multiple theaters, including against the Revolutionary Armed Forces of Colombia (FARC), Abu Sayyaf in the Philippines, and al-Qaida. Success occurs particularly where advances in information technology (IT) and structured analytical techniques are applied to the problem. Social network analysis, for example, is being successfully employed to determine high-value targets (HVT) associated with transnational groups. Its widespread use has contributed to the killing or capture of a significant number of terrorist operatives across the globe, including about three-fourths of al-

---

[1] National Commission on Terrorism, Report to the 105th Congress, *Countering the Changing Threat of International Terrorism*, 7 June 2000, URL: http://w3.access.gpo.gov/nct/, accessed on 12 April 2004.

[2] Defense Secretary Donald H. Rumsfeld, testimony before the Senate Armed Services Committee, 4 February 2004, URL: http://www.defenselink.mil/news/Feb2004/ n02042004_200402045.html, accessed on 12 April 2004.

Qaida leadership by late 2003.[3] Systems analysis has also gained traction as a way to understand the complex relationships between terrorist groups and their environment.[4]

The concept and process that links these intelligence efforts to military operations is intelligence preparation of the battlespace (IPB). IPB integrates intelligence analysis with operational planning and command decisionmaking. It is a structured, continuous four-phase analytical approach to defining the battlespace, describing battlespace effects, evaluating the adversary, and determining courses of action (COA). It meets the operational requirements of military forces tasked with combating all adversaries, including terrorists. Contemporary IPB doctrine and techniques are primarily oriented toward the conventional, nation-state adversary, with counterterrorism (CT) considerations receiving only nominal attention, if any.[5] Moreover, the ideas enshrined in current IPB doctrine are too limiting to accommodate the asymmetric character of the terrorist threat, focusing as it does on symmetric confrontations with nation-states.[6] This focus is understandable, given a law-enforcement approach to terrorism, the Cold War's legacy of superpower rivalry, and the attention given to rogue regimes in the post-Cold War period. In the context of GWOT, however, where the military's role and

---

[3] Written Statement for the Record of James L. Pavitt, Deputy Director for Operations, Central Intelligence Agency, before the National Commission on Terrorist Attacks upon the United States, Washington, DC, 14 April 2004, URL: http://www.cia.gov/cia/public_affairs/speeches/2004 pavitt_testimony_04142004.html, accessed on 14 April 04.

[4] For a complete systems analysis of terrorist groups, see Troy S. Thomas and William D. Casebeer, *Violent Systems: Defeating Terrorists, Insurgents and Other Non-State Adversaries,* Occasional Paper #52 (USAF Academy, CO: Institute for National Security Studies, March 2004).

[5] Joint and Service IPB doctrine offer supplemental guidance and checklists for dealing with asymmetric, unconventional and/or terrorist threats, which will be integrated with this study in subsequent sections. Joint Chiefs of Staff, Joint Publication 2-01.3, *Joint Tactics, Techniques, and Procedures for Joint IPB (JIPB)* (Washington, DC: Government Printing Office (GPO), 24 May 2000), viii, broadly asserts that "JIPB is a remarkably versatile process which can be adapted to support a wide range of joint activities applicable to countering an adversary's use of asymmetric warfare." Cited hereafter as Joint Pub 2-01.3. While the process is valid for the asymmetric threat, many of the specific techniques recommended in JIPB can be improved and added to for CT.

[6] A similar argument was made in a highly regarded 2002 RAND study for the US Army by Jamison Jo Medby and Russell W. Glenn, *Street Smarts: Intelligence Preparation of the Battlespace for Urban Operations* (Santa Monica, CA: The RAND Corporation, 2002), xiv. Their arguments with regard to the limitation of IPB in the urban environment apply equally well to the CT problem. They argue, for example, that IPB is limited "in part because of entrenched ideas about the types and locations of operations the US Army will conduct. Traditionally, IPB has focused on force-on-force operations against a known enemy on sparsely populated terrain."

the terrorist threat are heightened, applying IPB to the CT mission is not only needed, but past due.[7]

APPROACH

Mindful of these challenges and the evolving nature of the terrorist threat, the objectives of the present study are to:

1) Clarify the CT challenge and its intelligence demands;

2) Advance IPB tradecraft to meet CT requirements;

3) Apply enhanced IPB concepts and methods to terrorist threats.

The intent is not to replace current IPB doctrine and its associated tactics, techniques and procedures (TTP), but to modify them where necessary and add layers of best practices and emerging concepts as appropriate. The desired outcome is a core set of concepts and methods that reflect "state-of-the-art" thinking across government, business, and academia.

Note to Analysts

Regardless of rank or position, if you have a stake in delivering on-target intelligence for operations against terrorist groups, you may view this document as your guide. Although it is not a treatise on terrorism or a comprehensive rerun of IPB doctrine, it advances the latter to deal with the former. Detailed case studies of terrorist groups and tutorials on analytical techniques are not on offer; however, both are introduced and references to further detail in open-source literature are made throughout. The guide deals specifically with intelligence for military operations rather than being a primer on intelligence support to the full spectrum of CT efforts undertaken through the U.S. inter-agency process. Moreover, the non-state terrorist group is the unit of analysis even though state-sponsored terrorism remains deadly. This sub-state focus not only reflects the changing relationship between terrorists and states, but complements the current body of IPB doctrine. It bears repeating — the world of CT is larger than its military element. It includes diplomatic, informational, and economic instruments, most or all of which are more critical to the contest. Nonetheless, the military is certain to be engaged in this undertaking at all levels in conjunction with the other tools of state power.

---

[7] This conviction is consistent with a similar argument by Medby and Glenn, *Street Smarts*, 6, who claim "the tools traditionally used to conduct the IPB process have not kept pace with the varying types of operations and adversaries the Army encounters. Enemies, battlefields, and operations are different from what is traditionally envisioned."

Emphasis in this study is on the cognitive aspect of what is really a socio-technical issue; it involves both human and machine factors. That is, both enhanced mental skills and technology solutions are required to improve IPB. IT is a critical enabler, but long-lasting improvement requires that serious thought take root in organizational culture, through individual initiative as well as training and education programs. Once we understand how to structure the CT problem and develop the cognitive methods for working on it, IT can be brought to bear to improve horizontal intelligence sharing, battlespace visualization, data fusion and more. Since IPB in practice is often conducted on the field of battle, resources will be constrained, stakes will be high, and fog and friction will reign. IPB is an ally; it structures intelligence work even under tough conditions and when computers fail. Thus, the emphasis here is on improving the "brain piece" as a first step toward a more comprehensive socio-technical approach. In this sense, it embraces a common exhortation of former USMC Commandant, General Charles C. Krulak, to "equip the man, not man the equipment."[8]

This chapter introduces the core concepts of the book: terrorism, counterterrorism, and intelligence preparation of the battlespace. Given the difficulties associated with settling on a single definition for terrorism, the four core elements of terrorism are examined in sufficient detail so as to understand the challenges posed by the asymmetric, hybrid adversary. For its part, CT is examined in terms of its three interrelated mission levels — strategic, operational, tactical — and its fundamentally asymmetric character. The four phases of IPB are introduced and connected to the three levels of analysis, the intelligence cycle, and operational planning. As we move into the chapters, a consistent approach is used. First, current IPB doctrine is introduced and critiqued with emphasis on its objectives, core concepts, and basic methods. Concepts and methods with enduring value for CT are highlighted for retention. Each chapter also modifies current doctrine with new or improved methods for applying IPB to the terrorist threat and the CT mission. The final chapter summarizes the key outcomes for each phase and offers ten propositions to guide all CT.

VIOLENT THEATER

Terrorism is "violent theater."[9] "Tourists are terrorists with cameras; terrorists are tourists with guns."[10] While clever, and even accurate in a sense, these expres-

---

[8] Although repeated on many occasions, one documented example can be found in *Leatherneck Magazine*, May 1997, "Equipping the Man...Not Manning the Equipment," URL: http://www.usmc.mil/ cmcarticles.nsf/0/b214bdebbc9df9f6852564d70070efd3?OpenDocument, accessed on 14 April 2004.

sions are indicative of the problem with defining terrorism, a word that had already accumulated over one hundred official definitions two decades ago.[11] As pointed out by Bruce Hoffman, terrorism expert and author of *Inside Terrorism*,

> virtually any especially abhorrent act of violence that is perceived as directed against society — whether it involves the activities of anti-government dissidents or governments themselves, organized crime syndicates or common criminals, rioting mobs or persons engaged in militant protest, individual psychotics or lone extortionists — is often labeled terrorism.[12]

No doubt, we can generally agree terrorism is bad. But we need some precision, or at least recognition of terrorism's core elements to know what we are up against and how to avoid using it as a pejorative for any unwanted violence without also offering insight into the morality of the behavior, the legality of the act, or the appropriateness of a response.

The definitional problem exists in our own government. The FBI, for example, emphasizes the criminal aspect of terrorism as the "unlawful use of force or violence against persons or property to intimidate or coerce."[13] The State Department on the other hand draws attention to the political character of the actor and the noncombatant status of the target. This Department's definition has been used by the U.S. since 1983 to develop lists of Foreign Terrorist Organizations (FTO) and analyze terrorist attacks. It also enjoys a legal basis in Title 22 of the United States Code, Section 2656f(d), and is the most widely used:

---

[9] Brian Jenkins first introduced the idea of "terrorism is theater" in "International Terrorism: A New Mode of Conflict," *International Terrorism and World Security*, eds. David Carlton and Carlo Schaerf (London, UK: Croom Helm, 1975), 16.

[10] Anonymous.

[11] Alex P. Schmind, *Political Terrorism: A Research Guide to Concepts, Theories, Data Bases and Literature* (New Brunswick, NJ: Transaction Books, 1983), 119-152.

[12] Bruce Hoffman offers an excellent, concise discussion of the difficulties surrounding a definition of terrorism in, *Inside Terrorism* (New York, NY: Columbia University Press, 1998), 13.

[13] Hoffman, 38.

Premeditated, politically motivated violence perpetrated against non-combatant targets by subnational groups or clandestine agents, usually intended to influence an audience.[14]

The Department of Defense (DOD) definition ignores the actor entirely and focuses on the act as

The calculated use of violence or threat of violence to inculcate fear; intended to coerce or to intimidate governments or societies in the pursuit of goals that are generally political, religious, or ideological.[15]

With such divergence, it is no wonder the United Nations (U.N.) has been unable to reach a global definition as the basis for a convention against terrorism in all its forms. Instead, the current body of international law proscribes certain targets and specific tactics, thus whittling away at terrorism, but never attacking it head on.[16] Rather than attempting a new definition here, it is more important that we grasp generally accepted key elements: political motivation, violence with psychological impact, noncombatant target, and organized perpetrators.[17]

Violent Intellectuals

Terrorism is an intentional act resulting from the decision of an individual or organization. It is not momentary rage, impulse or accident.[18] *Political motivation* describes the purpose of the act, not the reasons for joining a group. Terrorism is always directed at changing or fundamentally altering the political order.[19] During the last half of the 20th century, many terrorist groups pursued the more conven-

---

[14] This definition is taken from the State Department's website and annual publication, *Patterns in Global Terrorism 2003*, URL: http://www.state.gov/s/ct/rls/pgtrpt, accessed on 15 April 04. Cited hereafter as State Department, Patterns 2003.

[15] Joint Chiefs of Staff, Joint Publication 3-07.2, *Joint Tactics, Techniques, and Procedures for Antiterrorism* (Washington, DC: GPO, 17 March 1998), I-1. Cited hereafter as Joint Pub 3-07.2.

[16] For a listing of the key terrorism conventions, see the United Nations website, URL: http://untreaty.un.org/English/Terrorism.asp, accessed on 15 April 04.

[17] The parsing of the key elements is drawn from Paul R. Pillar's, *Terrorism and U.S. Foreign Policy* (Washington, DC: Brookings Institution Press, 2001), 13. Pillar's text is highly recommended and reflects his extensive experience, culminating in service as the Deputy Chief of the Central Intelligence Agency's (CIA) Counterterrorist Center (CTC).

[18] Pillar, 13.

[19] Hoffman, 42. The exception to this maxim, as appropriately argued by Donald Hanle, is state repression terrorism, which seeks to reinforce an existing state order. Hanle cites the security services of Hitler, Stalin, and Saddam Hussein, which engaged is systematic terrorism against their populations. Interview with author, 20 May 2004, Washington, DC. See his chapter on "State Terrorism" in *Terrorism: The Newest Face of Warfare* (Washington, DC: Pergamon-Brassey's, 1989).

Figure 5. Embassy Bombing

Terrorists associated with al Qaeda detonated a large truck bomb outside the U.S. Embassy in Dar es Salaam, Tanzania, on 7 August 1998, just as another truck bomb exploded outside the U.S. Embassy in Nairobi, Kenya.

Source: FBI, URL: http://www.fbi.gov, accessed on 20 April 2004

tional goal of access to the halls of power, as exemplified by the statehood ambitions of ethnic separatist groups like the Basque Fatherland and Liberty Party (ETA). At the beginning of a new century, we must add to the equation an adversary not just seeking to shift power in the system, but pursuing an overthrow of the entire system from outside the system. Osama bin Laden may point to prior U.S. military presence in Saudi Arabia or the U.S. stance on the Israeli-Palestinian conflict as primary causes for global *jihad*. But in fact, a *fatwa* entitled "Declaration of the World Islamic Front for Jihad against the Jews and the Crusaders," released on 23 February 1998 in the *Al-Quds al-'Arabia* newspaper (based in London), calls for holy war against any non-Muslim coalition, declaring

to kill Americans and their allies, both civil and military, is an individual duty of every Muslim who is able, in any country where this is possible, until the Aqsa mosque [in Jerusalem] and the Haram mosque [in Mecca] are freed from their grip, and until their armies, shattered and broken-winged, depart from all the lands of Islam, incapable of threatening any Muslim.[20]

Going further, evidence suggests bin Laden and other members of this global *jihadist* cabal will not be satisfied with a U.S. retreat from the Middle East. On 15 November 2001, former Taliban ruler Mullah Mohammed Omar told the BBC that "the current situation in Afghanistan is related to a bigger cause—the destruction of America."[21] This is what Michael Ignatieff, Director of the Carr Center for Human Rights Policy at Harvard, calls "apocalyptic nihilism." He

---

[20] The fatwa is reprinted in part and analyzed by Bernard Lewis, *The Crisis of Islam: Holy War and Unholy Terror* (New York, NY: Modern Library, 2003), xxvii.

argues, "the apocalyptic nature of their goals makes it absurd to believe they are making political demands at all. They are seeking the violent transformation of an irremediably sinful and unjust world."[22] While not political in the conventional *realpolitick* sense, these statements do reflect "macroconcerns about changing a larger order" that can be considered "political" in a social, religious or even economic sense.[23]

Political motivation distinguishes terrorist groups from common criminals and lunatics. Criminals rely on violence often similar to terrorism in form, but with a material motive—money. Even when criminals threaten or use violence, the act of kidnapping, shooting or robbing is generally not intended to have "consequences or create psychological repercussions beyond the act itself."[24] With this in mind, terrorists regularly engage in criminal behavior and partner with transnational criminal organizations (TCO). In fact, the unholy alliance between extremism and organized crime is at the crux of the emergent threat landscape, earning its own label of narco-terrorism. Terrorism is also set apart from lunacy. Psychotics, like Charles Manson's "Helter Skelter" group, are motivated by abnormal behavior and individual values rather than a self-perceived public good.[25] Whether we can see the "good" in terrorist ambitions is irrelevant; Hezbollah, the Irish Republican Army (IRA) and others are convinced their actions are justified in terms of achieving "a greater good for a wider constituency."[26] In the apt words of Bruce Hoffman, "the terrorist is fundamentally a violent intellectual, prepared to use and indeed committed to using force in the attainment of his goals."[27]

---

[21] Transcript of interview with Mullah Omar conducted by BBC. Thursday, 15 November 01, 10:31 GMT, URL: http://news.bbc.co.uk/hi/english/world/south_asia/newsid_1657000/1657368.stm, accessed on 15 April 04.

[22] Michael Ignatieff, "It's War- But it Doesn't Have to be Dirty," *The Guardian*, 1 October 2001, URL: http://www.guardian.co.uk/Archive/Article/0,4273,4267406,00.html, accessed on 15 April 2004.

[23] Pillar, 14.

[24] Hoffman, 41

[25] Hoffman, 43.

[26] Hoffman, 43.

[27] Hoffman, 43.

Terror's Bad Name

Terrorism is a tactic—a form of warfare—by which violence or the threat of violence is intended to have a *psychological impact* on an audience. It **is** "violent theater," but the audience is not the victim of the attack. Terrorism earns its name when the normative values, or expectations, of the victim or target audience are violated.[28] Brian Jenkins, renowned terrorism expert, makes this point when he says

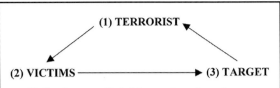

(1) Employment of lethal force or threat thereof.
(2) Results in communication of #1 to the target group.
(3) Results in the target's fear or terror of the terrorists.

Figure 6. Direct Targeting

Source: Alex P. Schmid and J. de Graaf, *Violence as Communication* (London: Sage Publications Ltd., 1982), 176, Hanle, *Terrorism,* 113.

> Terrorism is violence for effect; not only and sometimes not at all, for the effect on the actual victims of the terrorists. In fact the victims may be totally unrelated to the terrorists' cause. Terrorism is violence aimed at the people watching. Fear is the intended effect, not the byproduct of the [force employment].[29]

The classic relationship between terrorist, victim and target is shown in Figure 6, adopted from Hanle's text, *Terrorism: The Newest Face of Warfare*. The *target audiences* of the 11 September 2001 attacks were not its *victims*—airline passengers and employees or workers in the World Trade Center and Pentagon—but the American public and government. The takeaway insight is that the "true product" of terrorism is not the "physical attack on the victim, but the psychological impact upon the target."[30] Thus, choosing "victims" is among the most important decisions terrorists make. Misjudging the symbolic value of the victim and the expected target audience response can discredit a group and set back its goals. Religiously motivated terrorism adds an additional twist whereby both the mes-

---

[28] Hanle, 52.

[29] Quoted in Hanle, 112, from Brian Jenkins, *International Terrorism: A New Mode of Conflict* (Los Angeles, CA: Crescent Publications, 1975), 1.

[30] Hanle, 113.

sage and choice of victims may be secondary considerations to the transcendent, theatrical qualities of the act itself.[31]

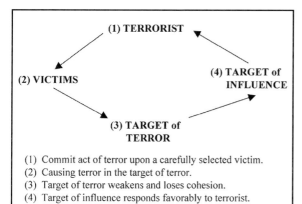

(1) Commit act of terror upon a carefully selected victim.
(2) Causing terror in the target of terror.
(3) Target of terror weakens and loses cohesion.
(4) Target of influence responds favorably to terrorist.

Figure 7. Indirect Targeting

Source: Hanle, *Terrorism*, 113.

There is more. Figure 6 represents the classical or *direct* form of terrorism. *Indirect* terrorism, as explained by Hanle, adds another target—the *target of influence*, which is distinct from the target of terror. The relationships shown in Figure 7 were on display in Iraq on 27 October 2003. Terrorists, possibly foreign *jihadists*, used suicide car bombs to kill innocent International Committee of the Red Cross (ICRC) workers. The targets of terror were ICRC and other non-governmental organizations (NGOs), but the targets of influence were not only NGO leadership, but the U.N., as well as Iraqi public and international opinion. Again, an accounting of the unique character of religious terrorism is warranted. While the terrorist organization may have an audience in mind when it sends out a suicide bomber, the audience of relevance to the actual bomber may very well be his or her family, or more significantly, god. That is, we must keep in our understanding the prospect of "Allah as audience." Under-

---

[31] According to Bruce Hoffman, for the religious extremists of Hamas, Islamic Jihad, and al-Qaida, violence is a "sacramental act or a divine duty executed in direct response to some theological demand or imperative." Thus, terrorism "assumes a transcendental dimension" and religion becomes the "legitimizing force." The religious sanction is essential as exemplified in an article entitled, "Sacrificing Oneself for God," by a Jewish rabbi from the West Bank, who argues, "suicide during wartime is permissible for the sake of victory of Israel." Hoffman, 94-95, 105. This perspective is reinforced, not only by the rhetoric of the terrorist's themselves, but in other key studies. Among these, I recommend a seminal inquiry into violence as a function of fantasy and "mystical longings" by James H. Billington, *Fire in the Minds of Men: Origins of the Revolutionary Faith* (New York: Basic Books, Inc., 1980). Recommended studies focused on the Islamic character of terrorism as a divine act, or fulfillment of a fantasy role, include Daniel Benjamin and Steve Simon, *The Age of Sacred Terror* (New York: Random House, 2003), M. J. Akbar, *The Shade of Swords: Jihad and the Conflict Between Islam and Christianity* (New York: Routledge, 2002), and Jessica Stern, *Terror in the Name of God: Why Religious Militants Kill* (New York: Ecco Publishers, 2003).

standing the relationships between terrorist, victim and target(s) is fundamental to all phases of IPB, but particularly the development of COA in phase four.

Innocence Lost

Noncombatants are the so-called "innocents" of war. The class is not limited to children, the elderly or the weak, but to all individuals who cannot defend themselves with violence.[32] We might also add those who choose not too defend themselves, such as conscientious objectors, and those whose profession prevents it, such as doctors.[33] In international humanitarian law (IHL), noncombatants are not clearly defined. Rather, the burden of distinguishing them is placed on combatants, who must determine the application of four standards whereby combatants, by definition: (1) are commanded by a person responsible for his subordinates; (2) have a fixed, distinctive emblem recognizable at a distance; (3) carry arms openly; and (4) conduct their operations in accordance with the laws and customs of war.[34] Anyone, including mercenaries, not meeting all these requirements is technically a noncombatant, and thus does not enjoy the "laws, rights and duties of war."[35] Of course, terrorists also fall short, and many messy, internal wars involve belligerents who avoid these symbols of professionalism to gain an asymmetric advantage. This does not make them noncombatants, but it does bring into question whether they should enjoy any of the rights of combatants when captured. The U.S. State Department adds further clarification:

> [T]he term "noncombatant" is interpreted to include, in addition to civilians, military personnel who at the time of the incident are unarmed and/or not on duty...We also consider as acts of terrorism attacks on military installations or on armed military personnel when a state of military hostilities does not exist."[36]

---

[32] Pillar, 14.

[33] Donald Hanle, interview with the author, 20 May 2004, Washington, DC.

[34] Article 1, *Hague Convention* (IV), "Respecting the Laws and Customs of War on Land, Annex to the Convention," 18 October 1907. Reprinted in, *The Laws of War: A Comprehensive Collection of Primary Documents on International Laws Governing Armed Conflicts*, eds. W. Michael Reisman and Christ T. Antoniou (New York, NY: Vintage Books, 1994), 41.

[35] *The Laws of War*, 43.

[36] State Department, *Patterns 2003*. The following are examples of non-combatants fitting State's definition: Col. James Rowe, killed in Manila in April 1989; Capt. William Nordeen, U.S. defense attaché killed in Athens in June 1988; the two servicemen killed in the Labelle discotheque bombing in West Berlin in April 1986; and the four off-duty U.S. Embassy Marine guards killed in a cafe in El Salvador in June 1985.

Whereas the bombings of commuter rail lines on 11 March 2004 in Madrid, Spain, clearly targeted non-combatant victims, the attack on the USS *Cole* in the port of Aden on 12 October 2000 is less clear. The USS *Cole* attack highlights the gray areas of the war-vs.-crime and terrorist-vs.-guerilla dilemma. Strategically located near the mouth of the Red Sea, Aden was undergoing a modest revival as a refueling stop when the USS *Cole* made its visit while en route to the Persian Gulf. Around noon, the USS *Cole* was in the middle of the harbor preparing to refuel at a floating station.

Figure 8. USS *Cole*

Seventeen Sailors aboard the USS *Cole* (DDG 67) were killed as a result of an explosion that left large hole in the port side of the Norfolk, VA-based destroyer.

Source: U.S. Navy Office of Information, URL: http://www.chinfo.navy.mil/navpalib/news/news_stories/images-cole1.html, accessed on 14 April 2004.

Small rubber boats went about securing the massive destroyer to the surrounding buoys with mooring lines. Two men in one of the boats apparently smiled and waved as they returned to its side. As sailors worked, a powerful explosion tore a 20-by-40 foot hole in the hull near the engine room and adjacent to eating and living quarters. Throughout the night and in to the next day, sailors fought to save their mates and boat. In the end, 17 sailors were killed and 39 injured.

Were they combatants or noncombatants? From Osama bin Laden's perspective, war had been declared in his *fatwa*, and the sailors of the USS *Cole* were instruments of the state engaged in military actions against the Muslim community. Thus, they were combatants. On the other hand, the U.S. did not consider itself at war, and the sailors of the USS *Cole* were not part of a logical causal chain designed to harm someone as part of a conflict. Moreover, their living quarters and mess were attacked, removing them even further from the fight. Based on the State Department clarification, they were noncombatants. The determining factor, which is beyond the scope of this book, is whether "war" exists with non-state groups at all. It *was* war in the sense that a political entity, an al-Qaida-affiliate, used lethal force for a political end; however, until 2001, the U.S. had never declared war on terrorists, and it is still unclear whether the international laws of war allow for it. If the bombing can be seen as a "salvo" in an on-going conflict, the engagement exists and war probably exists. To the sailors of the USS *Cole*, these distinctions are not relevant—the attack smelled, sounded and killed like war. In a way, the question poses a false dichotomy. Terrorism is simultaneously an act of war and a crime by the very nature, not only of the actions against the target, but most importantly, the tactic. To put it more directly, terrorism is criminal war.[37]

Fixing on Groups

Terrorism is collective violence carried out by *organized perpetrators*. The CIA's Counterterrorist Center (CTC) provides a specific definition for a terrorist group as "any group practicing, or that has significant subgroups that practice, international terrorism." Even though the State Department's definition leaves out the lone actor, IPB must include the solo terrorist as a CT target. For example, former CTC Deputy Director Paul Pillar argues that the four-year hunt to capture Mir Aimal Kansi following his shooting spree outside CIA headquarters was "always rightly regarded as a counterterrorist operation."[38] Several additional distinctions help characterize our adversary and provide general insight into capabilities and intentions.

First, terrorism is often state-sponsored. Examples of the latter include North Korea's 1987 in-flight bombing of a Korean Air Lines passenger jet, killing all 115 passengers, and Libya's sponsorship of the 21 December 1988 bombing aboard Pan Am 103 over Lockerbie, Scotland. During the Cold War, argues terrorism expert Martha Crenshaw, and particularly in the 1980s, the concept of state-sponsorship gained popularity because

> it simplified the problem of how to combat terrorism by making it an act of international aggression, even an act of war. The real ambiguity surrounding the causes of terrorism, which makes devising an appropriate remedy so hard, could be ignored by assuming that hostile states were the real cause.[39]

Since the end of the Cold War, state-sponsorship has declined and state-partnership, or even state-predation has increased. Hezbollah, for example, is no longer dependent on Iran, although coordination continues. JI preys on the state, or acts

---

[37] Two types of terrorism are not necessarily forms of war: state repressive terrorism and criminal terrorism. The former, because the population is not resisting (war is a duel), and the latter because the motivation is narrowly commercial, not political.

[38] Pillar, *Terrorism*, 14.

[39] Martha Crenshaw, "Thoughts on Relating Terrorism to Historical Contexts," in *Terrorism in Context*, ed. Martha Crenshaw (University Park, PA: Pennsylvania State University Press, 1995), 10.

outside its control throughout Southeast Asia. Indeed, contemporary terrorism erodes state sovereignty, taking advantage of "globalization cover" to transit porous borders and of "failures in governance" to exploit territory, resources and people. CT against states is certain to be part of our future; this is a reminder that IPB for military operations involving nation-states needs continuous updating to reflect the shifting security landscape.

	Defining Goals	Examples
Left	1) Anarchist—destroy the government 2) Marxist—foment worker's revolution 3) Socialist—economic restructuring	Argentinean Montoneros; German/Japanese Red Armies; Shining Path
Right	1) Racist—racial supremacy 2) Fascist- militant nationalism/ racism 3) Nationalistic	Ku Klux Klan; Neo-Nazis; Rumanian Iron Guard
Ethnic Separatist	1) Dispel foreign occupier 2) Create ethnically independent state	IRA ETA
Single Issue	1) Advance cause 2) Defend issue	Animal Liberation Front; Earth First!
Religious	1) Apocalyptic—cataclysmic destruction 2) Government—create religious government 3) Purity—purge heretical faiths	Aum Shinrikyo; Hezbollah; Hindu Nation

Figure 9. Terrorist Group Types

Source: Heather S. Gregg, "Defining and Distinguishing Traditional and Religious Terrorism," paper presented at International Studies Association Conference, March 2004, Montreal, Canada.

The shift in emphasis away from state-sponsorship is related to a second distinction. The "terrorist" label obscures a more fundamental identity, which is rooted in membership characteristics and shared motivations. Distinguishing groups in these terms leads to several simplified identity types: left, right, ethnic separatist, single-issue and religious extremist. Goals and examples for each are shown in Figure 9. Left-wing groups pursue anarchist, Marxist or radical socialist agendas and generally claim to represent the impoverished or disenfranchised.[40] Right-wing groups embrace racist, fascist, or fiercely nationalist agendas, while ethnic separatists pursue an autonomous or independent homeland. Single-issue groups have emerged in recent years as self-perceived champions of highly-focused causes—the term "eco-warriors" characterizes the many groups agitating for environmental reasons.

Religious extremism warrants further subdivision into three groups, as set forth by terrorism expert Heather Gregg: apocalyptic, religious government, and religiously pure state.[41] Apocalyptic groups are motivated by their faith system to hasten the end of the world or cause some other form of cataclysmic destruction, while individual terrorists in these groups are often motivated by an "Allah as audience" mind-set. Others seek the creation of a religious government, based on Islamic law or Reconstruction Theology for example, either within the confines of a state's borders, or transcending borders as in the pan-Islamic government desired by the Muslim Brotherhood.[42] Finally, several religious-based terrorist groups seek to cleanse, or purify, the state of so-called infidels.[43] By recognizing each of the types highlighted here, we gain immediate insight into general motivations, membership characteristics and even likely targeting strategies.

The U.S. *National Strategy for Combating Terrorism* offers a fourth distinction based on levels of operation by terrorist organizations, which serves as a basis for assessing the threat and structuring strategy. Groups on the first level operate primarily within a single state, such as the IRA (United Kingdom), ETA (Spain) or Abu Sayyaf (Philippines). By taking advantage of globalization, single-country groups can grow to have an impact on a regional or global level. Regional groups, such as JI (Southeast Asia) or the Salafist Group for Call and Combat (GSPC), in the Mahgreb region of North Africa, transcend at

---

[40] Bruce Hoffman offers a useful historical and contemporary examination of these group types in *Inside Terrorism*, 45-129.

[41] The figure and categories are adopted from a paper presented by Heather S. Gregg, "Defining and Distinguishing Traditional and Religious Terrorism," International Studies Association Conference, Montreal, Canada, 17-20 March 2004.

[42] According to Gregg, Reconstruction Theology is "one interpretation of Christian scriptures that calls for the creation of a Christian theocratic government in the U.S." Gregg, 8.

[43] Gregg, 11.

least one national boundary.[44] Groups at each level interact by: (1) cooperating to share intelligence, resources and personnel, and (2) promoting shared ideological agendas.[45] The high degree of interconnectedness, argues the *National Strategy*, necessitates pursuing "them across the geographic spectrum to ensure that all linkages between the strong and weak organizations are broken, leaving each of them isolated, exposed, and vulnerable to defeat."[46] These distinctions allow us to initially size up a group in terms of its relationship to the state, core identity, and operational reach. The most challenging groups will be those with global reach, a religious extremist identity and state(s) support. Al-Qaida epitomized this type of threat while the Taliban ruled Afghanistan, and Hezbollah continues to reflect these characteristics.

Hybrid Adversary

If terrorism is a form of warfare, we need to ascribe to the perpetrators an identity separate from the terror tactic. While blowing up a mosque earns the inglorious title of "terrorist," and a hit-and-run ambush by a small group of irregulars earns the label of "guerrilla," these terms mask the more complex reality discussed above. Going further, terrorists in Chechnya, Colombia, Iraq and elsewhere use forms of violence other than terrorism—they are hybrid adversaries. Like the FARC or al-Qaida, the most challenging groups are simultaneously criminals, terrorists, guerillas and soldiers. The forms of war—terrorism, guerrilla, conventional—are often confused with concepts like revolution, insurgency, *jihad*, and preemptive war. These strategic concepts refer to political strategies involving lethal force; they are politico-military constructs that will employ one or more of the forms of warfare. To avoid underestimating the multi-faceted, asymmetric capabilities of the terrorist group, the two additional dominant forms of warfare are succinctly addressed below. Of note, this discussion does not address cyberwar, which emerges in discussions throughout this work and warrants an independent IPB-oriented study.

---

[44] U.S., *National Strategy for Combating Terrorism*, February 2003, 8. Cited hereafter as National Strategy.
[45] *National Strategy*, 9.
[46] *National Strategy*, 9.

Maneuver and Mass

Conventional wars involve mechanized forces that rely on maneuver, mass and other principles to defeat the adversary in force-on-force battles. In the 2001 war in Afghanistan, Osama bin Laden fielded an "elite" force of Arab fighters with mechanized equipment as the 55th Arab Brigade. Other terrorist groups, such as the Liberation Tigers of Tamil Eelam (LTTE) in Sri Lanka, have occasionally fielded small armies. A conventional fight with terrorists is a rarity for at least four reasons. First, building and deploying it requires geo-political space. The terrorist must carve the territory from the state. In the case of al-Qaida, the Taliban provided the space. In the case of the FARC, former Colombian President Andres Pastrana ceded national territory as part of a peace process, allowing the FARC to consolidate its forces. In most cases, the terrorist must wrestle the space from the state, often as part of an internal war. Even when space is obtained, the terrorist group must be sufficiently mature and well-organized to recruit, train, equip and feed a conventional force, and it must have the professional skills to plan and execute operations. Third, acquiring conventional weapons and the infrastructure to support them is expensive and illegal unless there is access to resources resembling those of a state. States can build and sustain conventional forces the terrorist finds difficult to rival—a fact that is particularly true of industrialized states. Moreover, by building a conventional force, the terrorist is actually playing to the state's asymmetric operational advantages and thus setting itself up for almost certain defeat. Against an advanced industrialized foe, concentrating one's forces is an invitation to summary destruction.

Figure 10. Fighting al Qaeda

An Anti-Taliban Forces (ATF) fighter wraps a bandolier of ammunition around his body as ATF personnel help secure an al Qaeda compound against which the U.S. Marines had just conducted a Cordon and Search Raid in the Helmand Province of Afghanistan.

Source: U.S. Atlantic Fleet News, URL: http://www.atlanticfleet.navy.mil/ index.htm, accessed on 20 April 2004.

One Against Ten

Guerrilla warfare pits the weak against the strong. Of course, this is less a distinction related to the "will to fight" than it is of the ability to do so like a state. At its core is avoidance of direct confrontation, making it very similar to terrorism. The guerrilla's only chance of winning is to survive, preserving his smaller forces while simultaneously wearing down the adversary. Small, persistent attacks are intended to compel a weakening of the enemy's will. It takes advantage of asymmetries by directing what lethal force is available against the state's vulnerabilities. In the words of one of guerrilla warfare's primary architects, Mao Tse-tung, "the strategy of guerrilla war is to put one man against ten, but the tactic is to pit ten men against one."[47]

According to the DOD definition, guerrilla warfare involves "military and paramilitary operations conducted in enemy-held or hostile territory by irregular, predominantly indigenous forces."[48] This approach correctly highlights the military aspect of the operation, the obvious geo-political space (hostile) in which operations occur, and the irregular nature of the forces. However, whereas guerrillas were once principally indigenous forces, conflicts have witnessed a significant increase in the participation of non-indigenous forces from the time when the Afghan *mujahideen* welcomed the participation of Arabs to their fight against the Soviet Union. With victory against one of the world's superpowers in 1989, foreign fighters were emboldened and unemployed. Like the roving mercenaries of the pre-Westphalia period, they embraced bin Laden's call for a global *jihad* and fanned out across the globe to support a perceived defensive struggle by the Islamic community, or *umma*, against infidels and apostate regimes in the Balkans, Chechnya, Afghanistan again, and now Iraq. On the eve of the Iraq War of 2003, Syrians, Afghanis, Yemenis, Chechens, Saudis and others rushed to Iraq to join the fray.

Where the DOD definition comes up short is in addressing the distinctive targets and tactics of guerrilla warfare. In terms of targets, guerrilla warfare is distinguished from terrorism by its focus on the government rather than on noncombatants. Gray areas exist. Whereas most guerrilla operations throughout history have centered their targeting on the state's military, it is not uncommon to see guerrillas go after other government officials and related support facilities. In

---

[47]Quoted from Max Boot in his study of U.S. involvement in small wars during its history. *The Savage Wars of Peace: Small Wars and the Rise of American Power* (New York, NY: Basic Books, 2002), 112.

[48] Joint Chiefs of Staff, Joint Publication 1-02, Department of Defense *Dictionary of Military and Associated Terms* (Washington, DC: GPO, 12 April 2001, As Amended Through 17 December 2003), under "guerrilla war." Cited hereafter as Joint Pub 1-02.

the eyes of the guerrilla, these are legitimate targets given their association with the state's instruments of coercion; the further removed the target is from the causal chain of coercion, the more likely the attack is going to be perceived as terrorism. Of course, even when the targets are considered legitimate, the state is likely to employ the rhetoric of terrorism in an effort to discredit the guerillas.

The history of guerrilla warfare is replete with well-known theorists and practitioners, including Sun Tzu, Clausewitz, T.E. Lawrence, Charles Callwell (author of the influential *Small Wars: Their Principles and Practice*), Che Guevera and Vo Nguyen Giap.[49] All contributed to its development, but for the best articulation of its overall strategy and tactics we return to Mao as quoted in Bard E. O'Neill:

> What is the basic guerrilla strategy? Guerrilla strategy must be based primarily on alertness, mobility, and attack. It must be adjusted to the adversary situation, the terrain, the existing lines of communication, the relative strengths, the weather, and the situation of the people. In guerrilla warfare, select the tactic of seeming to come from the east and attacking from west; avoid the solid, attack the hollow; attack; withdraw; deliver a lightning blow, seek a lightning decision. When guerrillas engage a stronger enemy, they withdraw when he advances; harass him when he stops; strike him when he is weary; pursue him when he withdraws. In guerrilla strategy, the enemy's rear, flanks and other vulnerable spots are his vital points, and there he must be harassed, attacked, dispersed, exhausted, and annihilated.[50]

The choice between terrorism, guerilla and conventional war is largely one of capability and strategy, although issues of popular legitimacy also factor. The guerrilla seeks to preserve popular support by not intentionally killing civilians. The terrorist is often willing to kill civilians either to eradicate the adversary, or force a change in policy without regard to popular support. That said, carefully targeted terrorism can serve to mobilize support; not just among its core supporters, but among a sympathetic population.[51] In addition to the core elements of ter-

---

[49] Among the many histories of guerrilla warfare, I recommend: Robert B. Asprey, *War in the Shadows: The Guerrilla in History* (New York, NY: William Morrow and Company, 1994); Walter Laqueur, *Guerrilla Warfare: A Historical & Critical Study* (New Brunswick, N.J.: Transaction Publishers, 1998).

[50] Bard E. O'Neill is quoting from Mao's *On Guerrilla Warfare* (New York, NY: Fredrick A. Praeger, 1962) in, *Insurgency and Terrorism: Inside Modern Revolutionary Warfare* (Washington, DC: Brassey's, Inc., 1990), 25.

[51] See Hanle's chapter on Revolutionary Terrorism, 132-163.

rorism examined here, CT IPB must account for a hybrid adversary able to fight in multiple forms at once.

At this point, we should be able to size up a potential terrorist adversary by political motivation, targeting strategy, organizational characteristics and available forms of warfare. A quick look at the LTTE, for example, reveals a non-state, ethnic separatist group seeking autonomy by attacking noncombatants to terrorize the Sri Lanka public and influence the Sri Lankan government. LTTE uses guerrilla war and has even fought pitched battles with conventional forces. Although a single-country group, it has global reach in terms of its support infrastructure. These insights are not of the decision quality required by IPB, but they do serve as a point of entry for more nuanced analysis required by CT operations.

COUNTERTERRORISM

Combating terrorism entails all actions taken to oppose terrorism across the entire threat spectrum.[52] These actions come in two forms: anti-terrorism (AT) and CT. AT "is defensive measures used to reduce the vulnerability of individuals and property to terrorist acts, to include limited response and containment by local military forces.[53] We know it at as Force Protection (FP), and it generally involves hardening facilities, introducing layers of security, and implementing random measures to create uncertainty. When expected targets, such as embassies and military bases, are hardened, terrorists look elsewhere for softer, accessible targets, including housing complexes and commercial centers. Whereas AT is defensive, CT aims to "prevent, deter, and respond to terrorism."[54] Combating terrorism is examined in this section with emphasis on the missions and asymmetric character of CT.

The U.S. strategy for combating terrorism underwent a sea change on 11 September 2001. Prior to the attacks, the U.S. approach emphasized a mix of crime fighting and warfighting, with the law enforcement approach dominating. Crime fighting relies on investigation, forensics, prosecution and incarceration. Convicting criminals domestically is hard enough, where a robust law enforcement and judicial system exist. The international system is even less potent, suffering from voluntary participation, a weak Interpol, and a newly established international criminal court that does not yet enjoy universal participation. High-profile cases like Carlos the Jackal or Ramsi Youssef notwithstanding, terrorists are incredibly hard to arrest. And when arrested, convicting with proof beyond a reasonable

---

[52] Joint Pub 3-07.2, I-1.
[53] Joint Pub 3-07.2, I-1.
[54] Joint Pub 3-07.2, I-2.

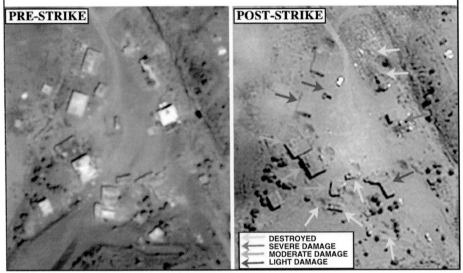

Zhawar Kili Al-Badr Terrorist Training Camp West: Severe Damage

PRE-STRIKE

POST-STRIKE

DESTROYED
SEVERE DAMAGE
MODERATE DAMAGE
LIGHT DAMAGE

Figure 11. Missile Strikes

According to the former Secretary of Defense, William Cohen, the capability to sustain terrorist operations from these facilities was significantly reduced. The anti-terrorist strikes on the terrorist camps in Afghanistan took place on 20 August 1998.

Source: DOD News Photo, URL:
http://www.defenselink.mil/photos/Jan1999/990113-O-0000X-001.html,
accessed on 17 April 2004.

doubt is difficult at best. Of the two Libyans tried in the Netherlands for the Pan Am 103 bombing, one, Al-Amin Kalifa Fahima, was released because the evidence failed to meet this standard. We also responded to the Khobar and USS *Cole* bombings with criminal investigations, although military options were considered. As a result of this police work, approximately 17 people had been convicted for these bombings through September 2001.

With a crime-fighting approach in use, overt military operations were applied sparingly in the last two decades of the 20th century. President Ronald Reagan used the military instrument in 1986 in the wake of the 5 April bombing of the LaBelle Club in Berlin. On 14 April, U.S. Air Force F-111s joined Naval aircraft in strikes in Tripoli and Benghazi, Libya, destroying a range of terrorist training and military targets. Just two years later, Pan AM 103 exploded in mid-air over

Lockerbie, Scotland, claiming the lives of all 259 passengers as well as 11 persons on the ground. The U.S. in 1993 responded to the attempted assassination by Iraqi agents of former President George Bush in Kuwait with missile attacks on Iraqi Intelligence Services headquarters. President Clinton replied to the 1998 embassy bombings in Kenya and Tanzania with cruise missile attacks on al-Qaida camps in Afghanistan and a suspected chemical factory in the Sudan. Public hearings by the National Commission on Terrorist Attacks upon the U.S. (the 9/11 Commission) in April 2004 substantiated U.S. planning of several covert operations, but also suggested a host of restraints, including an absence of "actionable intelligence," that precluded execution. By interviewing senior CT officials, Richard Shultz substantiated U.S. reluctance to employ Special Operations Forces (SOF) as a result of "nine mutually reinforcing, self-imposed constraints," including the criminalization of terrorism, not treating terrorism as a clear and present danger, concerns over legal authorities, aversion to risk, and a lack of actionable intelligence.[55]

With the GWOT well underway by February 2003, the Taliban regime in Afghanistan deposed, and al-Qaida under assault, the U.S. released its first *National Strategy for Combating Terrorism*. It enshrines a new approach, resting on the integration of crime-fighting and warfighting, but clearly elevating the role of the military. More directly, it declares

> Ours is a strategy of direct and continuous action against terrorist groups, the cumulative effect of which will initially disrupt, over time degrade, and ultimately destroy the terrorist organizations. The more frequently and relentlessly we strike the terrorists across all fronts, using all the tools of statecraft, the more effective we will be.[56]

The short history presented here highlights a substantive shift in U.S. CT policy, but we are reminded that the U.S. history of military-oriented CT extends back to the country's founding. During the administration of Thomas Jefferson, for example, the Barbary States of North Africa employed pirates to seize cargo and scuttle trading ships. After languishing in prisons, crews were ransomed or sold into slavery.[57] Jefferson responded in his first State of the Union address to Congress,

---

[55] Richard H. Shultz, "Showstoppers: Nine reasons why we never sent our Special Operations Forces after al-Qaida before 9/11," *The Weekly Standard,*" 26 January 2004, URL: www.weekly-standard.com, accessed on 17 April 2004.

[56] *National Strategy*, 2.

[57] Gerard W. Gawalt, "America and the Barbary Pirates: An International Battle Against an Unconventional Foe," (Thomas Jefferson Papers), np, URL: http://memory.loc.gov/ammem/ mtjhtml/ mtjhome.html, accessed on 14 April 2004.

to this state of general peace with which we have been blessed, only one exception exists. Tripoli, the least considerable of the Barbary States, had come forward with a demand unfounded either in right or in compact, and had permitted itself to announce war on our failure to comply before a given day. The style of the demand admitted but one answer. I sent a small squadron of frigates to the Mediterranean.[58]

Mission Analysis I

Mission analysis guides and informs IPB at all times. It frames the problem, reducing uncertainty and helping IPB zero in on the commander's decisionmaking needs—a problem well-defined is a problem half-solved. Framing begins with the commander's objectives and guidance, which helps us "understand the envisioned

---

Combating Terrorism Strategy Documents

National Security Strategy of the United States of America
Issued by the President, September 2002
National Strategy for Homeland Security
Issued by the President, July 2002
National Strategy for Combating Terrorism
Issued by the President, February 2003
National Military Strategy of the United States of America
Issued by the Chairman of the Joint Chiefs of Staff, 2004
National Military Strategic Plan for the War on Terrorism
Issued by the Chairman of the Joint Chiefs of Staff, October 2002
National Strategy to Combat Weapons of Mass Destruction
Issued by the President, December 2002
National Money Laundering Strategy
Issued by the Secretary of the Treasury and the Attorney General, July 2002
National Strategy to Secure Cyberspace
Issued by the President, February 2003
National Strategy for the Physical Protection of Critical Infrastructures and Key Assets
Issued by the President, February 2003
National Drug Control Strategy
Issued by the President, February 2002

Figure 12. Strategic Guidance

Source: Testimony of Raymond J. Decker, Director Defense Capabilities and Management, U.S. General Accounting Office, "Combating Terrorism: Observations on National Strategies Related to Terrorism," before the U.S. Congress, House of Representatives, Committee on Government Reform, Subcommittee on National Security, Emerging Threats, and International Relations, 3 March 2003.

---

[58] Gawalt, np.

military campaign or operation and desired end state."[59] Whereas current IPB doctrine and TTP include mission analysis as a sub-step in the first phase—describe the battlespace—its overriding importance to all phases argues for an initial treatment. Given the tough conditions and time constraints under which IPB is conducted in the field, IPB should never be started without first figuring out the mission, and continual reflection on the mission must follow the process to ensure analysis stays on track.

Like IPB analysis, CT planning and execution is carried out on three interrelated levels—strategic, operational, and tactical. The operational level "determines WHAT we will attack, in WHAT order, and for WHAT duration."[60] The operational level links tactical engagements to strategic objectives. Tactical engagements deal with how we fight, while the strategic level addresses "WHY and WITH WHAT we will fight and WHY the enemy fights us."[61] Although the levels of CT planning and execution are treated separately, we must think in terms of planning, operations and effects that transcend levels. That is, a tactical-level action can have strategic effects and strategic-level planning will shape tactical behaviors. Essentially, the levels provide a theoretical scaffolding to frame our work and understand the flow of action and effects across the battlespace. The IPB process is consistent for each level; however, specifics may vary considerably due to "obvious differences in missions, available resources," size of operational areas and other factors developed in Chapters 2-5.[62]

The Big Picture

GWOT is a strategic construct; CT policy objectives are established and national resources are developed and used to accomplish them.[63] Following the DOD definition, actions at the *strategic level* "sequence initiatives, define limits and assess risks for the use of military and other instruments of national power, develop global plans or theater war plans to achieve these objectives, and provide military forces and other capabilities in accordance with strategic plans."[64] Strategic-level CT integrates all the instruments of national power to achieve broadly defined security objectives that are consistent with the nation's *National Security*

---

[59] Air Force Pamphlet 14-118, *Intelligence*, "Aerospace Intelligence Preparation of the Battlespace (AFPAM 14-118)," 5 June 2001, 12. Cited hereafter as AFPAM 14-118.

[60] Air Force Doctrine Document (AFDD) 2, *Organization and Employment of Aerospace Power* (Maxwell AFB, AL: Air Force Doctrine Center, 17 February 2000), 3. Cited hereafter as AFDD 2.

[61] AFDD 2, 2.

[62] Joint Pub 3-07.2, I-7.

[63] Joint Pub 1-02, under "Strategic Level of War."

[64] Joint Pub 1-02, under "Strategic Level of War."

Strategy. U.S. strategic-level policy is currently enshrined in the *National Strategy for Combating Terrorism* although guidance can also be found in ten additional strategy documents shown in Figure 12. Among these are the *National Military Strategy* and *National Military Strategic Plan for the War on Terrorism* (classified). The former addresses a broad range of topics, including the need to create a global anti-terrorism environment. Its specific guidance includes:

> To defeat terrorists we will support national and partner-nation efforts to deny state sponsorship, support, and sanctuary to terrorist organization. We will work to deny terrorists safe haven in failed states and ungoverned regions. Working with other nations' militaries and other governmental agencies, the Armed Forces help to establish favorable security conditions and increase the capabilities of partners. The relationships developed in these interactions contribute to a global anti-terrorism environment that further reduces threats to the United States, its allies and its interests. For example, intelligence partnerships with other nations can take advantage of foreign expertise and areas of focus and provide access to previously denied areas.[65]

For the purposes of setting up IPB, the unclassified *National Strategy for Combating Terrorism* provides greater detail and is more than sufficient to outline key elements. While it is likely that policy will be refined in future years under subsequent administrations, we can expect strategic intent to remain generally consistent to "stop terrorist attacks against the United States, its citizens, its interests, and our friends and allies around the world and ultimately to create an international environment inhospitable to terrorists and all those who support them."[66]

U.S. strategic intent highlights the three core dimensions of combating terrorism: (1) causes, (2) capabilities and intentions, and (3) defenses. According to Pillar, these elements correspond to the life cycles of terrorism. The "cause" dimension focuses on root conditions and issues "that give rise to terrorists groups in the first place and motivate individuals to join them.[67] The second dimension centers on the intention and ability of groups to conduct terrorism, while the third focuses on defending against attacks. IPB for CT is focused primarily on the second dimension, although the joint force makes a significant contribution to the others.

---

[65] Joint Chiefs of Staff, *National Military Strategy of the United States of America 2004*, May 2004, 10. Cited hereafter as NMS.

[66] *National Strategy*, 11.

[67] Pillar, 29.

The three dimensions correspond to the four fronts of U.S. combating-terrorism policy: *defeat, deny, diminish and defend* (4Ds). Defeat and deny relate to terrorist capabilities (second traditional dimension), while diminish is akin to mitigating causes (first dimension), and defend (third dimension) is wholly about AT. In reverse order, the *defend* front "encompasses our nation's collective efforts to defend U.S. sovereignty, territory, and its national interests at home and abroad."[68] Recognizing the adaptive, asymmetric character of our adversary, it includes defending against attack with weapons of mass destruction (WMD) and the "cyber threat" in its many forms. Defend objectives include efforts to implement a homeland security strategy, develop domain awareness, or "effective knowledge" of the threat, protect physical and information-based infrastructure, protect citizens abroad, and ensure an integrated incident-management capability.[69] The *diminish* front works to mitigate conditions in the environment that give rise to and are exploited by terrorist groups. In addition to working on persistent, underlying problems, such as poverty, disease, and localized conflict, this front seeks to strengthen weak states, improve governance, and win the "war of ideas."[70]

On the *deny* front, the U.S. seeks to prevent terrorists from the "sponsorship, support, and sanctuary that enable them to exist, gain strength, train, plan, and execute their attacks."[71] Essentially, this front seeks to sever profitable relationships between terrorists and their stakeholders. Its corresponding objectives include ending state-sponsorship, establishing international standards of accountability, interdicting resources, eliminating sanctuaries, and strengthening international efforts by: working with willing and able states, enabling weak states, persuading reluctant states, and compelling unwilling states.[72] The *defeat* front is the most aggressive, seeking to defeat terrorists by *isolating* and *localizing* their activities and then destroying the organization through intensive, sustained action.[73] At the strategic level, all the instruments of national power are brought to bear to find and fix terrorists in order to disrupt their operations and ultimately, to terminate their functioning.

---

[68] *National Strategy*, 24.
[69] *National Strategy*, 24-28.
[70] *National Strategy*, 22-24
[71] *National Strategy*, 17.
[72] *National Strategy*, 17-21.
[73] *National Strategy*, 15.

Figure 13. Filipino Training

A U.S Special Forces soldier checks a Filipino scout ranger's target during marksmanship training. About 660 U.S. personnel deployed to the Philippines to assist Armed Forces of the Philippines forces during counter-terrorism training.

Source: US PACOM, URL: http://www.pacom.mil/philimagery/index3.shtml, accessed 14 April 2004

Joint forces are engaged on every front, and activity on one front will affect progress on the other. Although IPB for CT tends to focus on defeat and deny fronts, these military operations *will* impact our ability to diminish conditions and defend people and resources. Moreover, success in diminishing and defending will have cascading, positive effects on our ability to defeat terrorist groups. Opening a clinic in a Djibouti village improves living conditions, which can enhance efforts to "win hearts and minds," and thus shrink a potential terrorist recruiting pool, which changes the capabilities of the adversary. Military forces may actually help build the hospital, or they may provide security to defend workers. A more likely military CT mission is offensive action against a group seeking to disrupt construction. While tactical in nature, our ability to defeat the group and defend the clinic has strategic effects. The bottom line is that IPB for CT, while focused on defeating an adversary, must not be blind to the mutual exchange of effects across fronts and levels.

Campaigning

CT at the operational level entails planning, conducting and sustaining campaigns and major operations to accomplish strategic objectives within theaters or other operational areas.[74] Actions include "establishing operational objectives needed to accomplish the strategic objectives, sequencing events to achieve the operational objectives, initiating actions, and applying resources to bring about and sustain these events." Operational actions also suggest "a broader dimension of time or space" than tactics, enable "logistic and administrative support of tactical forces, and provide the means by which tactical successes are exploited to

---

[74] Joint Pub 1-02, under "Operational Level of War."

achieve strategic objectives."[75] The *National Military Strategy* is the bridging document that translates national security objectives into military strategy. More specifically to CT, the *National Military Strategic Plan for the War on Terrorism* and its successor link military objectives to national strategy and set the stage for operational planning by combatant commanders. According to press reporting, this first military CT plan is "more of a general framework of principles and objectives for military commanders than an attempt to define specific operations or tactical plans."[76] Although not detailed here due to its classified content, it must be treated as *mandatory* reading.

Objectives and missions at the operational level are certain to contain 4D parallels to be carried out by unified commands, component commands and joint task forces. Special Operations Command (SOCOM), for example, is charged to disrupt, defeat and destroy networked terrorist organizations. Their global approach to the problem covers the seams created by regional command boundaries, which is needed given the transnational character of modern terrorism. The *SOCOM Posture Statement* asserts that "SOF are specifically organized, trained, and equipped to conduct covert, clandestine, or discreet CT missions in hostile, denied, or politically sensitive environments."[77] Among the missions the IPB analyst might

Figure 14. Malian Training

Soldiers from the 1/10th Special Forces Group (Airborne) teach mounted infantry tactics to soldiers from the Malian Army in Timbuktu. The Pan Sahel Initiative (PSI) is a U.S. State Department-funded program in the northern African countries of Mali, Mauritania, Niger, and Chad designed to enhance border capabilities throughout the region against arms smuggling, drug trafficking, and the movement of trans-national terrorists. U.S. Army Special Forces, assigned to Special Operations Command Europe, are training selected military units in Mali and Mauritania on mobility, communications, land navigation, and small unit tactics.

Source: EUCOM Photos, URL: http://www.eucom.mil/ Photo_Gallery/index.htm, accessed 14 April 2004.

---

[75] Joint Pub 1-02, under "Operational Level of War."

[76] Bradley Graham, "Troops Could Stay for Months without Replacements," *Washington Post*, 23 January 2003, A12.

[77] US Special Operations Command, *Posture Statement 2003-2004*, 35, URL: http:// www.socom.mil/Docs/2003_2004_SOF_Posture_Statement.pdf, accessed on 17 April 2004.

support are "attacks against terrorist networks and infrastructures, hostage rescue, recovery of sensitive material from terrorist organizations, and non-kinetic activities aimed at the ideologies or motivations that spawn terrorism." Related missions include counter-proliferation, foreign internal defense (FID), civil-military affairs, counter-weapons of mass destruction, intelligence surveillance and reconnaissance (ISR), information operations (includes psychological operations), and direct action using unconventional forces.

The missions performed by SOCOM are integrated with the planning of regional unified commanders: Central Command (CENTCOM), European Command (EUCOM), Pacific Command (PACOM), Southern Command (SOUTH-COM), and Northern Command (NORTHCOM). All combatant commands, including SOCOM, develop and execute CT-related concept plans (CONPLAN) and operational plans (OPLAN). These classified documents integrate objectives, forces and mission at the operational level.[78] Likely missions include: promoting the capabilities of allied governments to combat terrorism, disrupting communications, interdicting terrorist resource flows, capturing or killing terrorist leaders, denying safe havens and sanctuary, and conducting information operations to influence perceptions. As an example, intelligence analysts supporting Joint Task Force-Horn of Africa (JTF-HoA) were credited in a 16 April 2004 DOD press release for "the capture of suspected terrorists and interdictions of drug shipments off the Horn of Africa."[79] According to CENTCOM, "a 'number' of suspected terrorists have been taken from dhows, traditional fishing vessels in the region, and 'pushed into the interrogation system because of their ties to al-Qaida.'"[80] Like the maritime interdiction operations (MIO) example here, mission analysis at the operational level requires understanding linkages to strategic objectives, desired outcomes, the capabilities of available friendly forces, the range of actors and factors capable of impacting the campaign, and "integrating tactical capabilities at the decisive time and place."[81]

Face-to-Face

The engagement with terrorists is joined at the tactical level—engagements are planned and executed to accomplish military objectives assigned to tactical units or task forces.[82] Forces are synchronized in time and space to achieve objectives

---

[78] An OPLAN identifies the forces and supplies required to execute the combatant commander's strategic concept and a movement schedule of these resources to the theater of operations, Joint Pub 1-02, under "Operations Plan."

[79] Kathleen T. Rhem, "Coalition Achieving Success in Horn of Africa," *American Forces Press Service*, 16 April 2004, URL: http://www.defenselink.mil/news/Apr2004/ n04162004_200404168.html, accessed on 17 April 2004.

[80] Rhem.

[81] Joint Pub 3-07.2, I-7.

in relation to anticipated adversary action. Combat examples might include a B2 Spirit bomber firing a precision weapon at a terrorist training camp, Special Warfare Combatant-craft Crewmen aboard a Mark Five boat interdicting smugglers, or Army Rangers capturing a key terrorist operative. CT at this level is not just hand-to-hand, but face-to-face. In fact, humanitarian, civil-military and information operations missions are likely to dominate. Thus, the IPB analyst is just as likely to support civil-affairs operations, humanitarian relief or psychological operations as well as the more traditional combat missions. Even while planning for highly specified engagements, we must keep in mind the potential strategic effects of tactical-level action.

Asymmetric Contests

Regardless of the mission level, CT is an asymmetric contest. In terms of both its type and the forms of violence employed, encounters between states and terrorists lack "a common basis of comparison in respect to a quality, or in operational terms, a capability."[83] Asymmetry does not equate to newness or something that is surprising, but rather directs our attention to the often dramatic differences between the state and terrorist in terms of a broad range of qualities. Among the many formal definitions of asymmetry, the most comprehensive comes from the U.S. Army War College:

> In the realm of military affairs and national security, asymmetry is acting, organizing, and thinking *differently* than opponents in order to maximize one's own advantages, exploit an opponent's weaknesses, attain the initiative, or gain greater freedom of action. It can be political-strategic, military-strategic, operational, or a combination of these. It can entail different methods, technologies, values, organizations, time perspectives, or some combination of these. It can be deliberate or by default. It can be discrete or pursued in conjunction with symmetric approaches. It can have both psychological and physical dimensions.[84]

At its core, asymmetry is about *difference*. CT is most challenging when there is a dramatic dissimilarity between opponents in several key areas, particularly when the belligerents are fighting different types of wars. For example, the Iraq War initially pitted the U.S. against the Iraqi conventional forces in a contest that was generally

---

[82] Joint Pub 1-02, under "Tactical Level of War."

[83] Montgomery C. Meigs, "Unorthodox Thoughts about Asymmetric Warfare," *Parameters* 33, no. 2 (Summer 2003), 4.

[84] Steven Metz and Douglas V. Johnson II, *Asymmetry and US Military Strategy: Definition, Background, and Strategic Concepts* (Carlisle, PA: Strategic Studies Institute, U.S. Army War College, January 2001), 5-6.

symmetric in terms of doctrine, weaponry, organizational structure, and the like, but that at the same time also reflected war-defining asymmetries in training, technology and cohesion to name a few. For example, the asymmetric air superiority advantage of the joint force not only kept the Iraqi Air Force on the ground, but led it to actually bury its aircraft in the sands (Figure 15). The asymmetries played to the U.S. advantage through the fall of Baghdad on 9 April 2003. As the war transitioned to an insurgency, the asymmetries grew, particularly in terms of strategy, weaponry, and tactics.

Figure 15. Buried Foxbat

A U.S. military search team examines a Cold War-era MiG-25R Foxbat B that lay buried beneath the sands in Iraq. Several MiG-25s and Su-25 ground attack jets have been found buried at al-Taqqadum air field west of Baghdad.

Source: DOD, URL: http://www.defendamerica.mil/ photoessays/aug2003/p080603b7.html, accessed 1 June 2004.

Among the various qualities forming the basis for an asymmetry, terrorism reflects an asymmetric strategy. Terrorists excel at "poor man's warfare." They rely on what military strategist Liddell Hart calls the *indirect approach*, attacking vulnerabilities while simultaneously avoiding direct physical engagements.[85] The contest is further complicated by mixing unconventional weaponry with their strategy; in fact, the one influences the other. In many cases, the weapons are among the most out-dated and cheapest on the black market, including man-portable surface-to-air missiles and backpack explosives. In one example of low-tech weaponry as part of an indirect approach, U.S. soldiers captured a donkey cart mounted with rocket-propelled grenades that had been used against the Iraqi Oil Ministry building and two hotels in November 2003.[86] Many other examples of innovative and unconventional tactics and weaponry exist, including cyber attacks and WMD.

Hanle breaks down wars into a classification scheme based on objectives and methods, further qualifying the asymmetric contest. A *total* political objective seeks the complete destruction of the adversary as a political entity, while the *limited* objective seeks only the abandonment of or a change in policy.[87] Examples of the

---

[85] The indirect approach is explained in B.H. Liddell Hart's classic study, *Strategy* (New York, NY: Signet, 1967).

[86] "Rocket strikes 'militarily insignificant'," CNN, 21 November 2003, URL: http:// www.cnn.com /2003/WORLD/meast/11/21/sprj.irq.main/index.html, accessed on 10 April 2004.

former can be found in the early positions of the Palestinian National Authority toward Israel, or more recently in the tapes of Osama bin Laden and *fatwas* of other extremists toward the U.S. A total military objective of *annihilation* pursues the destruction of the adversary's armed forces in decisive battle, and the limited objective of *attrition* leverages time to erode the adversary's will to fight.[88] Finally, military methods are either *positional*, using maneuver to seize or hold terrain (conventional war), or *evasive*, using maneuver to avoid the adversary's strength (guerrilla war and terrorism).[89]

Applying this framework to the insurgency in Iraq through early 2004, the militants were fighting a limited war of attrition using evasion. That is, they were seeking the limited objective of causing the U.S. and its allies to leave the country by eroding cohesion and will through a sustained series of knife cuts with car bombings, ambushes, and seemingly random attacks. As the weaker political entity, the insurgents "employ security and maneuver to evade the enemy's [U.S.] stronger armed forces, hitting only when and where local superiority can be assured."[90] Understanding that the Iraq War is informal and limited both in terms of political and military objectives provides insight to the key to insurgent victory—"making the cost of victory greater than the opponent is willing to bear."[91] On the other hand, al-Qaida is fighting a unique, *total* war of *annihilation* and *attrition* using *evasion* as part of its global *jihadist* insurgency strategy—the key to victory shifts. Drawing on Carl von Clausewitz, Hanle argues correctly that "In total war you erode your adversary's power base so that he becomes unable to fight, and in a limited war you maximize the cost(s) until he becomes unwilling to fight."[92] It is rare to find a terrorist pursuing a total war of annihilation, given their limited ability to generate the conventional force required to defeat a state's armed forces in open battle. Regardless of the military strategy, positional or evasive, victory always hinges on "destroying the enemy's will to resist."[93] In this asymmetric contest between the U.S. and terrorist organizations, Clausewitz's "will to resist" retains its value where terrorist organizations are concerned; however, CT adds the dimension of "will to support" as a critical aspect of the environment.

---

[87] Hanle, 62.
[88] Hanle, 62.
[89] Hanle, 62.
[90] Hanle, 57.
[91] Hanle, 59.
[92] Hanle, 59.
[93] Hanle, 61

PREPARING THE BATTLESPACE

The Chinese military strategist Sun Tzu offered one of the first documented expressions of IPB around 500 B.C., imploring commanders to:

> Know the enemy and know yourself; in a hundred battles, you will never be defeated. When you are ignorant of the enemy but know yourself, your chances of winning or losing are equal. If ignorant both of your enemy and of yourself, you are sure to be defeated in every battle.[94]

He directs attention to the value of not just estimating the threat, but understanding the action-reaction dynamic between adversaries. Noting the relational aspect of war, Carl von Clausewitz also argued, "war is nothing but a duel on an extensive scale."[95] As an example, it is not sufficient to know a terrorist leader is protected by thirty guards with automatic weapons before attempting a capture with Special Forces. Rather, we must also consider how the overall organization will respond to an invasion of their sanctuary, which will feed back into joint force operational planning. It is also possible, for example, that killing a specific leader will open the door for a more ruthless operative or remove a lucrative HUMINT contact. Similar thinking about delayed effects and adversary adaptability applies to operations for delivering relief aid or training allied security forces. The odds for knowing the adversary, knowing ourselves, and winning the duel are improved through IPB for all mission types.

IPB offers no magic solutions, nor does it eliminate the need for hard work. Instead, it serves as a mental model for structuring our thinking about a highly complex problem. It enables decision superiority by improving our ability to "get inside the adversary's observation-orientation-decision-action time cycle or loop" (OODA Loop).[96] IPB and the OODA Loop concept, developed by former Air Force Colonel John Boyd, are both focused on connecting intelligence and operations to provide "predictive intelligence to warfighters at the right time for use in planning and executing operations."[97] Thus, the practice of IPB is driven by the

---

[94] General Tao Hanzhang, *Sun Tzu's Art of War: The Modern Chinese Interpretation*, trans. Yuan Shibing (New York: Sterling Publishing Co., Inc., 1987), 100.

[95] Carl von Clausewitz, *On War: General Carl Von Clausewitz*, trans. Colonel J. J. Graham, (London: Routledge and Kegan Paul, 1966), 1.

[96] Colonel John R. Boyd, A Discourse on Winning and Losing, collection of un-numbered briefing slides from August 1987, URL: http://www.d-n-i.net/boyd/pdf/poc.pdf, accessed on 19 April 2004.

[97] AFPAM 14-118, 6.

integration of intelligence and operations, and therefore involves all stakeholders in the command decision-cycle.[98] IPB conducted in isolation will lead to ignorance of us and the adversary.

CT IPB has joint and service doctrine as its pedigree. The grandfather, Army Field Manual (FM) 34-130, *Intelligence Preparation of the Battlefield*, has been amended by the services and expanded in Joint Doctrine. While all variations have doctrinal similarities, and even involve similar TTPs and products, they are tailored to deal with their unique mission and mediums. The Air Force, however, asserts a more functional orientation as opposed to the geographical focus of the other services.[99] Whether this distinction remains accurate or not, all IPB must now think in terms of effects. That is, IPB must be focused on the effects joint forces can achieve, not just against the adversary directly, but in relation to the battlespace. This establishes an analytic environment that demands net assessment, which in turn invites serious thought about actual and potential asymmetries and their effects. For example, in the case of CT, where penetrating the organizational black box is difficult, accessible environmental effects for the "blue force" should be pursued to generate uncertainty and complexity, thus undermining terrorist group performance. As a further note, Joint Intelligence Preparation of the Battlefield, (JIPB) differs from service IPB in purpose, focus and level of detail.[100] JIPB focuses on the overall battlespace and adversary (terrorist organization) rather than on the mission or domain-specific interests of the Services.

Four Phases

IPB supports the decision cycle in four continuous phases: (1) defining the battlespace; (2) describing the battlespace's effects; (3) evaluating the adversary; and (4) determining adversary COA. The phases restated as objectives are shown in Figure 16. Phases one and two look outside the organization to salient environmental dynamics, while phases three and four seek to pierce the organizational black box of the adversary to uncover sources of strength and vulnerabilities. The first phase bounds the problem by clarifying the "arena of operations" as a func-

---

[98] John W. Bodnar argues the critical role of the "orientation" stage of the OODA Loop in warning analysis in *Warning Analysis for the Information Age: Rethinking the Intelligence Process* (Washington, DC: Center for Strategic Intelligence Research, Joint Military Intelligence College, December 2003).

[99] Quoting from AFDD 2, AFPAM 14-118, AFPAM 14-118, airmen "view the application of force more from a functional plan than geographic standpoint and classify targets by the effect their destruction/denial has on the enemy rather than where the targets are physically located," 9.

[100] Joint Pub 2-01.3, I-3.

tion of mission analysis, environmental dimensions, and knowledge requirements.[101] The output of phase one is analysis and collection focused on the battlespace characteristics most likely to influence the planned mission. Examples might include terrain, weather, demographics and culture. The nature of these influences is the purpose of phase two, where we are charged with figuring out the effects of the battlespace on friendly and adversary capabilities and operations. These effects are either direct or indirect and constraining or enabling, generating a dynamic situation in which comparative advantages can be exploited or lost. Moreover, the degree of complexity and uncertainty in the environment impacts a range of organizational factors, particularly the *orient* and *decide* elements of the adversary decision cycle.

Figure 16. IPB Objectives

Source: Adapted from JIPB by author.

In the absence of a structured IPB process, threat analysis usually begins and ends with phase three—evaluate the adversary. Given the ability of terrorists to blend into open societies or grow undetected in geographic hinterlands, determining strengths and weakness can be daunting. Nonetheless, threat analysis remains vital, and the old equation of "capabilities + intent = threat" still applies. IPB requires us to go beyond an accountant's approach to capabilities. Instead, we seek to uncover centers of gravity (COG), or sources of power, enabled by critical capabilities, which may or may not have critical requirements that equal vulnerabilities. This COG analysis translates description into prescription by pointing toward high-value and high pay-off targets. Finding terrorist COGs offer unique challenges; the present study offers some uniquely suited tools in Chapter 4. An essential aspect of phase three is *reverse IPB*; assessing friendly COGs as a means to understand potential terrorist COA,

[101] Naval Doctrine Publication (NDP) 2, *Intelligence* (Washington, DC: Naval Doctrine Command, no date), 31. Cited hereafter as NDP 2.

protect vulnerabilities, and leverage strengths. Reverse IPB also helps account for probable adversary denial and deceptions activities.[102]

Phase four brings it home with a forecast of adversary action based on what the environment affords, capabilities allow, and intent desires. Terrorist COAs are racked and stacked to identify most likely, unlikely and wildcard scenarios. Furthermore, the full range of COAs is evaluated to determine if any can be exploited to our advantage or influenced by our own deception efforts. A crystal ball is not proffered; however, methods for envisioning a wide range of creative, realistic COA options and assessing their probability are set forth. Phase four takes on the challenge of "predictive analysis" and seeks to help the commander "discern the adversary's probable intent and most likely COA."[103]

The phases and associated goals make up IPB doctrine, whereas their application to CT reflects tailored methods. The present work does not seek to tear down doctrine or discard relevant TTPs. Rather, doctrine is amended for the CT problem, and methods are recommended for accomplishing goals. Where existing methods work, they are retained, and where new ones are needed, they are introduced. As a final note of emphasis, mission analysis is part of every phase as shown in Figure 16. We must keep asking, what are we trying to achieve?

Three Levels

Our three familiar levels—strategic, operational, and tactical—shape the appropriate focus and detail for IPB and ensure time is not wasted. The levels apply to IPB as a whole and to each phase of the process. Focusing here on overall IPB, the strategic level considers a "global theater" and must weigh a broad range of factors, including the character of the international system, economics, culture, media, IT, space and many others. Analysis of the adversary focuses on strategic capabilities and intentions such as motivation, ideology dissemination and appeal, resource dependencies, demographics, forms of warfare, and general strategy. Operational level IPB focuses on a battlespace limited by the functional reach of friendly forces and the adversary, which may be country-specific, regional or transnational. It considers popular support, organizational structure,

---

[102] Per Joint Pub 2-01.3, I-6, the IPB analysis "should analyze the probability that the adversary may engage in 'counter JIPB' by deliberately avoiding the most operationally efficient (and therefore most obvious) COA in order to achieve surprise. Additionally, an adversary may deceive the JIPB analyst regarding the timing of an otherwise 'obvious' COA, through asynchronous attack preparations and by psychologically conditioning the JIPB analyst to accept unusual levels and types of activity as normal."

[103] Joint Pub 2-01.3, I-1.

operational planning, logistics, target selection, stakeholder relationships, training facilities, safe havens, communication assets, media roles, terrain and weather characteristics, and most importantly, COGs with any associated vulnerabilities. At the tactical level, IPB starts to focus on the location of the adversary, anticipated short-term actions, available weapon systems, personalities, usable vehicles, safe houses, local support, and highly specific strengths and weakness. Although COG analysis can be performed at all levels, it is primarily an operational-level function that informs tactical-level action. Even though mission analysis points to an operational level of planning and execution, keeping strategic and tactical level factors in mind is good practice—the worthy adversary does.

Linking Concepts

IPB is married to the intelligence cycle, operational planning, and command decisionmaking. In fact, this tight merging is leading to an evolution in the concept from IPB to what is being termed operational preparation of the battlespace. As an aside, all that is developed here remains relevant to this shift in focus, particularly our heavy operational emphasis. Sticking with IPB, it relates to the first phase of the intelligence cycle, planning and direction, by identifying "facts and assumptions" about the environment and priority intelligence requirements (PIR).[104] By determining PIR and likely COA, it sets up a collection plan—phase two—to close knowledge gaps and monitor indicators of possible COA execution. IPB improves the processing and exploitation phase by providing a "disciplined yet dynamic" structure for managing vast amounts of information and staying focused on relevant factors.[105] In support of the analysis and production phases, IPB fits with the more general goals of CT intelligence analysis as outlined by Mark Kauppi, Director of the CT Training Program at the Defense Intelligence Agency (DIA), in his primer, *Counterterrorism Analysis* 101: (1) improve threat awareness; (2) facilitate the disruption/ destruction of terrorist organizations and their activities; and (3) provide timely warning and accurate forecasting.[106] As a process and set of products, IPB supports dissemination and integration. Even when conditions do not allow for written intelligence estimates, IPB products can communicate judgments in a clear fashion. As a continuous process that constantly seeks to refine conclusions based on mission analysis and changing information, IPB epitomizes the evaluation and feedback phase of the intelligence cycle.

---

[104] Joint Pub 3-07.2, I-9.
[105] Joint Pub 3-07.2, I-10.
[106] *Counterterrorism Analysis 101*, Counterterrorism Training Program, Joint Military Intelligence Training Center, no date.

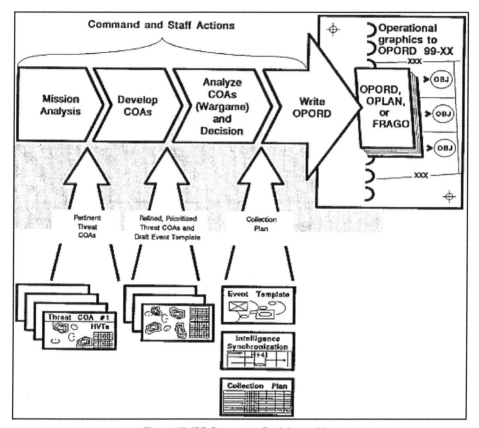

Figure 17. IPB Support to Decisionmaking

Source: US Army Field Manual 34-130, Intelligence Preparation of the Battlefield (Fort Huachuca, AZ: US Army Intelligence Center, 8 July 1994), np, URL: http://www.adtdl.army.mil/ cgi-bin/atdl.dll/fm/34-130/Ch1.htm, accessed 15 April 2004.

IPB support to operational planning and decisionmaking has been explained throughout; however, a more direct vision of the linkages is provided in Figure 17. Though tailored for conventional IPB against a nation-state in terms of products, the general structure of the relations remain in place for CT. IPB is both informed by and informs mission analysis by visualizing the battlespace, distinguishing known from unknown, and establishing "working assumptions regarding how adversary and friendly forces will interact within the constraints of the battlespace environment."[107] Terrorist group COG and COA shape friendly COA development, force selection and disposition, and target selec-

---

[107] Joint Pub 3-07.2, III-2.

tion. Analyzing COA development through wargaming is our typical method for "fighting the COA" to assess likely outcomes of engagements and discover additional opportunities or constraints. It leverages the action-reaction, or net assessment, approach of IPB to determine the optimal friendly COA. IPB support to decisionmaking continues through the *decide* and *act* steps of Boyd's OODA Loop by continuing to evaluate the battlespace and terrorists through additional PIRs and a synchronized collection plan to monitor progress, detect changes in adversary COA, and support further planning. This basic framework is also tailored to meet unique service and joint planning processes, including the Joint Air and Space Operations Plan.[108]

PARTING SHOTS

The terrorist threat is alive and killing. With the rise in religious extremism, the political motivations of terrorist groups are shifting to embrace more systems-shattering goals. Even as goals shift, terrorists continue to embrace the idea of "propaganda by deed," attacking symbolic targets to achieve a psychological impact on an audience. Increasingly, the audience is not just a nation-state, but popular opinion and even a supreme being. Innocents continue to be victims of choice, demonstrating the impotence of government while simultaneously indicting citizens for complicity. Even while states continue to sponsor terrorism, the era of globalization is witnessing the proliferation of non-state terrorist organizations that cross national borders and prey on states. Terrorist groups are adaptive, hybrid adversaries that pose a complex challenge to intelligence and operations.

By structuring this complex threat, IPB enables CT missions against terrorist groups and the environmental conditions in which they prosper. Broadly, CT seeks to defeat, deny, diminish and defend. Framed at the strategic level in national security documents, CT is planned and executed at the operational and tactical levels. Missions range widely, embracing operations typically characterized as Military Operations other than War (MOOTW) as well as direct combat. Importantly, the military finds itself in a vital, non-violent supporting role, shaping regional security relationships, building competent foreign security capabilities, and performing civil-affairs missions. For all mission types, IPB improves command decisionmaking by clarifying the operating environment, understanding the constraints and opportunities presented by the battlespace, assessing the threat in terms of capabilities and vulnerabilities, and forecasting likely courses of action. At the end of the day, the real value of this effort to forge CT IPB will be determined in the streets of Baghdad, the air terminals of the U.S., the jungles of Indonesia, or the wadis of the Sahel.

---

[108] For a thorough explanation of IPB integration with the Joint Air and Space Operations Plan and the Air Operations Center, see AFPAM 14-118, Chapter 6.

CHAPTER 2

TERROR'S SPACE

A *jihadist* rap video titled "Dirty Kaffir [Unbeliever]" is posted to the Internet by a London-based group, a thick jungle canopy cloaks an underground cocaine laboratory guarded by female guerrillas in southern Colombia, and boys and girls as young as twelve are abducted or sold into the ranks of Tamil rebels in Sri Lanka.[109] These images reflect characteristics of the modern CT battlespace, which is marked by an unprecedented degree of complexity and diversity. On one hand, the revolution in information technology enables a global recruiting campaign by religious extremists, while on the other, persistent socio-eco-

Figure 18. Colombian Jungles

Colombia employs an ongoing aerial eradication program involving turbo-thrush aircraft and ultra glyphosate (Roundup) herbicide to destroy coca crops.

Source: CIA, *Coca Fact Paper*, URL: http://www.cia.gov/ saynotodrugs/cocaine_o.html, accessed 24 April 2004.

nomic deprivation and failures in governance expand the recruiting pool. Single-country groups access transnational networks, and groups with global reach penetrate the dense physical terrain of mega-cities where governments fear to tread. It is

---

[109] I received a copy of the video via email on 4 February 2004, and I was able to confirm its posting by the head of the *Committee for the Defence of Legitimate Rights in Saudi Arabia*, a Saudi Arabian opposition group, Mohammed al-Massari. One of many articles on the video, including an interview with al-Massari, is by Antony Barnett, "Islamic Rappers Message of Terror," *The Guardian*, 8 February 2004, URL: http://www.guardian.co.uk/saudi/story/ 0,11599,1143646,00.html, accessed on 25 April 2004. According to BBC reporter Jeremy McDermott, up to 30% of the FARC is female. See, "Colombia's Female Fighting Force," *BBC News*, 4 January 2002, URL: http:// news.bbc.co.uk/2/hi/ americas/1742217.stm, accessed on 25 April 2004. For a short overview of the use of child soldiers by a the LTTE terrorist group, see Frances Harrison, "Analysis: Sri Lanka's Child Soldiers," *BBC News*, 31 January 2003, URL: http://news.bbc.co.uk/2/hi/south_asia/ 2713035.stm, accessed on 25 April 2004.

in this demanding environment, buffeted by the forces of globalization and extremism, that we perform IPB and execute CT missions.

Observing the battlespace and orienting on its salient features is the first phase of the IPB process. The objective of phase one—define the battlespace—is simple to state, but demanding to achieve. When successfully conducted, IPB yields a bounded problem focused on environmental factors that are most likely to influence the CT mission, whether it is to eliminate drug production facilities in the Colombian jungles or extend governance into the remote areas of urban sprawl in Karachi. As in subsequent chapters, we begin by examining current IPB doctrine and outlining its objectives and core concepts, including mission analysis, areas of operation and interest, battlespace dimensions, and collection priorities. Attention is next turned to achieving the phase's objectives and applying enduring IPB concepts to the CT battlespace. The "CT arena" presents unique challenges for delineating the battlespace and capturing its varied dimensions, necessitating the modification of current methods, introduction of new ones, and a general shift in emphasis toward the social dimension. Specifically, a multi-level framework for figuring out the contested battlespace and its mission-relevant characteristics is provided. It links the mission levels—strategic, operational and tactical—to nested battlespace levels, and stresses the increased importance of clarifying stakeholders and analyzing non-traditional features of the environment. To the abiding question of, "What are we trying to achieve?" this chapter adds—"What out there matters most?"

LOST IN SPACE

The first phase of IPB—define the battlespace—scopes the problem, focuses analysis, and shapes collection. It does this by looking out the window, beyond the organization, to the world around. It seeks to identify what is out there that can influence decisions and actions; what factors do we need to weigh in order to make good choices. Once these factors, or characteristics, are spotted, phase two seeks to explain how they will impact the performance of the joint force and terrorist groups. By the end of phase one, for example, we will recognize that weather, terrain, soldiering skills, local attitudes, and other factors will impact a six-month foreign internal defense mission; however, it is not until we complete phase two that we grasp how these factors impact mission success. Before determining constraints and opportunities afforded by the battlespace, we must first scan the environment and inventory the array of consequential variables—doing so is an enduring IPB requirement.

In this section, steps for defining the battlespace are discussed in turn. Joint and service doctrine is culled to determine the core concepts and methods that remain relevant to CT IPB. Where current thinking lacks consistency, divergences are highlighted and a common approach is recommended. Where current thinking proves valuable, it is championed and incorporated into the body of concepts and methods for CT. For example, the six general steps for phase one are retained in full, and existing guidance for analyzing the mission, managing time and resources, and closing knowledge gaps remains valid with only minor adjustments. The crux of phase one is mapping the battlespace and defining its main features. Contemporary thinking gets us underway, but modifications in terms of emphasis, concepts, and methods are needed as addressed here.

At first, the dizzying array of variables in the environment may seem overwhelming. Theoretically, the environment is everything outside the boundary of the organization; in our case, the joint or coalition force. Clearly, we are neither capable of sizing up the world, nor is every flap of a butterfly's wings salient to our mission. IPB helps us avoid drowning in a flood of information through a multi-step process. When successfully applied, the result is an entire IPB process centered on the aspects of the battlespace most likely to influence command decisions and COA implementation. Though ordered differently with slightly divergent terminology in joint and service doctrine, there is general agreement on these fundamental steps:

1) Analyze the mission;

2) Determine detail required and feasible in time available;

3) Identity limits of the battlespace;

4) Identify significant characteristics of the battlespace;

5) Evaluate existing databases and identify knowledge gaps; and

6) Act on intelligence requirements.[110]

Mission Analysis II

Mission analysis kicks off phase one and sticks with us through the end of phase four. Initial inquiry should seek to determine objectives and commander's intent appropriate to the mission level. The mission is most often defined at the

---

[110] To highlight contrasts within existing doctrine, Joint Pub 2-01.3 starts with "identify the limits of the joint force operational area," II-3, while AFPAM 14-118 begins with "mission analysis," 12. Field Manual 34-130, *Intelligence Preparation of the Battlefield* (Fort Huachuca, AZ: US Army Intelligence Center, 8 July 1994), np, URL: http://www.adtdl.army.mil/ cgi-bin/atdl.dll/fm/34-130/ toc.htm, accessed on 25 April 2004, hereafter cited as FM 34-130, begins with "identify significant characteristics of the environment."

operational level and guided by strategic-level national military strategy. A hypothetical CT example might be to deter an emergent ethnic separatist group in Bosnia Herzegovina from using violence, including terrorism. The coalition commander intends to support non-military efforts to influence the group's decisionmaking by strengthening security forces, disrupting illegal shipments of explosives, and supporting psychological operations that offer an alternative story to that preached by the group's leadership. Further clarification of the mission is likely to depend on the initial results of IPB, necessitating on-going cooperation between intelligence and operations staff. As planning progresses, analysis must go beyond objectives and intent to gain increased mission fidelity, including time available, roles for joint and coalition partners, operational constraints, and risks.[111] As the Bosnia scenario unfolds, additional intelligence of specific terrorism planning accelerates operational timelines, roles for North Atlantic Treaty Organization (NATO) partners are incorporated, and higher-level command authorities insist that operations involve Bosnian forces. As in this brief example, mission "adjustments" shape IPB, which in turn shapes the mission.

Getting it Done

Investing time and effort into mission analysis saves time and effort later. In this vein, step two is more about leadership than it is about analysis. Whereas strategic level IPB normally involves timelines extending into months and years, operational IPB occurs over days and weeks, while tactical IPB consumes only hours or days. Thus, a critical adjunct to mission analysis is an assessment of what can and must be accomplished given the time and resources available. The goal is quality, not quantity, and importantly, quality attached to the right step in the process. Four general options exist when time and resources are at a premium: command requirements, assumptions, pre-mission analysis, and reverse planning. When making trade-offs, the first and most important option is to engage the commander and staff to find out their requirements. Inquire as to the knowledge that is most lacking and what matters most to planning. Such an inquiry zeroes IPB in on the most important phases and the level of detail required. As detail decreases, assumptions increase. Assumptions must be surfaced early and often—an axiom reinforced by Secretary of State Colin Powell when he was Chairman of the Joint Chiefs of Staff, "Tell me what you know...tell me what don't know...tell me what you think...always distinguish which is which."[112] An operational assumption might be that another terrorist group will stay on the sidelines, or that elements of the local population will welcome a mil-

---

[111] JP 2-01.3, II-4.
[112] Quotation cited in AFPAM 14-118, 13.

itary presence. These assumptions and others have significant operational impact and strategic consequence, and they should be based on initial analysis of alternatives that is not refuted by available evidence (see Chapter 5 for application of the alternative competing hypothesis method). A third option for saving time is starting early. Intelligence professionals can draw on existing plans (OPLANs and CONPLANs), foreign terrorist organization (FTO) lists, and command guidance to start pre-mission IPB before an execute order is received.[113] The fourth option recognized throughout doctrine is to "plan backwards from the time when the information is required to determine the amount of time available for executing each step."[114] If all the steps cannot be completed in full, focus on the steps where the fog and operational needs are greatest.

Setting Limits

Step three is tough in part because it presupposes we know where the enemy is and will be. Unless we declare the world as our battlespace and judge every characteristic to be relevant, which would render IPB meaningless, we are stuck with the need to place limits. IPB doctrine offers three limited "areas" within the battlespace: area of operations (AO), operational area (OA), and area of interest (AI). The definitions for these are neither totally clear nor consistent in doctrine. Nonetheless, we can discern some general guidance from current doctrine that will serve us well on the CT front.

The battlespace is not the same as the environment. The environment consists of everything outside the boundary of the organization, but not everything "out there" is relevant to our CT mission. The concept of *battlespace* narrows the field by focusing on "the environment, factors, and conditions that must be understood to successfully apply combat power, protect the force, or complete the mission."[115] Thus, the battlespace is what is important about everything; determining "what is important" is the difficult task of IPB. It is a conceptual cut at what needs to be weighed when analyzing and selecting courses of action. It is a dynamic view, changing in relation to operational requirements, adversary actions, force availability, and other factors. It contracts and expands "in relation to the commander's ability to acquire and engage the enemy."[116] Given the complexity of CT, particularly in terms of diverse missions and threat

---

[113] The U.S. State Department maintains a current FTO list with listing criteria at URL: http://www.state.gov/s/ct/rls/fs/2003/12389.htm.

[114] AFPAM 14-118, 13.

[115] Joint Pub 1-02, under "Battlespace."

[116] Quoted from Field Manual 101-5-1/MCRP 5-2A, *Operational Terms and Graphics* (Washington, DC: Department of the Army and U.S. Marine Corps, 30 September 1997) in Medby, 16.

adaptability, shifts in battlespace contours are regular occurrences, if not a continuous quality. This dynamism demands a rejection of the linear thinking associated with the outmoded "battlefield." Think of the battlespace as the non-linear offspring of the battlefield, taking in areas of the operating environment beyond the physical surface of the planet to include air, space, cyber, and more recently, social dimensions. In turn, each of these dimensions must be considered across the levels of analysis and action—strategic, operational, tactical—and over time. Constructing the battlespace without factoring in time, available or required, is done at great peril.

Whereas the battlespace is a *mental construct of relevant factors over time*, the area of operations (AO) is an assigned space. It is typically defined by a higher headquarters and specified in the unified command plan (UCP), OPLANs, CON-PLANs, or operations orders (OPORD). The UCP, for example, carves the world into regional areas of responsibility as shown in Figure 19, which are often further broken down into AOs. The AO is a "geographical area, including the airspace above, usually defined by lateral, forward and rear boundaries, assigned to a commander...in which he has responsibility and the authority to conduct military operations."[117] An example is the assignment of responsibility to JTF-HoA for CT missions in the Horn of Africa area defined as "the total airspace and land areas of Kenya, Somalia, Sudan, Eritrea, Djibouti, Yemen, and Ethiopia and the coastal waters of the Red Sea, Gulf of Aden, and Indian Ocean."[118] Joint doctrine and Air Force doctrine, however, refer to an operational area (OA), which includes the geographically constrained AO plus the air, space and information areas through which coalition forces will operate.[119] OA embraces the idea of functional reach, or operational position of the joint force and the adversary. Given increased reliance on reach-back capabilities physically located in the U.S., the global reach of air, space and Special Forces assets, and the relevance of cyber capabilities, CT IPB is better served by the OA concept. Think of it as *where we operate with authority*. As a final note, assigning the AO and mapping the OA depends on IPB since they are a function of where the adversary is and will operate. Since terrorists are not normally assigned a geographic area, but

---

[117] FM 101-5-1, 1-10, in Medby, 14.

[118] CJTF-HoA Fact Sheet, CJTF-HoA Background, 19 March 2004, URL: http://www.cjtf-hoa.centcom.mil/factsheet.asp, accessed on 27 April 2004.

[119] AFPAM 14-118, 13 and Joint Pub 2-01.3, II-3.

rather stake one out, the OA concept also works better for visualizing where the enemy might be and where we want to be.

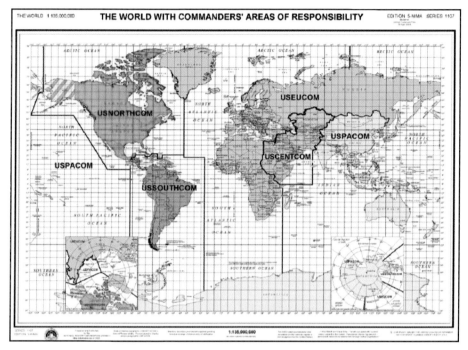

Figure 19. Unified Command Plan

Assigned areas of responsibility for five regional unified commands.

Source: DOD, URL: http://www.defenselink.mil/specials/ unifiedcommand/images/ areaof_responsibility.jpg, accessed 22 April 2004.

The *area of interest* is a second arena within the battlespace. Unlike AO/OA, there is generally concurrence in joint and service doctrine that the AOI is the "area of concern" to the commander,

including the area of influence, area adjacent thereto, and extending into adversary territory to the objectives of current or planned operations... An AOI is usually larger than an operational area, and encompasses areas from which the adversary or potential third parties can affect current or future friendly operations.[120]

Figure 20. Yemeni Special Forces

Yemeni Special Operations Forces practice maritime-based CT techniques learned from U. S. Marines.

Source: CJTF-HoA Official Photos, URL: http://www.cjtfhoa.centcom.mil/gallery.asp?photoid=1950202162003, accessed 24 April 2004.

Although referred to as a geographic area, it is more broadly the area "from which information and intelligence are required to permit planning or successful conduct of the command's operation."[121] It is limited by the adversary's ability to project power, the influence of third parties, the time expected to carry out the operation, and other factors that can be expected to impact the mission. Returning to the Horn of Africa, JTF-HoA's AOI most likely includes the Arabian Peninsula, and may extend geographically into Northern African or the Levant. Given the long-term mission of combating terrorism in the area, the AOI should also include transnational trade networks extending into Asia, the cyberspace where terrorists exchange information, and the cultural space where attitudes are formed. The OA is where we achieve direct effects, but the AOI is where indirect effects on our mission originate.

As highlighted in the AO vice OA discussion, the relationship between these constructs is not entirely clear in current doctrine. For example, Army FM 34-130 suggests "a command's battlespace generally includes all or most of the AO, as

---

[120] Joint Pub 2-01.3, II-5.
[121] FM 34-130, Chapter 2, 6.

well as areas outside the AO."[122] Any attempt to visualize relationships here in an operationally meaningful way is likely to cause brain lock. A RAND Corporation analysis seeks clarity based on cause and effect: the AOI influences the AO, which influences the battlespace. That is, the AOI consists of all "elements beyond the AO that might influence the mission in it," while the "battlespace is composed of the areas (or personnel) that are affected by ongoing operations within the AO.[123] Posing it as questions, the AO asks, where will I operate? The AOI asks, what can impact me outside the AO?[124] The battlespace asks "what will be impacted by me?" While helpful, it is still linear thinking: AOI => AO => Battlespace. Successful CT demands non-linear thinking and an appreciation for the feedback relationships inherent in these artificial "limits."

Going Three-Dimensional

Once the space we are dealing with is limited by OA and AOI, the next step is to identify its salient characteristics. In phase one, we are developing an inventory of characteristics that are of possible "significance or relevance to the commander's mission."[125] Each characteristic is evaluated in more detail during phase two to determine its effect on the COA available to friendly forces and potential adversaries. The importance of a characteristic is certain to vary over time as a function of mission, adversary behaviors, joint force capabilities, resource availability, and much more. Organizing the vast array of potential characteristics is the primary challenge of phase one and the focus of modifications to current IPB made in the next section.

As it stands, joint and service doctrine implores us to begin by considering all possible threat forces followed by incorporating a host of other factors into several dimensional buckets. Regarding threat forces, naming the adversary is easy when dealing with other nation-states (Soviet Union, North Korea, Iraq, etcetera), but it is far more complicated when non-state actors, including terrorist groups and NGOs, are added to the equation. In the case of CT, the adversary is most often a specified FTO, such as Hezbollah or Hamas, but in reality additional adversarial actors, attitudes and ideas are in the mix. Naming the enemy becomes more difficult as we move from tactical to strategic. At the time of this writing, there remains considerable debate over the adversary in the GWOT; is it terrorism, religious extremism, al-Qaida as movement, al-Qaida as corporation, al-Qaida as network, al-Qaida as pan-insurgency, al-Qaida as

---

[122] FM 34-130, Chapter 2, 5
[123] Medby, 15, 48.
[124] AFPAM 14-118, 19
[125] AFPAM 14-118, 17.

"evil" incarnate, or all the above? Some of this difficulty can be ameliorated through stakeholder analysis (introduced in the next section), but such ambiguity will always be present for CT.

The concept of *dimension* is used to carve up the battlespace into manageable chunks. Where terrain and weather features once dominated, today's multi-faceted missions demand consideration of surface, air, space, information and social dimensions. Service doctrine carves these up differently; however, the core dimensions of physical, information and social come across throughout. The physical dimension includes the geography of terrain, air, space, and weather. The information dimension consists of information, information systems, and information functions; it is "any medium adversary or friendly elements could use to transfer, defend or attack information."[126] The social dimension is the most diverse and difficult to assess, and yet it is the most critical to CT. Joint and Air Force doctrine refer to it as the human dimension, but since we are really talking about characteristics of groups of people and relationships among people, the term "social" is more apt. Regardless of the label, this dimension includes "militarily significant sociological, cultural, demographic and psychological characteristics of the friendly and adversary populace and leadership."[127]

What we Know and Don't Know

In these last two steps, we establish what we know and don't know. The former requires mining existing databases, exploiting available sources (classified reporting and databases as well as open sources), and communicating with accessible experts to determine the "state of our knowledge."[128] This can be a time-consuming process, suggesting the need for pre-mission homework, a ready inventory of known resources, a short list of experts, and access to the appropriate information systems. As a word of caution, we must avoid becoming bogged down here, searching for a 100% solution when a workable, 80% solution is needed. When time is constrained, elevate assumptions and pursue collection against knowledge gaps through the establishment of PIRs and collection operations.

REMODELING SPACE

This first phase of IPB deals with the dynamic nature of the CT battlespace by framing it in a way that ensures we capture its mission-relevant features.

---

[126] AFPAM 14-118, 17.

[127] Joint Pub 2-01.3, II-37.

[128] See forthcoming Joint Military Intelligence College (JMIC) book on exploiting open sources by Robert Steele.

Current guidance is concept-rich and method-poor. Among the enduring concepts presented here, the six-step process remains valid. By process completion, we should have a solid grasp on our mission, time and resource constraints for conducting IPB, a conceptual view of the battlespace with associated operational and geographic limits, a rough take on characteristics within each dimensional bucket that can influence the mission, and a plan for closing knowledge gaps. Thus far, the concepts have been modified only slightly, including a shift in terminology to deal with the social character of the battlespace. To improve its applicability to CT, further modifications are necessary. Applying net assessment to CT suggests a need to view the battlespace as a field of interaction, where OA and AOI for joint and adversary organizations are related in terms of operational positions and effects across levels. Moreover, dimensions are just the start. The modest terminology modifications initiated above are extended to further frame and structure the battlespace. Each dimension, for example, consists of several sectors, and all dimensions are nested in our strategic, operational and tactical hierarchy. Characteristics are also mapped against time—history matters and the future counts. Ideally, phase one provides the joint force with a comparative "situational awareness" advantage over the terrorist group, which can be exploited to minimize our uncertainty and maximize his. Building on the enduring concepts and refinements made in the last section, several modifications and new concepts are presented here. Specific recommendations include mapping stakeholders, incorporating dimensional sectors, positioning players, and nesting characteristics.

Mapping Stakeholders

Nailing down the adversary is the necessary first step of IPB overall and phase one specifically. As examined in Chapter 1 and discussed earlier in this section, naming and correctly identifying the terrorist group, particularly when dealing with contemporary Islamist extremist groups, is complicated by rapidly shifting, self-proclaimed group titles, multiple memberships by individual terrorists, and blurred connections between groups, movements and communities. The transnational nature of threat also requires cooperation across nation-states and with inter-governmental organizations like the U.N., European Union, Association of South East Asian Nations, and others. To the mix we will also add roles for private individuals, NGOs, neighborhood associations, religious communities, private security firms, and other violent non-state actors (VNSA). Placing these within a cultural or ideological context, fueled by the rapid dissemination of information, leaves a cauldron of complexity. IPB is charged with getting a fix on this mess, and a good place to start is by mapping out the stakeholders.

Figure 21. Afghan Officials

A corporal assigned to the Parwan Provincial Reconstruction Team talks with school teachers about the repairs needed for some of their classrooms in Gulbahar, Afghanistan, 4 May 2004.

Source: DOD Multimedia, URL: http://www.defenselink.mil/multimedia/, accessed 24 April 2004.

Stakeholders are individuals and organizations with an interest in the outcome of the contest. CT missions play out in a multi-centric world, where power and influence is diffused across actors. Civil-military affairs and psychological affairs missions, for example, are directly influenced by the presence of developmental and relief NGOs like NetAid or Refugees International, and the long-term influence of local leaders, including tribal chiefs, mayors, clerics, priests, shamans, elders, and school teachers (Figure 21). Even direct action missions to take down a sanctuary or capture a leader are likely to occur in a social context, possibly an urban battlespace, where families, businesses and entire communities become involved. As an example, Israel's targeted assassinations of two Hamas leaders in February and April 2004 roused vast street demonstrations, resulted in the deaths of civilians, and destroyed infrastructure. Mapping these diverse stakeholders is a form of social network analysis that results in a picture of the interorganizational network.[129]

The resulting stakeholder picture is a useful reminder that CT missions navigate a complicated terrain of multiple actors with shifting loyalties and varying degrees of influence. It provides initial insight into the relationships the terrorist may draw on to survive in the face of a concentrated CT effort. For example, it is widely held that the Revolutionary Guard of the Iranian armed forces maintains a stakeholder interest in the Hezbollah in Lebanon, providing a range of support services to include money, sanctuary and training. Strings are attached, although their strength remains a matter of dispute. In its 16 February 1985 foundational letter, Hezbollah asserted

---

[129] Mary Jo Hatch, *Organization Theory: Modern, Symbolic and Postmodern Perspectives* (Oxford: Oxford University Press, 1997), 65.

We, the sons of Hizb Allah's nation, whose vanguard God has given victory in Iran and which has established the nucleus of the world's central Islamic state, abide the orders of a single wise and just command currently embodied in the supreme Ayatollah Ruhollah al-Musavi al-Khomeini, the rightly guided imam who combines all the qualities of the total imam.[130]

With the death of al-Khomeini, the rise of more moderate political forces in Iran, and Hezbollah's growth into a dominant social, political, economic and military organization in Lebanon, it can be reasonably argued the Hezbollah no longer takes orders from Tehran. Therefore, the character of this important stakeholder relationship has changed.

In terms of methods for getting at these relationships, the task of phase one is to inventory all possible stakeholders, including, but not limited to those highlighted earlier as well as state sponsors, sanctuary or safe haven providers, individual financiers, charismatic leaders, weapons suppliers, diasporas, corrupt officials or agencies, sympathetic communities, financial institutions and other terrorist groups. As one example, the Tamil rebels in Sri Lanka, the Liberation Tigers of Tamil Eelam (LTTE), are supported by stakeholders among the Tamil Diaspora, including migrant communities, charitable NGOs and front companies.[131] When feasible, specific stakeholders must be identified such as in the case of Shun Sunder. Sunder is a medical practitioner in California who has provided an estimated $4 million to LTTE during the 1990s.[132] Notably, not all stakeholder associations are defined in terms of financial support. In many cases, such as celebrity support for an independent Tibet by the Beastie Boys, the association may provide more publicity than money. With all stakeholders inventoried, the next step is to estimate their potential influence on the mission—this is taken up in Chapters 3 and 4. This type of network analysis is revisited in future chapters as an important method for determining information and resource dependencies and critical capabilities and/or vulnerabilities. Too often, social network analysis only looks at the adversary's relationships, but when mapping the battlespace for CT missions, the entire

---

[130] Cited in *Amal and the Shi'a: Struggle for the Soul of Lebanon*, by Augustus Richard Norton (Austin, TX: University of Texas Press, 1987), 168-169.

[131] The full extent of Diaspora support to the LTTE is superbly detailed in Daniel Byman and others, *Trends in Outside Support for Insurgent Movements* (Santa Monica, CA: RAND Corporation, 2001), 42-55

[132] Byman, 51.

network, including friendly and neutral actors, should be addressed to get at the relational nature of the contest.

Dimensional Sectors

Stakeholders operate within and across the dimensions of the battlespace. The position staked out in the three dimensions—information, physical, and social—is the OA; an ecological niche in the ecosystem we call terror's battlespace. The dimensions are big buckets for organizing the mission-relevant characteristics in the environment. Their relative importance and the uncertainty level of their contents shift depending on the CT mission. Civil-affairs missions weigh the social dimension as more important, but the information and physical ones are not ignored. Direct action to capture an operative in an urban setting requires extra attention to the physical characteristics of the battlespace, for example. This represents a good start, but dimensional buckets are too abstract for the demands made by current IPB guidance, which declares:

> A joint force's battlespace must encompass all characteristics of the environment, factors, and conditions that must be understood to successfully apply combat power, protect the force, or complete the mission. The friendly and adversary use of the electro-magnetic spectrum, the capabilities of both sides to use satellites for communications and intelligence gathering, friendly and adversary information systems capabilities and vulnerabilities, and the perceptions and attitudes of the leadership and population both inside and outside the operational area are examples of non-geographic characteristics that must be considered when determining the full, multi-dimensional spectrum of the joint force's battlespace.[133]

The three dimensions provide orientation and balance, but they fall short of the fidelity required to ensure we observe and orient on all the relevant features. For greater precision and to help get organized, we add the idea of "sectors" nested within dimensions.[134] Think of dimensions as a strategic-level construct and sectors as the operational equivalent. Dimensions frame our work. Sectors fill out the frame by grouping and relating characteristics in sub-categories that we aggregate later to provide a more holistic picture. The reductionist process of breaking

---

[133] Joint Pub 2-01.3, II-6.

[134] Dimensions and sectors have enjoyed prominence in political and organizational theory for many years. In organizational theory, the following sectors are identified: industry, raw materials, human resources, financial resources, markets, technology, economic conditions, government, socio-cultural, and international. See Daft, 137.

down the battlespace is ultimately complemented by an inductive process of linking tactical "facts" to strategic "theories."

Figure 22. Dimensional Sectors

Source: Author.

Devising sectors and their labels is more art than science. Therefore, the sectors identified in Figure 22 are a guide, or rules-of-thumb; open to modification based on the CT mission in question. That said, these sectors do capture the dozens of characteristics highlighted throughout force protection, asymmetric conflict, information operations, MOOTW, and other appendices found in joint and service doctrine. For example, the Force Protection (an AT mission, not CT) attachment to AF doctrine suggests that the following elements, at a minimum, be addressed: geography, terrain, weather, demographics, religious beliefs, political belief, transportation, communication networks, rules of engagement, treaties, crime, environmental hazards, and civil unrest.[135] Moreover, they reflect an appreciation for the complexity of the problem, including the diversity of CT missions, terrorist groups, and environmental dynamics. The intent is not to present the universe of relevant characteristics, but to ensure we are not neglecting any important galaxies. Time allowing, each characteristic is further broken down into four core elements: agents, space, information, and resources. For example, the transshipment of an illegal commodity such as heroin involves specific people, occupying and moving through physical space, transferring information and resources. Getting specific about these four core elements is the real grunt work of IPB in phase one.

The physical dimension is well-developed in current IPB guidance and includes geography, weather, and artifacts. Geography encompasses the land, maritime, air, and space domains as well as hazards and diseases originating in the natural world. The land domain "concentrates on terrain features such as surface materials, ground water, natural obstacles such as bodies of water and mountains, the types and distribution of vegetation, and the configuration of surface drainage" to name a few.[136] The maritime domain is the sea and littoral environ-

---

[135] AFPAM 14-118, 166.

ment, while the air domain reaches from the surface to the atmosphere's edge where space takes over. Rarely will terrorist groups have a space presence; however, it is increasingly common for adversaries to rely on commercial imagery and the telecommunications systems resident in space. Weather refers to conditions in the atmosphere. Finally, artifacts are man-made features: buildings, roads, bridges, harbors, tunnels, airfields.

The information dimension is less developed than the physical, but has nonetheless received considerable attention as cyberspace, cyber security, cyber attack, information operations, computer network attack, information assurance and other "informational" concepts have come to the fore in the national security dialogue. In terms of IPB, Air Force doctrine is the most detailed, breaking the informational domain into the information itself, the technology used to collect, exploit, assess, and disseminate it, and the cognitive style of individuals and groups.[137] "Information" serves as a generic label for a hierarchy of knowledge, beginning with measurements and observations known as data.[138] When data are placed in context, indexed, and organized, they become information, and information turns into knowledge when it is understood and explained. The effective application of knowledge is wisdom.[139] Technology includes the tools used to collect, exploit, and create information and knowledge. IT ranges from computer chips to satellite dishes to cellular phones. In the words of "informational" expert Bruce Berkowitz, "information technology has become so important in defining military power that it overwhelms almost everything else."[140] The "brain" sector refers to the "OOD" of the OODA Loop. The ability of terrorist groups to observe (collect intelligence), orient (develop situational awareness and fix on salient features), and decide is so important to CT that it is discussed in more detail during phase three—evaluate the adversary. For now, it is sufficient to note that phase one requires us to inventory the decisionmakers, which flows from stakeholder analysis, for further psychological evaluation.

The social dimension consists of at least three primary sectors, each placing collection, analysis, and operational demands on the joint force and terrorist group. Demographics, as developed in Chapter 3, usefully characterize the dimension overall. The political sector focuses on the distribution of power in

---

[136] Joint Pub 2-01.3, II-10.

[137] AFPAM 14-118, Attachment 4, "Aerospace Intelligence Preparation of the Battlespace for Information Operations,"130-146.

[138] Edward Waltz, *Knowledge Management in the Intelligence Enterprise* (Boston: Artech House, 2003), 62.

[139] Waltz, 62.

[140] Bruce Berkowitz, *The New Face of War: How War will be Fought in the 21st Century* (New York: The Free Press, 2003), 2.

the system and the rules that govern political interaction. Depending on the mission level, relevant characteristics might include the role of inter-governmental organizations (IGO), international laws and treaties, criminal court jurisdiction, rules of engagement, and failures in governance due to incapacity, illegitimacy or excessive coercion.[141] The form of government, democracy vs. authoritarianism, the extent of civil society, and on-going conflict resolution measures are just a few additional considerations. The economic sector will include the availability of goods and services, market tendencies, rules governing trade, illegal commodities (drugs, guns, humans), unemployment, bank accounts, money laundering schemes, exchange rates, and many more factors related to the trade in goods and services.

The culture sector is the least understood and yet the most important as we deal with today's terrorists. Cultural intelligence is gaining prominence, and intelligence professionals are increasingly called on to understand the sociology and psychology of their opponent. Attempts at "actionable" cultural intelligence often fall short, resulting in interesting histories, customs and folklore. Cultural intelligence deserves more attention and increased study.[142] As operationalized here, cultural intelligence looks at the norms and values that shape individuals, groups, and communities. Breaking it down, "norms make explicit the forms of behavior appropriate for members" of the group being evaluated.[143] To determine if a norm is a property of the group or community in question, the following criteria must be met: 1) there is evidence of beliefs by individual members that certain behaviors are expected; 2) a majority of group members share the belief; and 3) there is general awareness that the norm is supported by most of the group's members, not just the leadership.[144]

---

[141] For a discussion of "failures in governance" as a key to the formation of violent non-state actors, see Troy S. Thomas and Stephen D. Kiser, *Lords of the Silk Route: Violent Non-State Actors in Central Asia*, Occasional Paper 43 (USAF Academy, CO: Institute for National Security Studies, May 2002), 45-47. For further insight into state failure, see Chester Cocker, "Why Failing States Endanger America," *Foreign Affairs*, September-October 2003, 32-45, Donald Snow, *Uncivil Wars: International Security and the New Internal Conflicts* (Boulder, CO: Lynne Rienner Publishers, 1996), and reporting by the State Failure Task Force, University of Maryland, URL: http://www.cidcm.umd.edu/inscr/stfail.

[142] Of note, the USMC has engaged in an on-going cultural intelligence effort through its Center for Emerging Threats and Opportunities at the Marine Corps Warfighting Lab. More information can be found at http://www.ceto.quantico.usmc.mil/projects.asp.

[143] Troy S. Thomas and William D. Casebeer, *Violent Systems: Defeating Terrorists, Insurgents, and Other Non-State Adversaries,* Occasional Paper 52 (USAF Academy, CO: Institute for National Security Studies, March 2004), 32, quoting from Daniel Katz and Robert L. Kahn, *The Social Psychology of Organizations* (New York: John Wiley & Sons, 1978), 385.

[144] Katz, 386.

Collectively, values constitute the group's ideology and provide a more "elaborate and generalized justification both for appropriate behavior and for the activities and functions of the system."[145] Values become norms when they are operationalized by the group members in terms of specific behaviors. Despite a broad range of terrorist group types introduced in Chapter 1, two value systems tend to dominate: transcendental and transactional.[146] Religious extremist, single issue, and ethnic separatist groups embrace a transcendental value system, which places emphasis on morality, sacred duty, the supernatural, and symbolism. Transcendental values are difficult to inculcate, but are more effective in sustaining loyalty. Transnational criminal organizations (TCO) and warlords with private militias epitomize the transactional or pragmatic value system with their emphasis on amassing wealth or power. The transactional value system can be rapidly developed, but it is also more susceptible to disruption and defection in the face of a superior threat or more lucrative alternatives for members. The most effective groups foster a dual-value system, manipulating symbols and delivering tangible value. Dual-value systems have the added advantage of offering reinforcing sources of adaptability; faith can often be sustained even when cash runs short.

Culture emerges from the evolution and propagation of norms and values. Diagnosing culture is exceedingly difficult, but when successful, cultural insight provides answers to practical issues, including: who matters, where are boundaries, why and how does work get accomplished, what are problems, and what is most important to the community or terrorist group.[147] Cultural strength, or the extent to which members share the norms and values, is the community's glue. It is a strong and often overlooked source of cohesion and survivability in social organizations. A terrorist group with a strong culture, such as the IRA or Hezbollah, is more likely to enjoy greater member commitment. An organization with an inflexible or weak culture will have greater difficulty dealing with environmental turbulence.

As characteristics are dumped into sector buckets, three additional aspects must be weighed. First, each characteristic has a history and a future. Time matters. Like my old, run-down Jeep, machines have histories that suggest an optimal life-span. Cultures are the product of a history that can motivate into the future well after a charismatic leader passes—today's event is tomorrow's mythology. Second, every sector serves as a source of information and/or resource to the stakeholders. In phases two and three, the information and resource dependencies

---

[145] Katz, 385.

[146] Katz, 388.

[147] Thomas G. Cummings and Christopher G. Worley, *Organization Development and Change* (Cincinnati, OH: South Western College Publishing, 1997), 480.

of each sector are examined as forms of (1) constraint or opportunity and (2) vulnerability or strength. Therefore, it is important to identify the salient feature of each sector and inventory the information and resources it provides. These buckets have holes, and it is not always clear where to put the info. At this point, we are less concerned with filling the right buckets than we are with ensuring we capture most of the relevant characteristics.

Positioning Players

Dimensions enable us to visualize and map the "terrain" of the battlespace, ensuring we pay appropriate attention to all mission-relevant features. Now, we return to limiting the space in a way that sharpens focus and identifies the footprint of stakeholders on the terrain. Armed with an assessment of the positions for all key players in the battlespace, the commander and staff can start to think in terms of maneuvering in the battlespace to exploit dimensional advantages and maximize adversary constraints.

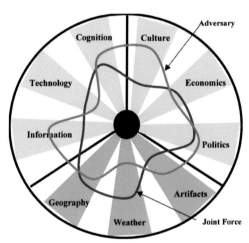

Figure 23. Positioning Players

Source: Author.

A theoretical relative positioning of a terrorist group and the joint force is shown in Figure 23. The "blobs" represent the OA for both. The lines do not necessarily represent a place on a map, but can represent the extent to which sector characteristics affect our CT mission and terrorist goals—this is essentially an initial cut at phase two of IPB. Returning to the JTF-HoA example, geography and weather have more of an impact on American forces than on indigenous groups. Artifacts are limited outside the sprawling urban areas, reducing their impact to both sides. In the social dimension, political factors, particularly failures in governance and the devolution of power to tribal groups, has significant impact, where cultural factors seem to impact terrorists more than the joint force. This last assessment invites debate, revealing the value of this basic positioning method for testing assumptions, visualizing assessments, and generating discussion.

Such "blobology" is also useful for making comparisons and thinking through how the OA might change to improve advantage relative to the adversary. From this perspective, the blobs provide insight to a functional position within the battlespace. The AO is assigned based on geography, but the OA is where we choose to operate. The OA offers greater flexibility and allows us to re-position forces and actions relative to the terrorist group's OA. If the Somali-based *Al-Ittihad al-Islami* (AIAI), for example, is directly impacted by access to information regarding future targets (NGOs, embassies, shipping) using the Internet, the joint force will want to increase its presence and influence within the information dimension. Given the limited IT infrastructure in the region, such dependence may represent vulnerability. On the other hand, AIAI is more likely to rely on human agents rooted in kinship groups for information, which reinforces the need for JTF-HoA to persist in its efforts to build bridges in the culture sector. Taking this tack, interaction exists where the two OAs overlap. When we work in other players, a picture develops of what features are relevant to CT as a function of their impact on these other stakeholders. If a relief NGO is critical to a humanitarian-centered CT mission, and if the NGO is directly affected by infrastructure, such as roads and bridges, the joint force is well served by working with the NGO to overcome this battlespace constraint. Positioning players in the battlespace based on OA is an improvement over existing IPB methods, which highlight the need to consider other stakeholders, but do not expect us to map out their position in relation to ours.

Following the positioning of players, we overlay the AOI and conceptualize the entire battlespace. The AOI is what is "outside" the joint force OA—geographically and functionally—that can affect the mission indirectly. If the terrorist group's OA exists outside the joint forces', then those areas should become part of our operating area as well. The AOI also includes other characteristics of each sector that may be outside both the terrorist and joint force OA, but can still influence the engagement. Identifying these characteristics is made easier by re-introducing time. For an operational mission lasting 30-60 days, changes in the technology sector are unlikely to fall within the AOI whereas a multi-year mission requires continuous evaluation of changes in telecommunications, computing and sensors. There is utility in augmenting current doctrine in two additional ways. First, adding an analysis of the adversary's AOI opens the door to creating additional uncertainty in the battlespace for the terrorist and further assessing relative capabilities. Second, our dynamic view of the environment means the AOI-OA interface is one of mutual feedback and influence. The terrorist group, for example, acts in a way to reinforce conditions that contribute to prosperity—this "systems thinking" approach tracks with the mutual influence experienced by the three levels of analysis and action. The battlespace emerges from the overlapping of the time-constrained AO (geography), OA (operational effects) and AOI (indirect influence) for all relevant stakeholders.

Nested Characteristics

Mission analysis orients us to the appropriate level for performing CT IPB. As argued in Chapter 1, IPB has value at every level. At the strategic level it directs us to broad global trends: the diffusion of power in a multi-centric system; the advancement of technology; and patterns in terrorist group attributes and behaviors. Strategic-level characteristics shape operational-level considerations, including the infrastructure of the physical dimension, the web of social relationships in which the terrorist group is embedded, and the role of information technology in sharing information. In turn, the tactical level is focused on the specific terrain, social groups, and technologies. The levels serve as mental scaffolding, focusing analysis on the right amount of detail and salient dynamics, while also helping us to think in terms of vertical effects. That is, the levels are nested, and analysis and action at one level will influence the same at another. When working at the tactical level, for example, it is important to understand how (1) tactical effects will cascade at the operational and strategic levels and (2) strategic-level trends and operational dynamics will shape tactical options. This modification to current IPB thinking helps us understand reinforcing influences across levels. With the inclusion of nested levels, the battlespace picture becomes more like a hologram than a painting. The joint force and terrorist group, along with other stakeholders, are positioned in relation to each other in the (1) dimensions, (2) over time, and (3) across levels. Another way to conceptualize nesting in relation to dimensions and player positions is shown in Figure 24. Ideally, the joint force will achieve influence on all levels while isolating the adversary to the tactical level.

Urban Battlespace

The urban battlespace offers an important final example of nested levels of characteristics as they relate to dimensions. Although terrorists inhabit the entire landscape of the physical dimension, the urban space, and its associated features in the information and social dimensions, is certain to be dominant terrain for CT.[148] The following

---

[148] The detailed example of the urban battlespace is adopted and updated from a previous article that is particularly relevant to both the concept of nested levels and the dominant terrain of CT. An abbreviated version of the article is available, Troy Thomas, "Slumlords: Aerospace Power in Urban Fights," *Aerospace Power Journal* (Spring 2002), 57-68. See also *The City's Many Faces*, ed. Russell W. Glenn (Santa Monica, CA: RAND Corporation, 2000), and Alan Vick, *Aerospace Operations in Urban Environments: Exploring New Concepts* (Arlington, VA: RAND Corporation, 2000).

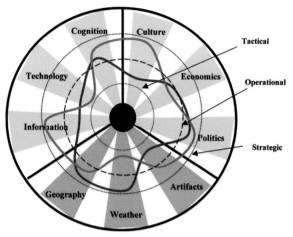

Figure 24. Mapping Levels

Source: Author.

example links the nested strategic and operational level dynamics to the three battlespace dimensions as an example of how IPB for CT missions in urban terrain might proceed.

Strategic Urbanization

Urbanization is the relevant strategic-level trend. In the industrial and post-industrial era, cities have become the center for economic growth. As of 2003, 74.5% of the populations of advanced countries lived in urban areas.[149] While developed countries can handle urbanization, trends in developing countries are threatening government capacities. According to the UN Population Division (UNPD):

> Population growth will be particularly rapid in the urban areas of less developed regions, averaging 2.3 per cent per year during 2000-2030. Migration from rural to urban areas and the transformation of rural settlements into urban places are important determinants of the high urban population growth anticipated in the less developed regions. Almost all the growth of the world's total population between 2000 and 2030 is expected to be absorbed by the urban areas of the less developed regions. By 2017, the number of urban dwellers will equal the number of rural dwellers in the less developed regions.[150]

The social impact is considerable. Unemployment in much of the developing world exceeds 50 percent; subsistence activities or informal jobs make up 75 percent of urban employment in sub-Saharan Africa and 30-50 percent in Latin America.[151] While poverty traditionally exists principally in rural areas, we are

---

[149] UN Population Division (UNPD), *World Urbanization Prospects: the 2003 Revision* (New York: UNPD, 1999), 5.

[150] UNPD, *World*, 5.

[151] According to the 1999 UNPD *World Urbanization Prospects, 3.* Hereafter cited as UNPD, *World 1999*.

witnessing a shift to urban areas that is particularly devastating for women, children and the elderly. According to World Bank estimates, 1.3 billion people survive on less than $1 a day and women die during childbirth at rates up to 100 times that of the developed world.[152] Rapid urban growth in excess of government capacity results in civil strife, possibly conflict, and certainly humanitarian crises. As a contributor to a failing state, rapid urbanization is a principal causal factor for the dramatic increase in civil war over the past decade. When combined with increasingly nationalistic ethnic separatist groups, the result is a watershed change in the nature of armed conflict and a plentiful harvest for terror's sales force.

WORLD'S LARGEST CITIES (in millions)

2000		2015 (projected)	
1 Tokyo	26.4	1 Tokyo	26.4
2 Mexico City	18.1	2 Bombay	26.1
3 Bombay	18.1	3 Lagos	23.2
4 São Paulo	17.8	4 Dhaka	21.1
5 New York	16.6	5 São Paulo	20.4
6 Lagos	13.4	6 Karachi	19.2
7 Los Angeles	13.1	7 Mexico City	19.2
8 Calcutta	12.9	8 New York	17.4
9 Shanghai	12.9	9 Jakarta	17.3
10 Buenos Aires	12.6	10 Calcutta	17.3
11 Dhaka	12.3	11 Delhi	16.8
12 Karachi	11.8	12 Metro Manila	14.8
13 Delhi	11.7	13 Shanghai	14.6
14 Jakarta	11.0	14 Los Angeles	14.1
15 Osaka	11.0	15 Buenos Aires	14.1

Figure 25. World's Largest Cities

Source: Anne-Marie Lizin, "City-to-City Networking to Fight Poverty," Choices Magazine (UNDP, September 2002), 21.

Potentially more important to CT is the way urbanization is occurring. The most dramatic growth is seen in the "million cities," or those with populations between 1 and 10 million. By 2015, there will be 516 of these cities compared with only 270 in 1990.[153] Because these cities are not among the handful of 10 million plus mega-cities (see Figure 25), they are not always getting priority for limited state resources. Moreover, the growth is not occurring in the city core, but along the fringes, resulting in so-called "unintended" urban slums that are beyond the reach of government services and control. As seen on the periphery of Baku, Casablanca, Aden, Istanbul, or Cairo, this new urban sprawl constitutes its own highly complex battlespace.[154]

Urban areas also have strategic value to terrorists due to their location, symbolism, and power.[155] Cities exist in areas that sustain populations due to the proximity of

---

[152] Charles W. Kegley, Jr., and Eugene R. Wittkopf, *World Politics: Trend and Transformation,* 8th ed. (New York: Bedford/St. Martins, 2000), 126.

[153] UNPD, *World 1999,* 2.

[154] All visited by author in 1994, 1995, 2003 or 2004.

resources and lines of communication that are vital for economic prosperity: Istanbul straddles the Bosporus Strait, Tashkent bridges Asia along the ancient Silk Road, Seoul hugs the Han River, Buenos Aires overlooks the Rio de la Plata, and Singapore guards the Strait of Malacca.[156] As hubs for air, land and sea travel, these cities and others are hard to avoid. Cities are symbols that transcend their socio-economic role; such symbolism is derived from the cultural, religious, political, and social factors. Given the link to identity, control often becomes the object of struggle even when the costs are excessive; think of Jerusalem, Najaf, Fallujah, Kandahar, Grozny and even Hue, Vietnam. Insurgents, terrorists and criminals thrive in the symbolically target-rich urban environment. Some of the darkest days of the conflict in Northern Ireland involved the Irish Republican Army (IRA) bombing campaign in London during October 1981.[157] As pointed out in a previous study,

> cities are centers of power. They are often the seat of government, the commercial epicenter, the industrial backbone, and the information hub for states, regions and even non-state actors. Their control brings ready access to resources, technologies, information, and the population.[158]

Operational Space

The trends in urbanization highlight the changing character of a principal CT battlespace. Given the complexity and instability in many monster cities of the developing world, it also creates a highly uncertain battlespace. That said, even the urban battlespace lends itself to operational-level analysis across dimensions. For example, the physical dimension of an urban area consists of five spaces. First, there is the airspace above the ground. Second, there is the super surface space, which consists of structures above the ground that can be used for movement, maneuver, cover and concealment and firing positions.[159] Iraqi insurgents in Fallujah, for example, used minarets to gather intelligence and target U.S. marines. Third, the surface space consists of the exterior areas at the ground level to include streets, alleys, open lots, and parks—the surface space is routinely shattered by car bombings.[160] The fourth space is the subsurface, or subterranean level, consisting of those sub-systems existing below ground to include subways, sewers, utility structures and others.[161] Although

---

[155] Three reasons adapted from an assessment by the DOD Joint Staff, J-8, Dominant Maneuver Assessment Division, "The Role of Urban Areas in Military History," *Handbook for Joint Urban Operations* (Washington, DC: DOD, 17 May 2000), I-5. Cited hereafter as *Joint Urban*.

[156] Joint Publication 3-06, *Doctrine for Joint Urban Operations* (Washington DC: GOP, 16 September 2002), I-4. Cited hereafter as Joint Pub 3-06.

[157] *Joint Urban*, IV-39.

[158] Joint Pub 3-06, I-4.

[159] Joint Pub 3-06, I-4.

[160] Joint Pub 3-06, I-4.

often overlooked, the subsurface space is more often exploitable because these sub-systems exist as part of a city's planned infrastructure; therefore, they have relation-ships that are knowable. A fifth type of space, which brings in the informational dimension, is the telecommunications infrastructure and other means for disseminat-ing information, from sophisticated sensors or wide-eyed children using cellular phones or beating drums.[162] In Mogadishu, communication between clan members was often conducted by the pounding of make-shift drums.

The physical dimension of five spaces can be further modeled using terrain zones. As proffered by the Joint Warfare Analysis Center (JWAC), "Cities are artifacts. Humans design, build, maintain, and alter them—by and to plans. All aspects of the urban terrain—the location, size, and materials making up the physical components are recorded and archived... And that makes cities the most understandable and militarily exploitable..."[163] While this is true for urban areas under government control, it is not always the case in the unin-tended and unregulated slums of the developing world. Although the relation-ships and nodes in these slums are harder to discern, they still exist within the context of a terrain that can be sorted into rough categories that have opera-tional and tactical relevance.

ZONE	DESCRIPTION	CITY AREA
I.	Attached and closely spaced buildings	Core
II.	Widely spaced high-rise office buildings	Core and periphery
III.	Attached houses	Boundary
IV.	Closely spaced industrial/storage buildings	Core and LOCs
V.	Widely spaced apartment buildings	Periphery
VI.	Detached houses	Boundary and periphery
VII.	Widely spaced industrial/storage buildings	Boundary and LOCs

Figure 26. Urban Terrain Zones

Source: Alan and others, *Aerospace Power in Urban Environments: Exploring New Concepts* (Arlington, VA: RAND Corporation, 2000), 74-80.

---

[161] Los Angeles, for example, has over 200 miles of storm sewers, which could readily be used for movement. Marine Corps Combat Development Center, Marine Corps Warfighting Publication (MCWP) 3-35.3, Military Operations on Urbanized Terrain (MOUT) (Washington, DC: Headquarters USMC, 1998), 1-3.

[162] Joint Chiefs of Staff, Joint Publication 3-13, *Joint Doctrine for Information Operations* (Washington, DC: GPO, 9 October 1998), GL-7.

[163] JWAC, *Air Power in MOUT: A JWAC Experiment* (Science Applications International Corpo-ration, CD-ROM, August 1998), Slide 4.

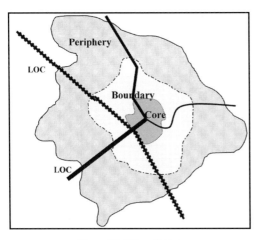

Figure 27. Urban Space

Source: Troy Thomas, "Slumlords: Aerospace Power in Urban Fights," *Aerospace Power Journal* (Spring 2002), 62.

"Terrain zones" are a useful frame for assessing the physical structure and its operational impact. One method of distinguishing terrain zones is by function, distinguishing between administrative, industrial, commercial and residential areas.[164] But if we are to stick to a strictly physical characterization at this point and how it might relate to mission execution, it is better to think in terms of height and density. The higher and more densely packed the structures, the more difficult it is to conduct surveillance, provide security, find sanctuaries and weapons caches, and target terrorists. For example, "residential" implies suburban housing developments to most Americans, which suggests a type of order and structural character that is inconsistent with much of the world. Residential in Seoul, South Korea, means high-rise apartment buildings, while residential in Aden, Yemen, means tin and clapboard shantytowns.[165] To our benefit, rigorous research on terrain zones has already been initiated based on the study of fourteen diverse cities and the seven zone types shown in Figure 26.[166]

Each of the zones described here tends to be located in concentric fashion as shown in the simplified graphic of Figure 27. The core is the heart of the city, normally located at the center of the urban area and home to the most important economic, political and social structures—also where the government tends to exert greatest control. The boundary links the core to the periphery, usually consisting of critical lines of communication (LOC) and a mix of industrial, commercial and

---

[164] Functional categorization is used by the USMC in MCWP 3-35.2 and the *Urban Generic Information Requirements Handbook*, Marine Corps Intelligence Activity, December 1998.

[165] Observations based on authors multiple visits to Seoul in 1998/1999 and three-day walking tour of Aden, Yemen, in 1995.

[166] The research was conducted by Dr. Richard Ellefsen, a geography professor at San Jose State University who also worked as a consultant for the Naval Surface Warfare Center and Aberdeen Proving Ground. The data were generated from detailed examination of maps, aerial photography, and visits. Dr Ellefsen picked his cities to reflect diversity in terms of population, geographic location, climate, terrain, port services, political importance, and development process. His research is effectively summarized and critiqued in Vick, 74-80.

residential structures. The periphery extends out from the core, transitioning into the surrounding landscape. The periphery can be an orderly mix of functional areas or an unruly sprawl that exceeds the capacity for governance. An example of operationally-relevant intelligence analysis resulting from a terrain zone break-down is that only 1-3 percent of urban areas are characterized by Zone I and II terrain and that these zones dominate in the developed cities where CT is less likely.[167] In fact, over 60 percent of urban areas consist of Zones V and VI where height and density are not as great, but where complexity and instability increase. Linking this back to trends in urbanization, many cities in the developing world are dualistic, with small modern cores and unintended primitive peripheries. During a recent walk through Casablanca, shanty towns nestled with new buildings in the urban core, suggesting an alternative, integrative trend.

The urban battlespace also has cross-cutting functional features that bring the city to life and serve as social, infor-mation and physical networks for terrorist activity. Among other functions, IPB must consider services, communi-cation, transportation, and utility networks that enable resources to flow throughout the city. The service network consists of government build-ings, universities, diplomatic offices, medical facilities and other activities that provide

Figure 28. Peshawar, Pakistan

Source: Author.

for governance and basic human needs. Roads, subways, waterways, railroads and sea and airports are a few of the elements of the transportation network. The U.S. and its adversaries rely on these links to move forces, weapons and supplies. The Mogadishu International Airport was critical to airlifting and staging supplies and forces during Operation RESTORE HOPE in Somalia. In Seoul, the Han River bridges serve as chokepoints, potentially channeling refugees and forces.[168] The communication network controls the flow of information through the infor-mation dimension. It can be manipulated by the joint force, adversaries and third

---

[167] Vick, 77.

[168] In June 1950, the destruction of the bridges substantially disrupted the momentum of a press-ing North Korean Army. Unfortunately, it also trapped an entire South Korean division in the city core.

parties, affecting the perceptions of noncombatants and combatants alike. The utility network provides energy, water and sanitation. Each network is also critical to the noncombatants who are dependent on utilities for cooking, heat and sanitation.

There are formal and informal variations on each of the functional subsystems that have implications for how military forces are employed—another initial cut at phase two. In the developed cities, functions are characterized by centralized administration, industrial or post-industrial technologies.[169] The Washington, DC Metro, for example, is managed by a large bureaucracy, utilizes advanced computer technologies and consists of a defined network of rail lines and transfer stations. Formal functions are easier to collect against given their common characteristics, the availability of documentation on their operations, and their susceptibility to remote sensor surveillance and reconnaissance. Informal functions are less "knowable" because they exist outside the reach of government. They are characterized by decentralization, often including the absence of any central managing authority. Primitive or adaptive technology dominates, and the network generally consists of patterns of individual or small group activity. Notably, informal functions are more survivable under conditions of turbulence and conflict. The periphery of Peshawar or Karachi, Pakistan, for example, is a seemingly endless sea of urban squalor. Public transportation, power and water are infrequent, trash is piled high in the streets, and lawless sectarian groups fight in the streets.[170] There are no blueprints. Given the subtlety of their informal relationships, direct surveillance and reconnaissance, such as human intelligence (HUMINT), are essential to understand and ultimately exploit the informal side of the battlespace.

---

[169] Thomas, 62.
[170] Based on author's driving and walking tour of Peshawar in 1994.

Figure 29. Sarajevo, Bosnia-Herzegovina

Source: US Army, URL:
http://www.tfeagle.army.mil/Units/Eagle/MWR/mwrweb/
tours/sarajevo/Photos/sarajevo9.jpg, accessed 2 June 2004

At the risk of oversimplification, the social architecture of cities can be divided into three rough types: hierarchal, clan and multicultural.[171] Hierarchical cities are the most familiar. They are characterized by a unified citizenry that live according to agreed rules of interaction.[172] The city consists of chains of command that operate within an accepted legal framework.[173] Most of the cities of North American and Europe qualify, as do many in Asia such as Singapore, Kuala Lumpur and Tokyo. At the opposite end of the spectrum are clan cities that manifest from rapid urban growth and associated impoverishment.[174] Relationships are governed by loyalty and revenge. Restless young men fight over limited resources and control of the government. Clans form and fight, while many citizens simply struggle to survive the crossfire. CT missions in a clan-based urban system will find it difficult to distinguish friend from foe and identify patterns of activity. The examples are many: Kinshasa, Republic of Congo; Dushanbe, Tajikistan; and areas of Lagos, Nigeria. Multi-cultural systems exist between these extremes in which "contending systems of custom and belief, often aggravated by ethnic divisions, struggle for dominance. They are, by their nature, cockpits of struggle."[175] Clan-type interactions can gain momentum and drag the city into brutal violence. Jerusalem is a good example of a multi-cultural city that oscillates between hierarchal order and clan-oriented conflict. Sarajevo is an example of city that descended into a factional hell and is still on the path to recovery.[176]

---

[171] Adapted from the work of Ralph Peters, "The Human Terrain of Urban Operations," *Parameters* (Spring 2000), 4.

[172] Peters, 5.

[173] Peters, 4.

[174] Peters, 8.

[175] Peters, 5.

[176] Visited by the author in February 2004.

PARTING SHOTS

In an era of globalization, the linear approach to describing the battlespace is stuck in the era of disco and domino theory. In this chapter, the goal of phase one—define the battlespace—is achieved by building on existing IPB doctrine and methods. A six-step process is retained, beginning with mission analysis and ending with collecting against knowledge gaps. Important modifications and new methods are made for steps dealing with defining the limits of the battlespace and identifying its salient features. With regard to the former, the enduring concepts of AO, OA, AOI and battlespace are modified to account for multiple players, CT missions, and the relative positioning of stakeholders in the battlespace. In the case of the latter, dimensions are sorted into three main categories of social, physical and information, and further broken down into three sectors each. Dimensions and sectors help organize our effort, ensure balance across dimensions, and provide a landscape on which to position players. Given the many relevant players in CT, mapping stakeholders and characterizing their relationships is an added requirement. Positioning stakeholders in relation to each other across dimensions and levels and in consideration of time horizons offers the most complete visualization of the battlespace possible. Though tough to accomplish in the face of high levels of uncertainty, phase one handles the first "O" of the OODA Loop—observe—and begins work on the second—orient. In doing so, it provides the commander with the best situational awareness possible and sets up the more challenging analysis of battlespace effects in phase two. When successfully performed phase one answers the question, "What out there matters most?"

CHAPTER 3

BATTLESPACE EFFECTS

The global diffusion of information technology allows a bin Laden speech to shape terrorist targeting strategy in Iraq, reconstruction efforts in an Afghanistan village enables access to fresh intelligence on the location of weapons stores, and heavy February rains complicate the monitoring airborne drug trafficking in the Andean region.[177] These simple examples are indicative of the types of effects the battlespace can have on counterterrorism (CT). The joint force and terrorist do not operate in a vacuum, but

Figure 30. Afghan Village

A soldier with the 450th Military Police converses with boys during an Adopt-A-Village Program in Gulbahar, Afghanistan, 4 May 2004.

Source: DOD, URL: http://www.defenselink.mil/multimedia/, accessed 24 April 2004

within an increasingly dynamic arena that affords constraints and opportunities. When confronting transnational networks of terrorist cells, which prosper in the shadows of sovereignty and are fueled by the digitally scattered rhetoric of zealots, the traditional emphasis on geography and weather fails to capture the full spectrum of mission-relevant effects originating from the environment. Rather,

---

[177] An audio-tape attributed to Osama bin Laden surfaced in February 2003 in which the speaker stated, "We have been following anxiously the preparations of the crusaders to conquer the former capital of Islam and steal their wealth and impose a puppet regime that follows its masters in Washington ad Tel Aviv...We also want to clarify that whoever helps America...either if they fight next to them or give them support in any form or shape, even by words, if they help them to kill the Muslims in Iraq, they have to know that they are outside the Islamic nation," and thus subject to punishment. Transcript reprinted in Daniel Benjamin and Steve Simon, *The Age of Sacred Terror: Radical Islam's War Against America* (New York: Random House, 2003), 459-460. According to Lieutenant General David Barno in a February 2004 interview with the BBC, "Where our units interact with the same elders, the same leaders on a regular basis, our intelligence will improve dramatically, and we've seen indications of that in the last two months," including the seizure of weapons caches or stores. Andrew North, "Village Life Benefits US Troops," BBC News On-line, 20 February 2004, URL: http://news.bbc.co.uk/2/hi/south_asia/3507141.stm, accessed on 16 May 2004.

understanding the external influences on CT operations requires analysis of effects that range across the battlespace dimensions. Where the information dimension enables communication and forges perceptions, the social dimension guides behaviors and determines attitudes. When integrated as part of a net assessment, all three dimensions shape the courses of action (COA) available to the joint force, terrorist group, and other stakeholders.

Building on our orientation to salient battlespace features in phase one, intelligence preparation of the battlespace (IPB) continues in phase two by describing the effects these features have on operations. Phase two is essentially a continuation of the "Orient" step in the OODA Loop that bleeds over into the "Decision" step; it clarifies command options. It answers a key question—how do the features of the battlespace impact the ability of the joint force, the terrorist group, and other stakeholders to accomplish their respective objectives? Phase two does not focus on how the adversary will impact the joint force; rather, the important relational dynamics among stakeholder courses of action is central to phase four. That said, a net assessment of how the environment treats all players in relation to each other is performed here.

As before, we begin by examining current IPB doctrine to determine enduring concepts and improve their application to CT. Analysis reveals a rich body of doctrine and tactics, techniques, and procedures (TTP) against a nation-state adversary for the physical dimension, a developing roadmap for the information dimension, and spotty guidance for the increasingly vital social dimension. The first section also fills a gap in current doctrine by fleshing out the concept of "effects," which is at the core of phase two and fundamental to CT IPB as a whole. The second section builds on current doctrine by unveiling concepts and methods for evaluating effects across all sectors and for the battlespace overall. The newly introduced concepts of uncertainty, nesting, affordances, and dependencies are complemented with techniques for evaluating the underdeveloped social dimension. Recommendations and examples of the types of IPB products likely to be useful for CT decisionmaking are sampled throughout. Taken as a whole, this chapter offers the IPB analyst a set of tools whose specific utility will vary by mission, decision requirements, and time available. To the questions of "What are we trying to achieve (mission analysis)?" and "What out there matters most (define the battlespace)," we now add "How does it impact us?"

SPECIAL EFFECTS

The second phase of IPB—describe battlespace effects—molds CT options by painting a clearer picture of what the environment allows. Armed with this understanding, the commander is able to exploit the battlespace to the joint force's advantage. When awareness of opportunities for environmental leverage are integrated with insight into adversary vulnerabilities (phase three), the result is an asymmetric knowledge and capability advantage. Absent good work in phase two, opportunities will be missed, constraints will be misjudged, and the terrorist will obtain unexpected advantages.[178] In this section, joint and service doctrine are again harvested to determine the concepts and methods that remain at the core of CT IPB. Specifically, the enduring concepts of effects and COA are developed, and the basic steps of phase two are introduced: (1) analyze the mission-relevant effects of each dimension and (2) describe the effects on adversary and friendly capabilities and COA.[179]

Figure 31. Night Vision

Combat Controllers from the 20th Special Forces Group use a variety of night vision devices to direct fire from an AC-130U Gunship at the Tonopah Test Range during an exercise.
Source: JFCOM, URL:
http://www.jfcom.mil/newslink/photolib/
mc02/af/0731/0731/0731af1_JPG.html/,
accessed 10 May 2004.

Before tackling doctrine and TTPs, three points must be made. First, phase two presupposes some knowledge of adversary capabilities and plans. This is a good reminder that the IPB process is iterative. In practice, we may only be able to describe general battlespace effects at first, requiring us to revisit phase two after completing our analysis of COA in phase four. At this point, we are dealing in general plans for all players. Examples: provide security for NGO relief work (joint force); publicly protest presence of U.S. military trainers (activist); transfer explosive materials to urban cell (terrorist).

Second, the effects of the battlespace are dynamic, and they will routinely shift as terrorists seek new advantages to counter our latest CT move or due to changes in battlespace conditions. For example, U.S. forces, particularly Special Forces, routinely leverage our lead in night operations, resulting from advantages in night vision and infrared technology. Terrorists and insurgents such as those confronted

---

[178] Per FM 34-130, Chapter 2, the consequences of failing to perform phase two include the commander's failing "to exploit the opportunities that the environment provides," and the opponent's finding and exploiting "opportunities in a manner the command did not anticipate," 9.

[179] Joint Pub 2-01.3, II-9.

during fighting in Fallujah, Iraq in early 2003, countered by exploiting the dense urban infrastructure to avoid exposure to U.S. surveillance. At the strategic level Al-Qaida relied on the global financial network to rapidly move money through wire transfers, credit transactions, and multiple bank accounts; however, increased international cooperation to disrupt terrorism financing—reflecting increasing advantage in the informational domain—forced a shift in strategy emphasis by Al-Qaida financiers to an informal banking system known as *hawala*.[180] By some estimates, the *hawala* system of unregulated, informal remittance transfers delivers $2.5 to $3 billion annually into Pakistan alone.[181]

---

[180] According to terrorism expert Rohan Gunaratna, as of 2003 Al-Qaida's "banking network operates feeder and operational accounts, transfers from the feeder accounts to the operational accounts usually taking place through several bank accounts in order to disguise their true purpose...Al-Qaida also siphons funds from legitimate Islamic charities and NGOs that it infiltrates, while its extensive web of front, cover and sympathetic organizations include businesses ranging from diamond-trading, import-export, manufacturing and transport. Al-Qaida's clandestine penetration of legitimate public and private organizations included one charity that became the unwitting target of such activities and whose board at the time included President Pervais Musharraf of Pakistan." *Inside Al-Qaida: Global Network of Terror* (New York: Colombia University Press, 2002), 62-63; Gunaratna, Associate Professor, Institute of Defence and Strategic Studies, Nanyang Technological University, interview by author, 24 February 2004, Sarajevo, Bosnia Herzegovina, and 19 March 2004, Montreal, Canada.

[181]Gunaratna, 63. According to E. Anthony Wayne, Assistant Secretary for Economic and Business Affairs, the "h*awala* is a system used extensively throughout the world to transfer value outside banking channels and until 9/11, this system was in many jurisdictions completely unregulated, and only minimally so in others. The quantity of funds that flows annually through *hawala*-like channels internationally, though very hard to measure, is very large. Most such funds are believed to be related to the legitimate remittance to families at home of earnings by expatriate workers, many from South Asia, Latin America, and the Philippines, or to the conduct of legitimate trade. As with charities, however, this sector, since it is less transparent than the formal banking sector, has frequently been abused by terrorist financiers and other criminals to move funds in every corner of the world. Along with our Departments of Treasury and Justice partners in the USG, as well as our partners in the anti-terrorist coalition, we have worked to broaden foreign regulatory standards on alternative remittance systems such as *hawala*. Testimony to the House Committee on International Relations, Subcommittee on International Terrorism, Nonproliferation and Human Rights, "International Dimension of Combating the Financing of Terrorism," 26 March 2003, URL: http://www.state.gov/e/eb/rls/rm/2003/19113.htm, accessed 16 May 2004

A third practical consideration, which applies to all IPB phases, is an appreciation for the analytical "pitfalls" commonly associated with attempts to understand any complex phenomena, including effects. Complex problems are often dealt with through simplification strategies known as heuristics, which are helpful, but prone to error. Of these cognitive biases, *mirror-imaging* is our tendency to fill in gaps in our knowledge by "assuming that the other side is likely to act in a certain way because that is how the U.S. would act under similar circumstances."[182] With terrorist groups, mirror-imaging blinds us to unexpected strategies and tactics, such as using commercial airlines as missiles or religious groups forging alliances with secular, criminal organizations. When evaluating COA and terrorist perceptions of the environment, mirror-imaging can be minimized through awareness and creative methods, including red teaming, alternative futures generation, and old-school brainstorming. A second cognitive bias relevant to assessing effects is known as the *fundamental attribution error*, which is a tendency to explain behaviors in terms of individual traits rather than environmental conditions. For example, to explain the absence of a major terrorist attack on the U.S. for over two years after 9/11 as the result of a deliberate choice by Al-Qaida leadership is probably an attribution error. Although we cannot know for certain, it is more likely that changes in the international CT environment (invasion of Afghanistan, international cooperation, new technologies) forced Al-Qaida to shift to a regionally-based strategy where softer targets exist. As argued by judgment expert Max Bazerman and others,

---

[182] In his seminal book, *The Psychology of Intelligence Analysis*, Richards J. Heuer, Jr. argues that "mirror-imaging leads to dangerous assumptions, because people in other cultures do not think the way we do... Failure to understand that others perceive their national interests differently from the way we perceive those interests is a constant source of problems in intelligence analysis... The U.S. perspective on what is in another country's [or terrorist groups] national [or stakeholders] interest is usually irrelevant in intelligence analysis. Judgment must be based on how the other country perceives its national interest. If the analyst cannot gain insight into what the other country is thinking, mirror-imaging may be the only alternative, but analysts should never get caught putting much confidence in that kind of judgment." Center for the Study of Intelligence, Central Intelligence Agency (Washington, DC: GPO, 1999), 70. Also available at URL: http://www.cia.gov/csi/books/19104/art9.html, accessed on 17 May 2004.

It is critical to realize that heuristics provide time-pressured managers and other professionals with a simple way of dealing with a complex world, producing correct or partially correct judgments more often than not. In addition, it may be inevitable that humans will adopt some way of simplifying decisions. The only drawback is that individuals frequently adopt these heuristics without being aware of them. The misapplication of heuristics to inappropriate situations, unfortunately, leads people astray.[183]

Among the many cognitive biases to which analysts routinely fall victim, mirror imaging and the fundamental attribution error are the most relevant to phase two of IPB. They rear their heads in subsequent phases, and thus deserve our continued attention.

Effects

What is an effect? Although existing IPB doctrine asks us to describe effects, it offers no definition of the concept. Fortunately, effects-related thinking is gaining sufficient traction in operational doctrine to get us started. Per the DOD, an effect is "the physical, functional, or psychological outcome, event, or consequence that results from specific military or non-military actions."[184] This definition makes sense when we think from the organization out. That is, the definition works when an effect, such as diminishing the roots causes of terrorism, is the result of joint force actions; of course, this may also be a form of the fundamental attribution error. This line of thinking is the basis for effects-based operations (EBO), which is the

> process for obtaining a desired strategic outcome or "effect" on the enemy, through the synergistic, multiplicative, and cumulative application of the full range of military and nonmilitary capabilities at the tactical, operational, and strategic levels.[185]

---

[183] Max H. Bazerman, *Judgment in Managerial Decision Making* (New York: John Wiley and Sons, Inc., 1994), 7. See also Paul C. Nutt, *Making Tough Decisions: Tactics for Improving Managerial Decision Making* (San Francisco: Josey-Bass Publishers, 1989), and Morgan D. Jones, *The Thinker's Toolkit: Fourteen Skills for Making Smarter Decisions in Business and in Life* (New York: Random House, 1995).

[184] JFCOM Glossary, under "Effects," URL: http://www.jfcom.mil/about/ glossary.htm#E, accessed 14 May 2004.

[185] JFCOM Glossary, under "Effects-based Operations." For an analytical approach, see Paul K. Davis, *Effects-based Operations: A Grand Challenge for the Analytical Community* (Santa Monica, CA: RAND Corporation, 2001).

This definition and the EBO concept fit with our examination of CT IPB thus far with one important exception—IPB requires us to reverse the cause-effect directional arrow. In addition to thinking about how we impact the battlespace, we are asked to figure out how the battlespace affects us. In reality, the relationship between the organization and the environment is open and dynamic. From a systems perspective, the organization is continually exchanging energy and information with the environment; organizational behaviors are shaped by environmental conditions, and the environment is in turn shaped by the organization.[186] The trick for the IPB analyst is to think in both directions all the time. Later in this chapter, several concepts and methods are introduced to characterize the complex relationship between the battlespace and relevant organization.

Thinking in terms of effects begins with a seemingly simple question: Does the battlespace feature identified in phase one have an impact or not? Will persistent sandstorms restrict operating windows, or will local opinion allow intelligence

---

[186] IPB is a form of systems analysis, which has its roots in the General Systems Theory of biologist Ludwig von Bertalanffy, *General Systems Theory* (New York: George Braziller, 1968). As explained by Francis Heylighen, editor of the Principia Cybernetica Project, Bertalanffy and other systems theorists emphasize all systems are "open to, and interact with, their environments, and that they can acquire qualitatively new properties through emergence, resulting in continual evolution. Rather than reducing an entity (the human body) to the properties of its parts or elements (organs or cells), systems theory focuses on the arrangement of and relations between the parts which connect them into a whole (holism). This particular organization determines a system, which is independent of the concrete substance of the elements (particles, cells, transistors, people). Systems analysis, developed independently of systems theory, applies systems principles to aid a decisionmaker with problems of identifying, reconstructing, optimizing, and controlling a system (usually a socio-technical organization), while taking into account multiple objectives, constraints and resources. It aims to specify possible courses of action, together with their risks, costs and benefits." Principia Cybernetica Project, URL: http://pespmc1.vub.ac.be/SYSTHEOR.html, accessed 20 May 2004. The Systems approach informs much of my work and will be applied further as a way to evaluate organizations in phase three of IPB.

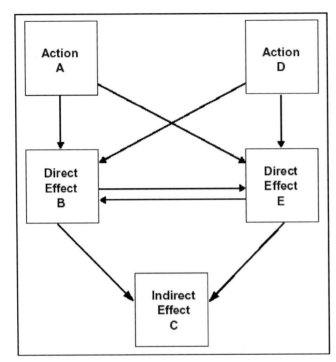

Figure 32. Direct and Indirect Effects

Source: USAF Doctrine Center briefing, "Strategic and Indirect Effects: Defining and Modeling," reprinted in T.W. Beagle, "Effects-Based Targeting: Another Empty Promise," (Maxwell Air Force Base, AL: Air University Press, December 2001), 6.

gathering? Yes or no? Such simplicity is an important start, but it is of limited utility to a commander seeking to understand how the feature will impact operations, whether the effect represents a constraint or opportunity, and how all the effects interact to create comparative advantage or disadvantage relative to the adversary. To get beyond binary answers to a laundry list of factors, we begin by distinguishing between direct and indirect effects.

Direct effects have an immediate, usually recognizable impact in time and space with no intervening effect or mechanism between act and outcome.[187] Conversely, *indirect effects* tend to be delayed in time and space, resulting from an intermediate effect or mechanism to produce the final outcome; they are much more difficult to recognize (Figure 32).[188] Indirect effects are less important for tactical level action, but become increasingly important as we move through the operational to the strategic level. As an example of a direct effect that cannot be discarded during planning, consider the relationship between a group targeted by a psychological operations message and the behavior of an influential religious

---

[187] JFCOM Glossary, under "direct effects."

[188] T.W. Beagle, "Effects-Based Targeting: Another Empty Promise," School of Advanced Airpower Studies thesis (Maxwell Air Force Base, AL: Air University Press, December 2001), 6.

leader in the region. In the sectarian cauldron of violence that is Kaduna, Nigeria, it would be foolish to ignore the relevance of Islamist firebrand, Ibraheem Zakzaky, located farther north in Zaria, who declares, "If we want a million people out on the streets on any issue we can do that."[189]

While Zakzaky may have a direct effect on operational planning, an indirect effect might emanate out of Al-Qaida's support to a local extremist group, such as the *Ja'amutu Tajidmul Islami* (The Movement for Islamic Revival). Effects are a two-way street, impacting friendly forces and the adversary. For example, a direct effect against a terrorist group, such as the Moro Islamic Liberation Front (MILF) in the southern Philippines, is the disruption of training caused by an attack on their jungle camp. The indirect effect of disrupting training is likely to be a decrease in attacks down the road, or even a longer training program with smaller throughput due to increased concealment requirements. According to a MILF field commander, codenamed "Congressman," the destruction of their main camp, Abu Bakr, in 2000 by the Philippine Army has forced them to break up into smaller, more mobile guerilla units and confine leaders to secret locations, combining to make training more difficult.[190] Battlespace features in the operational area are also more likely to have a direct effect than those in the area of interest; in fact, distinguishing between direct and indirect effects helps delineate the battlespace. An initial cut at direct and indirect effects focuses IPB on what must be considered now without blinding us to beyond-the-horizon forces.

---

[189] Dan Isaacs, "Nigeria's Firebrand Muslim Leaders," BBC News, 1 October 2001, URL: http://news.bbc.co.uk/2/hi/africa/1573491.stm, accessed on 27 April 2004.

[190] Orlando de Guzman, "The Philippines' MILF Rebels," BBC News, 6 May 2003, URL: http://news.bbc.co.uk/2/hi/asia-pacific/3003809.stm, accessed on 27 April 2004.

Figure 33. Nigerian Officers

Nigerian Army officers participate in a Ministry of Defense workshop for Public Affairs Officers, learning the "better we are at keeping the public informed, the more support we can expect from them. Alternatively, the less information we provide, the less support we should expect."

Source: The Embassy of the United State, Nigeria, URL: http://usembassy.state.gov/nigeria, accessed 24 April 2004.

Courses of Action

Once an effect has been classified as direct or indirect, the next task is to determine its specific impact on COA under consideration by the joint force, terrorist group(s) and other stakeholders. A COA is simply a specific plan intended to accomplish the CT mission.[191] If the joint force's CT mission is to disrupt the airborne shipment of drugs in the Andean region, COA might include: (1) selectively deploy security personnel to key airfields used by light aircraft; or (2) use airborne command and control aircraft to monitor and direct intercepts of suspect drug aircraft. If a feature of the environment has an effect on the ability of the joint force or its allies to carry out the COA, then it must be identified and assessed. The sheer volume of potential runway surfaces, for example, has a direct effect on the ability of security services to secure them; whereas a steep rise in the price of aviation fuel may have an indirect effect on the number of flights over time. Determining and describing the specific nature, or quality, of the direct or indirect effect on the COA is the yeoman's work of phase two. That is, answering the questions of WHY and HOW is tougher than dealing with WHAT. Existing methods are highlighted below; however, new

---

[191] DOD offers a more detailed definition: "1. A plan that would accomplish, or is related to, the accomplishment of a mission. 2. The scheme adopted to accomplish a task or mission. It is a product of the Joint Operation Planning and Execution System concept development phase. The supported commander will include a recommended course of action in the commander's estimate. The recommended course of action will include the concept of operations, evaluation of supportability estimates of supporting organizations, and an integrated time-phased data base of combat, combat support, and combat service support forces and sustainment. Refinement of this data base will be contingent on the time available for course of action development. When approved, the course of action becomes the basis for the development of an operation plan or operation order." Joint Pub 1-02, under "Course of Action."

Figure 34. Peru Airstrip

Clandestine airstrips in Peru are usually located in the far eastern areas, where aircraft can depart before the Peruvian air force can catch them. Here, the airstrip at Campanilla is being blocked and dismantled by Peruvian National Police.

Source: William W. Mendel, "Colombia's Threats to Regional Security," *Military Review,* May-June 2001, 16.

concepts and methods are developed in the next section to get us beyond the physical dimension to full-dimensional analysis.

Step-by-Step

Equipped with our new insight into effects and COA, we can get down to work. Joint and service doctrine reflect general consistency on phase two's core steps: (1) analyze the mission-relevant effects of each dimension, and (2) describe the effects on adversary and friendly capabilities and COA. The allocation of effort to each step and degree of detail required "will vary depending on the mission, the general capabilities of both friendly and adversary forces, and the relative significance or importance of each battlespace dimension to the specific military operation being planning."[192] As a rule-of-thumb, missions that anticipate hostile action will require more detail than those occurring in a benign set-

---

[192] Joint Pub 2-01.3, II-9.

ting, such as civil affairs missions to receptive villages or foreign internal defense (FID) training on a secure range. Missions in complex geography, such as the suburbs of Manila, will require more detail than missions in unpopulated and/or less densely vegetated terrain. The operational area demands more work than the area of interest, and a skilled, transnational adversary like Hezbollah requires more effort than a localized, nascent group like the Pattani United Liberation Organization (PULO) of southern Thailand.[193] This last rule-of-thumb warrants a word of caution. We bear the responsibility of avoiding overestimating or underestimating the adversary. While ground truth on adversary capabilities is not possible, success in phase two and for the CT mission overall depends on good work in phase three—evaluate the adversary. As with COA, phase two requires some preliminary work on adversary capabilities; therefore, we continually revisit the initial assessment of battlespace effects based on refined phase three and four work as well as changes in the battlespace itself. The IPB process is feedback-oriented, requiring circular systems thinking rather than habitual linear thinking.

---

[193] Analysts have identified PULO as a possible behind-the-scenes instigator of attacks by Muslim youth against security forces in the southern Thailand provinces of Songkhla, Yala, Pattani. Over 100 of the attackers were killed in the fighting, which Thai Prime Minister Thaksin Shinawatra blames on local gangs involved in smuggling and drug trafficking. Analysts, however, point to the arrest in Thailand of JI operations chief, Hambali, in 2003 and evidence that "many members of Thailand's Islamic groups, especially PULO, were given training by militant organizations in Afghanistan and Pakistan." Kate McGeown, "Who was behind the Thai attacks?" BBC News Online, 30 April 2004, URL: http://news.bbc.co.uk/2/hi/asia-pacific/3670537.stm, accessed on 18 May 2004.

Step One

Capitalizing on our inventory of mission-relevant features identified in phase one, we next analyze them to determine effects on operations. Joint and service doctrine uses three buckets—terrain, weather, "other" factors—that we have realigned into the dimensions and sectors shown in Figure 35, which elevates the importance of social and information factors to better fit CT requirements. In the paragraphs that follow, presently available methods for analyzing effects for these dimensions are introduced with initial commentary on their fit with operations against terrorists. As with all

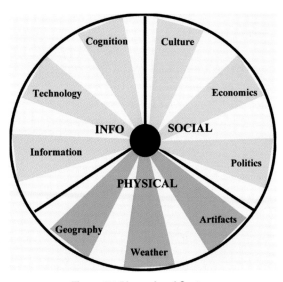

Figure 35. Dimensional Sectors

Source: Author.

recent IPB doctrine, the preponderance of guidance is for combat against a nation-state, relying on conventional forces in non-urban terrain. Finally, it bears repeating, IPB analysis is not an end in itself. Rather, "it is the means to determine which friendly COA can best exploit the opportunities" the battlespace provides and how the battlespace affects the adversary's available COA.[194]

The *physical dimension* includes geography (land, maritime, air and space), weather, and artifacts. As developed in phase one, analysis is directed to those features and their effects that are germane to the mission. The effects of the maritime space are relevant, for example, to JTF-HoA's mission to disrupt the trans-shipment of weapons into Somalia, but they can be filtered out for an unconventional operation against a Taureg supply route in the deserts east of Timbuktu. Joint and service IPB doctrine are robust on this front, offering time-tested methods for the weather and land components of geography and relatively new, but equally useful methods for dealing with the maritime, air and space domains. Artifacts, or man-made structures and infrastructure, are generally factored into these existing methods, which works equally well for CT; however, there is a

---

[194] FM 34-130, 11.

pressing need for the development of methods dealing with terrain where artifacts outweigh natural features, such as urban settings.

The militarily relevant aspects of geography are analyzed using the OCOKA methodology: observation and fields of fire (effects of lethal or non-lethal weapons); concealment and cover; obstacles; key terrain; and avenues of approach. As each is examined in turn, CT requires keeping a diverse array of missions and stakeholders in mind. The OCOKA method was developed by the U.S. Army to deal specifically with the land component, but it has gained credence in the maritime and air domains and has some limited applicability to space. Highlights of weather analysis close out this section after additional considerations for the space, air, and maritime domains are addressed.

Observation and *fields of fire* serve related purposes. Observation is "the ability to see (or be seen by) the adversary either visually or through the use of surveillance devices."[195] A field of fire is "the area that a weapon or group of weapons may effectively cover with fire (effects of lethal or non-lethal weapons) from a given position."[196] Reflecting the combat orientation of current IPB, their evaluation allows us to:

(1) Identify potential engagement areas, or "fire sacks" and "kill zones;"

(2) Identify defensible terrain and specific system or equipment positions; and

(3) Identify where maneuvering forces are most vulnerable to observation and fires.[197]

For direct action CT missions to disrupt or destroy terrorist infrastructure or capture a high value target (HVT), these effects retain their full relevance. Parallels for non-combat CT missions at the tactical and operational level also exist. Observation in particular should be expanded to include the ability of the joint force to monitor activities of NGOs, community leaders, or coalition forces. Where transparency of joint force activities is at a premium, possibly when trying to build trust in a local community, reverse observation analysis is warranted to ensure the desired psychological effect. Determining "engagement areas" is probably the most important for CT. This is where we expect to encounter the terrorist or another key stakeholder. It might include planned distribution points for relief supplies, a front business in a suburb where money is laundered, or a target we expect the terrorist to attack. Both observation and fields of fire deal with vision

---

[195] Joint Pub, 2-01.3, II-10.

[196] FM 34-130, 11.

[197] FM 34-130, 12.

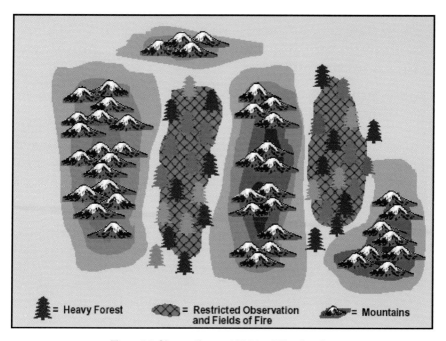

Figure 36. Observation and Fields of Fire Overlay

Source: Joint Pub 2-01.3, 11.

in the battlespace; what we can see or affect without obstruction. Where obstructions to line-of-sight (LOS) observation or direct fires exist, vision is limited and vulnerabilities increase. When combined, the result is a graphic depiction of how the physical features of the OA/AOI restrict vision and fires, as shown for wilderness terrain in Figure 36; similar examples for urban, jungle, desert and other complex terrains are needed.

Concealment and *cover* are the inverse of observation and field of fire. Concealment refers to anything that offers protection from observation, while cover is protection from direct and indirect effects from lethal and non-lethal weapons.[198] Typically, we think in terms of artifacts, such as buildings or tunnels, or natural features like a jungle canopy or glacial crevice. For CT, we must again think more broadly. Consider domestic laws that protect individual terrorists from monitoring or arrest, or front business and charities that mask illegal fundraising, or kinship communities that protect suspected operatives. Real-world examples abound for each, ranging from legal restrictions against wire-tapping to the Pashtun tribal code in western Waziristan that deters Pakistan's Inter-Ser-

---

[198] Joint Pub, 2-01.3, II-11.

vices Intelligence (ISI) from rooting out *jihadists*. Cover and concealment not only pose advantages to the terrorists, but they help the joint force identify avenues of approach, defensible positions, locations for surprise actions, and assembly, staging, or dispersal areas.[199]

Obstacles are at the core of the OCOKA model. Simply, obstacles are any natural and/or manmade obstructions that disrupt, fix, turn, or otherwise shape mobility.[200] Obstacles exist across every sector and dimension and are highly relevant to all CT missions. Among many other examples, land obstacles include artifacts and natural terrain features; air obstacles include balloons, wires, towers, smoke and other obscurants; space obstacles include satellites, meteors, space debris and other sun-related effects (solar winds, radiation); and maritime obstacles include flotsam, reefs, icebergs, harbors, and straits. Moving beyond the physical, the information dimension experiences firewalls, cognitive impairments, and bandwidth obstacles among others, and the social dimension confronts cultural norms, resource scarcities, and political alliances that obstruct a much broader conception of mobility—our ability to navigate a particular aspect of the battlespace. Obstacles are classified as unrestricted, restricted, or severely restricted in terms of their impact on mobility.[201] Their respective consequences are currently geared toward the movement of combat units; however, they have equal utility for movement related to CT missions.

---

[199] FM 34-130, 15.

[200] Joint Pub, 2-01.3, II-11, and FM 34-130, 15.

[201] Unrestricted indicates terrain free of any restriction to movement. Nothing needs to be done to enhance mobility. Restricted terrain hinders movement to some degree. Little effort is needed to enhance mobility but units may have difficulty maintaining preferred speeds, moving in combat formations, or transitioning from one formation to another. Severely restricted terrain severely hinders or slows movement in combat formations unless some effort is made to enhance mobility. This could take the form of committing engineer assets to improving mobility or of deviating from doctrinal tactics, such as moving in columns instead of line formations or at speeds much lower than those preferred. FM 34-130, 17.

Key terrain, when appraised broadly across dimensions, is any locality that "affords a marked advantage" to stakeholders as a result of its control.[202] Critical at all levels, key terrain is evaluated by assessing the impact of its control upon the results of the engagement.[203] Due to its importance, key terrain is often identified as an objective; however, we are cautioned against thinking of physical space as an "end" itself, particularly in the CT arena:

> Key terrain is decisive terrain if it has an extraordinary impact on the mission. Decisive terrain is rare and will not be present in every situation. To designate terrain as decisive is to recognize that the success of the mission depends on seizing or retaining it.[204]

Rather, the control of key terrain facilitates mission accomplishment by providing advantages in surveillance, reconnaissance, mobility, defense, and influence. Key terrain also exists at each of our levels of action and analysis—strategic, operational, and tactical.

Figure 37. Kandahar

Marines on patrol in Afghanistan squeeze their way through the narrow streets of a village south of Kandahar.

Source: USMC, URL:
www.usmc.mil/marinelink/mcn2000.nsf,
accessed 21 May 2004.

By way of an example, the entire country of Afghanistan represented strategic key terrain in the physical dimension in the CT contest with Al-Qaida. Opera-

---

[202] FM 34-130, 18.

[203] Joint and Army doctrine cast this in more conventional, combat-oriented terms: "key terrain is evaluated by assessing the impact of its seizure by either force upon the results of the battle." CT missions, particularly those geared toward mitigating conditions and influencing perceptions, are more likely to control, influence or leverage key terrain than "seize" it. Joint Pub, 2-01.3, II-13.

[204] FM 34-130, 19-20.

tional key terrain included the city of Kandahar and the mountainous caves around Tora Bora. At the tactical level, key terrain included key intersections, dominant buildings, and unobstructed fields of fire near tunnel openings. Parallels exist for the other dimensions, and more importantly, for integrated arenas of the battlespace. Depending on the mission, CT actions directed toward the Wahhabist cleric, Sheikh Salman bin Fahd al-Awda, for example, might have to contend with the key terrain of the mosque in his home city of Buraydah, Saudia Arabia (physical dimension), linked to his actual rhetoric and chokepoints for the distribution of his tapes (information dimension), and to the cultural norms of both his core supporters and the malleable masses (social dimension).[205] The critical point to grasp here is, we must not only think of key terrain for the non-physical dimensions (Internet server, psyche of a specific operative, religious sermon, scarce resource), but we must also think in terms of mobile terrain such as aircraft, trains, ships or even nomadic communities. Key terrain is an enduring concept when more generally applied for the other dimensions.

The final element of OCOKA, *avenue of approach*, is air, space, land or sea routes that lead any of the stakeholders to its objectives. They are most important when the COA under consideration involves the maneuver of forces. Avenues are evaluated by first identifying mobility corridors, which are "areas relatively free of obstacles where a force can capitalize on the principles of mass and speed, but is canalized due to restrictive terrain."[206] Whether a mobility corridor exists, or is free of obstacles, depends on the type of force and mission. For CT missions to seize suspected weapons or contraband hidden beneath the floor of a hut, for example, analysis of possible mobility corridors will consider cover, concealment, and observation. Second, mobility corridors are categorized like obstacles as unrestricted, restricted, or severely restricted. When two or more mobility corridors can be grouped together, an avenue of approach exists. In turn, the overall avenues should be prioritized based on their ability to support the mission and in terms of access to key terrain, degree of canalization, ease of movement, concealment and cover, observation and fields for fire, and directness to the objective.[207] Anti-terrorism missions rely heavily on avenues of approach analysis, particularly in an era when suicide car bombs

---

[205] Al-Awda and Sheikh Safar bin Abd al-Rahman al-Hawali are known as the *dawa*—religious awakening—sheikhs for their fiery rhetoric, which among other proclamations, has "insisted that the government [Saudi Arabia] undertake a broad program of reform to bring Saudi life into accordance with the requirements of *sharia*, which was violated by, among other things, banks that had 'usurious' policies, the unequal distribution of public resources, and a foreign policy that did not advance Islamic concerns." Benjamin, 107-108.

[206] Joint Pub, 2-01.3, II-15.

[207] FM 34-130, 22.

are a primary terror weapon. Likewise, CT missions require the joint force to evaluate avenues for terrorist and stakeholder movement. Importantly, terrorist movements are not limited to actual attacks, but include surveillance, recruiting, financing, and service (medicine, food, education) delivery operations. Finally, the concept of avenues has parallels in cyberspace and social networks.

Figure 38. Noble Eagle

An F-15C Eagle from Langley Air Force Base, VA, flies over Washington during an early morning combat air patrol mission in support of Operation NOBLE EAGLE.

Source: USAF, URL: www.af.mil/photos, accessed 21 May 2004.

We have gone into some detail explaining the OCOKA methodology, which was developed for the land domain, but which applies to the other geographic spaces and to CT missions directly. Still, OCOKA does not address all the effects originating from the maritime, air, and space environments; an evaluation of their "uniqueness" is required. The *maritime space*, for example, affects operations in the open three-dimensional space of the sea and the more constricted areas of the littorals. Among sources of "maritime effects," are chokepoints, natural harbors, ports, sea lines of communication (SLOC), and the "hydrographic and topographic characteristics of the ocean floor and littoral land masses."[208] SLOCs, like the Red Sea passage between Eritrea and Yemen, for example, provide opportunities for land-based observation or attack, constrain mobility, and suggest key terrain for interdicting the movement of terrorists and/or weapons into the Horn of Africa. Closer to the shores of Somalia, characteristics like littoral gradient and composition, coastal infrastructure, levels and locations of commercial fishing, and tides all impact the ability of the terrorist to move secretly, or of the joint force to interdict.

Military operations in the *air space* are even less constricted than those at sea. Nonetheless, air operations are impacted by land and sea characteristics (urban density, mountains, ocean currents). Air Force doctrine recommends a four-step process for assessing air effects: (1) assess air-related operating locations and facilities (targets, airfields, missile launch site, aircraft carriers, anti-aircraft artil-

---

[208] Joint Pub, 2-01.3, II-17.

lery, radars, etcetera); (2) plot weapons systems threat ranges and service ceilings or operating altitudes; (3) incorporate analysis of other dimensions (terrain, weather, air corridors, aviation rules); and (4) synthesize results in graphic displays (step two below).[209] Since the 1950s, air space factored into CT primarily as (1) a medium through which retaliatory strikes were executed (Operation ELDORADO CANYON against Libya in 1989 and the cruise missile strikes in response to the African embassy bombings in 1989), or (2) the result of commercial airline hijackings. Regarding the latter, Bruce Hoffman asserts that the

> advent of what is considered modern, international terrorism occurred on 22 July 1968. On that day three armed Palestinian terrorists, belonging to the Popular Front for the Liberation of Palestine (PFLP), one of the six groups then comprising the Palestine Liberation Organization (PLO), hijacked an Israeli El Al commercial flight en route from Rome to Tel Aviv.[210]

The attacks of 9/11, when civilian airliners were hijacked and converted to fuel-laden missiles, sparked a paradigm shift in both our understanding of the threat and the nature of combating terrorism. Your author and many other intelligence professionals entered uncharted waters when we begin performing IPB to support missions to defend (AT) or intercept (CT) civilian aircraft posing a potential threat. As part of Operation NOBLE EAGLE, intelligence professionals added to the mix of battlespace considerations the effects of Federal Aviation Administration rules, the locations and capacities of commercial airports, and the range of civilian aircraft types. From the terrorist's perspective, air space effects are also critical, particularly given the heavy lifting performed by airborne surveillance and reconnaissance platforms to find, fix and track terrorists, and the precision-strike capabilities of air-delivered weapons.

---

[209] AFPAM 14-118,25-26.
[210] Hoffman, 67.

Figure 39. Statute of Liberty

A 60-centimeter natural color image of the Statue of Liberty collected by QuickBird on 2 August 2002.

Source: DigitalGlobe, URL: www.digitalglobe.com, accessed 21 May 2004.

Because few terrorist organizations control their own space assets, space is underappreciated by intelligence analysis for CT. And yet, not only are space-based systems integral to joint force capabilities, but they are accessible to the terrorist. For example, a well-financed terrorist organization can work through legitimate front companies to purchase commercial satellite imagery (Figure 39). Additionally, terrorists are known to use satellites for communication, although bin Laden stopped using satellite phones in 1997 on suspicion that the National Security Agency (NSA) could track his communications via satellite intercepts and detect his location based on a "voiceprint."[211] For CT IPB, space "begins at the lowest altitude at which a space object can maintain orbit around the earth (approximately 93 miles) and extends upward to approximately 22,300 miles

---

[211] Peter L. Bergen, *Holy War, Inc.: Inside the Secret World of bin Laden* (New York: Free Press, 2001), 229. Also interviewed by the author, 16 January 2004, Washington, DC.

(geosynchronous orbit).[212] Key effects to analyze include orbital mechanics, propagation of electromagnetic energy, orbit density and debris, and solar and geomagnetic activity.[213] Impacts are most likely to be felt on satellite communications, high-frequency operations, radar systems, satellite control and tracking, satellite anomalies, spacecraft charging, satellite disorientation, and manned space flights.[214] A more practical approach for the CT analyst in the field is to assess the operational impact of space access by an adversary, gaps in joint force space-based ISR, and a loss in access to space systems.

Weather's relevance is intuitive and further "official" clarification risks unnecessary complication. At a minimum, it is worth knowing that weather is the "state of the atmosphere regarding wind, temperature, precipitation, moisture, barometric pressure and cloudiness."[215] Weather patterns expressed over many years for a specific region constitute a climate. Weather affects military operations in two ways: (1) it interacts with and modifies the other dimensions of the battlespace, and (2) it can have a "direct effect on military operations regardless of the battlespace dimension."[216] At a minimum, IPB should establish thresholds for understanding when deteriorating conditions in visibility, winds, precipitation, temperature, and cloud cover "can be expected to have favorable, marginal, or unfavorable effects on specific types of operations and equipment."[217] Keep in mind that unfavorable effects for the joint force may prove profitable for the adversary. Sandstorms can grind high-tech U.S. equipment to a halt and restrict ISR operations; however, these same conditions may afford a conditioned group, such as the GSPC in Algeria, cover and concealment. Among other examples used by adversaries, back-lighting can undermine night-vision goggles and unexpected heat sources can throw off infrared sensors.

Information Dimension

The effects of the information dimension cover a wide swath, from human perception to data fusion. Rather than distinguishing between information, technology, and cognition, joint and service doctrine focus on cyberspace, the electromagnetic spectrum, and human factors.[218] The terminology distinctions are less important than understanding how their interplay can affect military oper-

---

[212] Joint Pub, 2-01.3, II-28.

[213] Joint Pub, 2-01.3, II-29.

[214] For the only thorough treatment of IPB for space, see AFPAM 14-118, Attachment 3, 117-129.

[215] Joint Pub, 2-01.3, II-39.

[216] Joint Pub, 2-01.3, II-39.

[217] Joint Pub, 2-01.3, II-41.

[218] Joint Pub, 2-01.3, II-34.

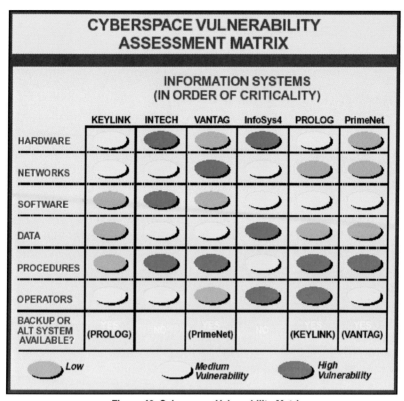

Figure 40. Cyberspace Vulnerability Matrix

Source: Joint Pub 2-01.3, II-38

ations. Not only is information superiority, and now decision dominance, at the core of the joint force's vision and capabilities, but terrorists are increasingly reliant on cyberspace. To date, terrorists have used information, particularly the media, as a force multiplier, extending the reach and impact of its message on target audiences. IT also serves organizational purposes, including coordination, information sharing, and recruiting. Rarer are actual information attacks, although as discussed in the next section, the threat of mass disruption in cyberspace is real enough.

Looking first at cyberspace, which links the three sectors, joint doctrine recognizes the growing importance of integrated hardware, software, networks, data, procedures, and human operators to the joint force and the adversary. Insight into effects springs from an analysis of the information systems on which the joint force, terrorist, and other stakeholders depend to determine how critical they are to performance. The more critical the information system, the more damaging the impact of system failure, data loss, or operator error is to capabilities and COA execution. Crossing system prioritization against vulnerability results in a matrix—shown using notional systems in Figure 40—that can be used to get an initial snapshot of the potential effects of system disruption.[219] The Services contribute less to this discussion in open sources than one might think. Rather than describing informational effects, the Air Force focuses its IO appendix on the effects other dimensions will have on the IO activities of gain, exploit, attack, and defend.[220] Where the information dimension is discussed, we are asked to assess effects by answering the following questions: (1) How does information technology assist or hinder ISR operations; (2) How dependent are they [adversaries] on information systems?[221] These two questions represent the only attempts to get beyond identifying what cyber-capabilities exist and into an analysis of how information systems relate to performance. The absence of well-developed concepts and methods for this aspect of the information dimension does not reflect a lack of progress or effort, but rather the difficulty of figuring out these relationships.

The electromagnetic spectrum relies on technology (radio, radar, laser, electro-optic, and infrared equipment) to emit information. It offers an "operating medium for communications; electro-optic, radar, and infrared imaging; signals intelligence (SIGINT), measurement and signature intelligence (MASINT); and electronic warfare (EW) operations.[222] These operations are not the sole purview of the joint force; terrorists, IGOs, NGOs, and others rely on high frequency radios, radar, listening devices, and radio controls. In one of the most basic, yet ingenious examples of a contest within the electromagnetic spectrum, the Provisional Irish Republican Army (PIRA) pioneered the use of radio controls from model aircraft to detonate bombs from a distance. According to Bruce Hoffman, the British Ministry of Defense developed sophisticated electronic countermeasures and jamming techniques, which the PIRA was able to thwart with a sophisticated network of electronic switches after five years of its own research and development.[223] While evaluating its effects is often beyond the skills of most IPB analysts, communications experts can help figure out how changes in the electromagnetic environment (interference, skip zones, radio

---

[219] Joint Pub, 2-01.3, II-38.

[220] AFPAM 14-118, 130-146.

[221] AFPAM 14-118, 135.

[222] Joint Pub, 2-01.3, II-31.

[223] Bruce Hoffman, "Responding to Terrorism Across the Technological Spectrum," *In Athena's Camp: Preparing for Conflict in the Information Age*, eds. John Arquilla and David Ronfedt (Santa Monica, CA: RAND Corporation, 1997), 354.

dead space, attenuation, or equipment failures) impact the ability of any stakeholder to utilize the medium.

The human mind is at the core of the CT challenge. Not only does terrorism render a psychological wound, but the cognitive abilities, predispositions, and perceptions of all players are critical within the contest of wills. Recognizing this, current doctrine stresses the need to evaluate individual psychology, but leaves little else with which to work. At minimum, the IPB analyst is encouraged to pursue a psychological profile of leaders in terms of biographical data such as family background, education, belief, values, character traits, and decisionmaking style.[224] Ideally, such analysis will yield rare insight into strategy, motivation, or even the holy grail of intelligence work, intention. Organizational-level thinking is essentially ignored, but the importance of public opinions, belief, and values (which cross into the cultural sector) are not. As for group-wide effects, morale and regime loyalty are highlighted as key variables that can impact performance and susceptibility to psychological operations.[225] Although relevant, they are only part of the cognitive sector, which also includes considerations of narrative, rationality, and perception.

Social Dimension

The social dimension serves as a catch-all for what current doctrine calls "other factors," but which is developed only partially. Effects stemming from the political sector span the levels, from alliances to rules of engagement. The economic sector shapes commerce, finances, land use patterns, industry, public services, employment and other characteristics that may provide opportunities or constrain options. Finally, culture affects behavioral norms and worldviews. Collectively demographic analysis might reveal the role of ethnicity, age, religion, income and other population qualities in shaping public opinion, socio-economic development, or the use of violence. From current doctrine we can embrace the "strong emphasis placed on demographic analysis" for MOOTW, which includes CT.[226] Joint doctrine comes closest to giving CT-relevant guidance, proffering the following for effects-based evaluation as applied to special operations or civil-military affairs missions:

---

[224] Joint Pub, 2-01.3, II-37.

[225] Joint Pub, 2-01.3, II-39.

[226] Joint Pub, 2-01.3, V-I.

Figure 41. Destroyed Drug Lab, Colombia

Source: Department. of State, U.S. Embassy Colombia,
URL: usembassy.state.gov/colombia/www.snasc.shtml,
accessed 19 May 2004.

(1) Issues motivating political, economic, social, or military behaviors of groups;

(2) Economic or social programs that could cause desired changes in population behavior;

(3) The goals and strategies of political organizations and special interest groups capable of influencing the mission;

(4) The formal and informal political, economic, and social power structure;

(5) The history and nature of political violence in the country; and

(6) The attitudes, values, and motivations of the civil populace.[227]

While each is a source of effects, this listing is more reflective of phase one analysis than it is of phase two's requirement to explain how attitudes, history, or social conditions shape COA. Nonetheless, it provides a baseline for the modest attempt at improvement later in the chapter.

---

[227] Joint Pub, 2-01.3, IV-8, IV-15.

Step Two

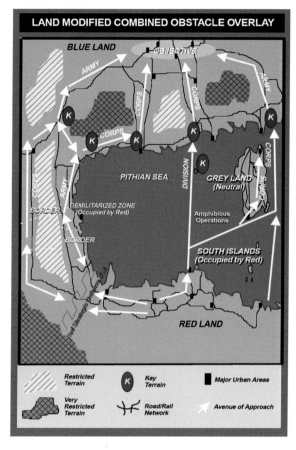

Figure 42. Land MCOO

Source: Joint Pub 2-01.3, II-18

Step two relates effects to specific COA and attempts to communicate them to commanders in an accessible, graphic way that enables good decisionmaking. The current methodology is inductive, building up from each dimension and then integrating for a holistic picture of what the battlespace allows. COA are tested against the integrated battlespace picture to determine how the battlespace will or will not support their execution. Since most sectors will afford both advantages and disadvantages, the challenge is to compare both within each sector and then for the OA and AOI overall. Certain COA suggest their own emphasis. A COA to find and destroy a drug lab in the jungles controlled by the FARC, for example, will require an evaluation of each dimension, although information and social effects are likely to take a back seat to physical effects related to tactical execution. That said, an awareness of the decisionmaking style and values of the adversary cannot be overlooked if combat is likely, capture possible, or political effects are likely to constrain the role of U.S. forces.

The trick for the IPB analysis is to describe the effects of each dimension, and if possible, the overall battlespace on the COA. Many formats are possible; however, graphic depictions are preferred. The most common graphic display is known as the military combined obstacle overlay (MCOO). Figure 42 is a joint doctrine example of land MCCO, which captures the results of an OCOKA

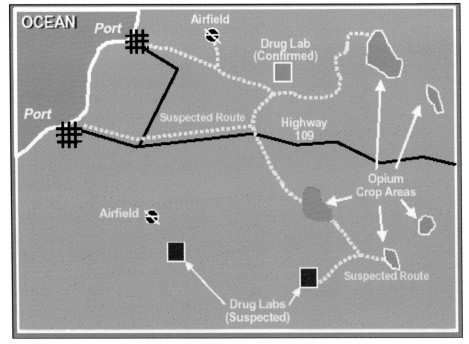

Figure 43. Infrastructure Overlay (Illegal Drugs)

Source: Joint Pub 2-01.3, II-18

assessment for a conventional fight against a nation-state. Figure 43 offers an alternative graphic for counter-drug operations, which is more akin to the type of product suited for CT. Ideally, the infrastructure overlay of Figure 42 is combined with a MCOO. Given the complexity of overlaying effects from multiple sectors, it may be necessary to use sector-only graphics, allowing each to suggest an optimal COA, and reserving an integrated assessment for verbal or written communication. In addition to those shown here, joint doctrine recommends an impressive list of graphics with applicability to CT, including association matrices, event templates, legal status overlays, pattern analysis plot sheets, population status overlays, and time-event charts.[228] Rather than showing each of them here, these and others will be integrated with modifications in the next section and subsequent chapters as appropriate. At the end of the day, the result of step two is a preliminary prioritization of COA for the joint force, terrorist, and key stakeholders based on how well each is supported by the battlespace.[229]

---

[228] Joint Pub, 2-01.3, V-9-27.
[229] Joint Pub, 2-01.3, II-44.

TOTAL EFFECTS

As the last section makes clear, several concepts and methods from existing doctrine are helpful for CT IPB, especially in application to the physical dimension. In this section, additional concepts for an improved methodology are presented to color in the white spaces of the social and information dimensions. The transition from existing doctrine to the new concepts is approached first through the idea of *net effects*. All of the ideas presented here are not valuable all of the time. Net effects of the battlespace, for example, may not be relevant to a particular tactical-level mission; more likely, only one or two of the ideas will prove suitable for the task at hand. As elsewhere in this guide, the ideas presented here should be thought of as a set of tools we can use to solve specific CT problems.

Net Effects

The inverse of the inductive approach sketched above is a deductive method based on a more generalized portrayal of the battlespace. Rather than looking from the organization out, we think from the environment in—Can we describe the overall battlespace in a way that lends insight to probable impacts on all participants? How the joint force or adversary responds to these overall dynamics determines who derives the most advantage. Political and organizational theory offer some useful concepts toward achieving this goal, and here they are applied to assess effects related to *uncertainty, nesting, stakeholders, dependencies,* and *affordances*. All five concepts are of potential use; however, mission and resource availability will drive what can be accomplished in the time allotted. At a minimum, we should seek to get a general fix on how messy the situation is, who the major players are, and what constraints and/or opportunities are presented.

Uncertainty Principle

The CT battlespace is turbulent, creating uncertainty for the joint force and adversary.[230] Uncertainty, commonly attributed to the environment, is actually experienced by decisionmakers. It is akin to the Clausewitzian "fog of war." The denser the fog, the greater the risk of mission failure to all participants. Uncertainty is a more useful concept than its seeming ambiguity suggests. It has specific components, *complexity* and *change*, that are evaluated to characterize the environment and suggest implications for the organizations in it. As one benefit, an initial diagnosis of the degree of uncertainty helps gauge the challenges ahead in terms of workload, information requirements, and extent of assumptions.

---

[230] The seminal work on the turbulent character of the contemporary international system is James N. Rosenau's, *Turbulence in World Politics* (Princeton, NJ: Princeton University Press, 1990).

The degree of uncertainty is influenced by a simple-complex axis (see Figure 44), which "refers to the heterogeneity, or the number and dissimilarity of external elements relevant to an organization's properties."[231] More directly, how cluttered are each of the sectors with things of concern to our COA? As the numbers of relevant features and other organizations (friendly, neutral, or adversarial) in the battlespace increase, so does the complexity. For example, the battlespace in Afghanistan during Operation Enduring Freedom gained complexity as relief NGOs, outside terrorist organizations, such as the Islamic Movement of Uzbekistan (IMU), and additional coalition forces poured in. Moreover, changes in weather, the influence of the heroin trade, refugee flows, and attacks on cultural objects like the Buddhist statutes at Bamiyan, and a host of other variables added to the complexity even before the operation began.

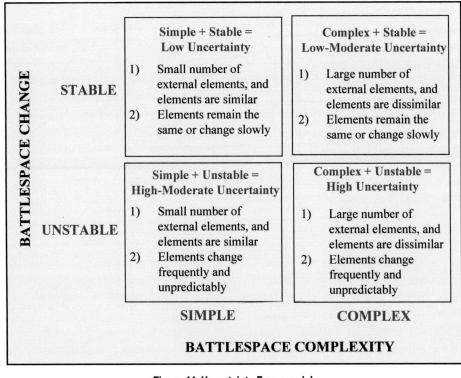

Figure 44. Uncertainty Framework I

Source: Adapted from Robert B. Duncan, "Characteristics of Perceived Environments and Perceived Environmental Uncertainty," *Administrative Science Quarterly* 17 (1972), 313-327.

---

[231] Richard L. Daft, *Organization Theory and Design*, (Mason, OH: South-Western, 2004), 141.

Uncertainty is also influenced by a stable-unstable axis, which refers to whether elements in the environment are dynamic.[232] Are things changing? In a stable battlespace, the mission-relevant features experience little change over time. At the other extreme, the unstable environment is characterized by abruptly changing and shifting features. Instability in Afghanistan was increased by rapidly shifting alliances between tribes, a prison revolt in Mazar-i-sharif, unexpected levels of resistance in the Tora Bora region, and other dynamic features. Figure 44 pulls these two axes together in a way that allows us to quickly size-up the degree of uncertainty faced. CT missions gain uncertainty as timelines, vulnerabilities, hostile interference, stakeholders, and other factors increase. IPB seeks to reduce our uncertainty relative to the terrorist, while CT missions seek to increase adversary uncertainty to undercut performance.

The degree of uncertainty in the battlespace has general effects on decision-making, organization, and COA development. Change and complexity impact decisionmakers by altering their intelligence demands. Meeting shifting requirements consumes resources and energy, and the resulting availability of needed intelligence can enable or hinder decisionmaking. A complex-stable battlespace, for example, can result in information overload. A complex-unstable environment generates an "overwhelming amount of information, but [decisionmakers] will not know which information to attend to due to constantly changing circumstances."[233] To get a clearer picture of whether uncertainty breeds indecision or poor judgment among blue, red or other decisionmakers, this net assessment should be integrated with the psychological profiling of specific decisionmakers if possible. Some commanders and terrorist group leaders are capable of good judgment under uncertainty, but many are not.

Uncertainty also drives organizational structure. Drawing again on systems thinking, the *law of requisite variety* states that

> for one system to deal with another it must be of the same or greater complexity. In organizational terms this means that organizations map perceived environmental complexity with their internal structures and management systems. There is a theoretical limit to this, of course, since if the organization ever realized the full complexity of its environment, it would be that environment.[234]

In CT terms, this means the battlespace will influence the command and control structure and functions of us and our adversaries. A failure to fit one's organiza-

---

[232] Daft, 142.
[233] Hatch, 90.
[234] Hatch, 90.

tion to the environment can result in a lack of adaptability, missed intelligence, and ultimately, decreased performance. Think of it this way: If the Intelligence Community were to fail to build capacity to collect HUMINT or conduct cultural analysis, it would not be adapting to the realities of CT.

What structures result? A stable-simple battlespace fosters a *mechanistic* organization, marked by formalized rules and procedures, clear hierarchy of authority, rigidly defined tasks, centralized planning and decisionmaking, and vertical communication.[235] It is the epitome of the modern bureaucracy, a veritable Kafkaesque castle. The mechanistic organization improves efficiency, but it also reduces the ability to adapt and pursue alternative strategies. Mechanistic organizations are generally rigid and rational, which makes them vulnerable. Where uncertainty reigns, *organic* organizations prove more successful—communication is horizontal, knowledge is diffused, control is lessened, hierarchies are flattened, tasks shift to reflect new demands, and decisionmaking is decentralized.[236] Organic organizations are a better fit for terrorists, often resulting in an asymmetric command and control advantage until nation-states and military forces adapt.

By way of an example, the al Aqsa Martyr's Brigade debuted as a terrorist group on 12 October 2000 during a paramilitary parade in Nablus, Palestinian Territories.[237] According to *Jane's Intelligence Review*, the brigades were "a loose coalition of irregulars, hurriedly trained in basic individual combat and equipped with privately owned small arms. Operatives wore plainclothes and limited their activities to roadside shootings..."[238] During this early phase, their organizational structure was organic; however, efforts to create a formal military organization, establish infrastructure, acquire arms, develop tactical leadership, and attract recruits to their secular version of the Hamas suicide squads made them increasingly mechanistic. Ultimately, a cell-based structure emerged under the senior command of Marwan Barghouti with an intelligence division, military logistics division, special combat teams, suicide bomber volunteer forces, and chapters in at least six West Bank towns.[239] This left the Brigades vulnerable to direct mili-

---

[235] Daft, 149.

[236] Daft, 149. See also Tom Burns and G. M. Stalker, "Mechanistic and Organic Systems," *The Management of Innovation* (Oxford: Oxford University Press, 1994). Reprinted in *Classics of Organization Theory,* eds. Jay M. Shafritz and J. Steven Ott (Fort Worth, TX: Harcourt College Publishers, 2001), 201-205.

[237] David Eshel, "The Rise and Fall of the Al Aqsa Martyrs Brigades," *Jane's Intelligence Review,* 14, No 6 (June 2002): 20.

[238] Eshel, 21.

[239] Chapters included Nablus, Jenin, Tulkarm, Ramallah, Bethlehem and Hebron. Eshel., 23.

tary action, as evidenced by the temporary destruction of their infrastructure and capture of senior leaders during Israeli military operations in April 2002. In the case of the Brigades, the remaining organic aspects of the structure, including a decentralized organization, diffused supplies of arms, and ready access to external resources, including willing martyrs, enabled it to survive.[240] Organic structures can survive uncertainty, while mechanistic organizations find it difficult to navigate such turbulent waters.

Uncertainty also impacts COA development. Planning and forecasting is increasingly important as instability and complexity go up. In a placid environment, organizations are free to focus on current problems and operations—the day-to-day efficiency of garrison training. Turbulence, on the other hand, creates the need for more detailed COA development, increased COA options, improved forecasting of adversary COA (phase four), and the ability to respond quickly. Response speed refers to the ability to execute a COA without delay when the

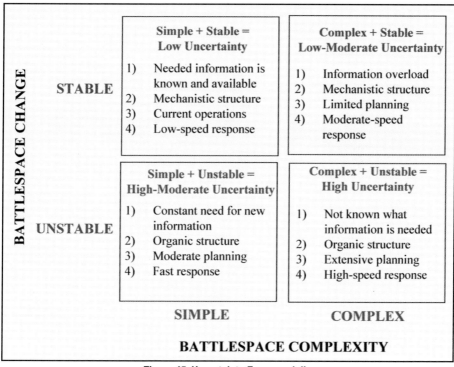

Figure 45. Uncertainty Framework II

Source: Adapted from Richard Daft, 152, and Mary Jo Hatch, 91.

---

[240] Eshel, 22.

battlespace affords optimal advantages. The effects of uncertainty on information requirements, organizational structure, and COA development are summarized as rules-of-thumb in Figure 45.

Figure 46. Friday Mosque, Andijan, Ferghana Valley, Uzbekistan

Source: Author.

Nesting Effects

The idea of vertical effects was introduced in Chapter 2 as a discussion of nested battlespace characteristics using the urbanization example. Likewise, effects cascade across our levels of analysis and action—strategic, operational, and tactical. Conventionally, effects cascade "when they ripple through an enemy target system, often influencing other target systems as well. Typically this can influence nodes that are critical to multiple target systems."[241] These indirect effects do not just influence targets, but they influence all stakeholders and the battlespace itself, usually flowing from the higher to lower levels of conflict; however, tactical-level effects can have strategic consequences—My Lai and Abu Graib.

---

[241]FCOM Glossary, under "cascading effects."

To help understand the cascading influences of nested effects, consider the following brief examples. Within the cultural sector of the social dimension, for example, an operational consideration in targeting a training camp is whether we have insight into the school of Islamic thought embraced by the camp's protectors, which has implications for how prisoners of war (POW) are treated.[242]

This operational-level analysis informs tactical-level evaluation of specific religious and tribal leaders who have a stake in protecting or supporting the camp. The convictions of a specific Islamic school of thought, such as Wahhabism, influence a global trend in the resurgence of a more fundamentalist, or even radical approach to Islam, which in turn forges a global movement of *jihadists* that embolden and support the initial school of thought at the operational level.[243] Globalization is a strategic-level dynamic of the social and information dimension that impacts communication infrastructures among belligerents at the operational level, which shapes the types of specific devices—cell phones, email, courier—used at the tactical level. Trends in developing world socio-economic development, such as increasing disparity between the poor and wealthy or rising infant mortality rates, translate into failures in governance at the operational level, which enables terrorist groups and other criminals to operate with impunity in the

---

[242] Once captured, the Muslim commander has several options, which differ according to the Islamic school of thought (*madhab*) followed by the commander. According to the Shafi'i *madhab*, the commander is allowed four options; execution, enslavement, or release with or without ransom. The Maliki *madhab* does not allow for gratuitous release; that is, without ransom, while the Hanafi madhab forbids release under any condition until the war is terminated. The controversy surrounding the treatment of captives springs from contradictions among *Qur'anic* verses and inconsistent practices by the prophet Mohammad, and points to the need to thoroughly understand the prevailing *madhab* of any potential adversary to discern expected actions. There is general consensus, however, that the commander is not authorized to force the enemy to embrace Islam. Indeed, the POW must be kept alive and ultimately released, unless the Muslim commander follows the Maliki *madhab*. See Troy Thomas, "Prisoners of War in Islam: A Legal Inquiry," *The Muslim World* (January 1997), 47.

[243] Islamic laws regarding international relations, known as *siyar*, have real implications for CT missions against Islamist extremists. There is urgency in understanding, for example, what siyar has to say about a POW, given the frequency of conflicts in which participants invoke jihad, and the continued likelihood of American and allied warriors becoming POWs. The need is further accentuated by the reality of conflict involving groups like al-Qaida, the IMU, or Abu Sayyaf. War with non-state actors exists outside the body of contemporary international law—war is traditionally the circumstance of states, and international law is the law of states. Even if we extended the laws of war to non-state actors like Al-Qaida, they reject the system on which these very laws are predicated. These groups as well as hostile Islamic states, however, are bound by the legal maxims associated with jihad, which entitles their adversaries, including the U.S., to certain expectations of conduct. Armed with this understanding, individual warriors can assert rights even where the jurisdiction of international law ends, and policymakers are better positioned to leverage international opinion against those who violate the same laws they claim to enforce.

state's hinterlands. The not-so-new "idea" here is that our analysis of battlespace effects must move vertically as well as horizontally.

Webs of Influence

Stakeholders were introduced in Chapter 2 as fundamental to CT analysis. They are inventoried in phase one and evaluated in phases three and four. Here, they are related to one other in order to paint a picture of overall influence. Three "influences" are useful, particularly when we start to limit the battlespace by OA and AOI. First, is the stakeholder likely to have a direct or indirect influence on the mission? A direct influence indicates the stakeholder impacts decisions or actions immediately—a religious leader can withhold divine sanction for a terrorist act, or an ally can veto an operation. Indirect influence may degrade performance in the near-term, but is more likely to impact decisions or actions down the road. A regular weapons supplier who backs off the sale of black-market, shoulder-launched surface-to-air missiles will not stop tomorrow's attack on a civilian airliner, but he may be able to undermine future planning.

Second, is the influence likely to be adversarial, friendly or unknown? Of course, these generic labels can mean many things, ranging from active support with intelligence or combat force to passive support by acquiescence to a CT mission in neighboring territory—Russian tolerance of U.S.-supported CT operations in the Pankisi Gorge, Georgia in 2002. More detailed methods for analyz-

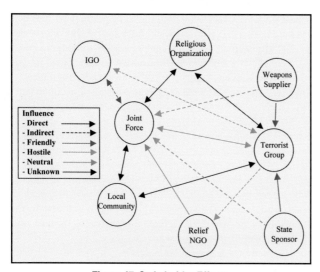

Figure 47. Stakeholder Effects

Source: Author.

106

ing orientation is pursued in phase three. Finally, toward what other stakeholders is the influence likely to be exerted? How we label these characteristics is less important than understanding who the relevant players are beyond the named terrorist group and what impact they are likely to have on the mission. A simplified, conceptual example of stakeholder mapping to reveal the interorganizational network of influences is shown in Figure 47. Of note, this map only shows a few stakeholders and their relationship to the joint force or the terrorist group; a more accurate map will also show relationships among the stakeholders. Furthermore, mapping external relations is probably one of the most difficult tasks in the CT analysis business, so it is important to highlight degree of certainty.[244] The result is a *web of influence* that provides insight into the effects other players are likely to have on COA in terms of assistance, interference, or neutrality. Thus armed, the joint force can seek to exploit alliances, flip or disrupt hostile parties, or persuade the uncommitted. Moreover, it suggests how the terrorist or another stakeholder might respond to one of these moves based on their direct or indirect relationships.

Figure 48. Urban slums, Ferghana, Ferghana Valley, Uzbekistan

Source: Author

Dependencies

A fourth option for thinking about net effects is the concept of dependency. Dependency moves us closer to an organizational perspective, but still offers a general concept for identifying and defining the influences of the battlespace. The idea is that the battlespace is the source of scarce resources that are critical to survival, or less dramatically, COA execution. The concept has its roots in resource dependency theory, which argues in its simplest form that the environment is a powerful constraint on organizations. Thus, resource dependencies must be effectively managed to guarantee the organization's survival and "to secure, if possible, more

---

[244] A RAND Corporation study stresses the difficulty of collecting intelligence on external relations. Bonnie Cordes, Brian M. Jenkins, Konrad Kellen, *A Conceptual Framework for Analyzing Terrorist Groups* (Santa Monica, CA: The RAND Corporation, June 1985).

Figure 49. Toma Suburb, Casablanca

Source: Driss Benjelloun, Urba-Systèmes, interview with the author,
7 May 2004, Rabat, Morocco.

independence and freedom from external constraints."[245] For the purposes of
CT, "resources" is a broad term, encompassing information, money, technology,
divine sanction, allies, skilled operatives, and others.

Dependency is measured in terms of criticality and scarcity. *Critical* resources
are vital to system function. Individuals committed to suicide bombing are a critical resource of Hamas and Islamic Jihad now and the LTTE (Sri Lanka) in the
past. *Scarce* resources are not widely available in the environment, causing
intense competition for them—diamonds and plutonium are scarce, landmines
are not.[246] Unfortunately, willing suicide bombers are also abundant. Resources
that are critical and scarce demand the greatest organizational attention and may
represent a critical vulnerability (more on this in phase three). Critical resources
that are widely available, or scarce resource that are not critical, create less vulnerability, while non-critical, abundant resources do not constrain COA. As we

---

[245] I.M. Jawahar and Gary L. McLaughlin, "Toward a Descriptive Stakeholder Theory: An Organizational Life Cycle Approach," *The Academy of Management Review* 26, no. 3 (July 2001). From
ProQuest.
[246] Hatch, 79-80.

analyze each sector, we should ask whether we or the terrorist group are dependent on any resources whose disruption could undermine COA implementation. For civil-affairs missions, a dependent relationship is likely to exist with community leadership; whereas, the capture of a terrorist cell leader may be dependent on an unobstructed route in and out of the hideout in the labyrinthine suburb slum of Toma, Casablanca.

Affordances

The final "net effect" option builds on our discussion of battlespace positioning in Chapter 2 by capturing an overall assessment of what the battlespace affords. In that discussion, we looked at how blobs can be used to get a sense of the extent to which sector characteristics affect our CT mission and terrorist goals as shown in Figure 50. Regardless of how we choose to display relative positioning for each sector, the key is to size up whether each sector affords advantages (opportunities) or disadvantages (constraints). If, for example, our analysis in phase one suggests the attitudes of the local population will directly impact COA execution in the operating area, phase two assesses whether existing attitudes are favorable (opportunity) or unfavorable (constraint). Figure 50 suggests a mixed bag, with the joint force and the terrorist group enjoying some degree of favorable support with no clear advantage for either. Of course, the challenges associated with collecting accurate intelligence about attitudes and intentions make it difficult to have a high degree of confidence in the results; the goal is a general sense of what each sector and dimension affords as the basis for more targeted intelligence collection and analysis. In this net assessment of opportunities and constraints we must incorporate an appreciation for the inherent limits of human perception. The argument that what we perceive about the battlespace is more important than what it actually presents is rooted in *affordance theory*. The perception theorist James J. Gibson invented the word "affordances" to refer to "the offerings of the environment, roughly the sets of threats (negative affordances) and promises (positive affordances) that characterize items in the environment relative to organisms."[247] That is, we see constraints where none exist, and we fail to recognize opportunity when it knocks. What we think we see is more relevant to the COA we choose than what is really out there. Essentially, it is another cautionary tale against mirror-imaging, reminding us that the terrorists and stakeholders may behave in unexpected ways and charging us to creatively turn obstacles into opportunities.

---

[247] Andrea Scarantino, "Affordances Explained," *Philosophy of Science* 70, no. 5 (December 2003), 950.

Dimensional Effects

In addition to adopting the five general concepts and methods for analyzing net effects, CT IPB should also tend to sector and dimension-specific effects that are not adequately covered in current doctrine. As noted, the OCOKA method is robust and appropriate for CT when modified as discussed. On the information and social fronts, additional work is needed. Therefore, the paragraphs that follow focus on several effects particularly relevant to CT missions in the information dimension, which are then linked to the demographic and cultural effects of the social dimension. Additional effects from the physical dimension are not ignored, but integrated throughout.

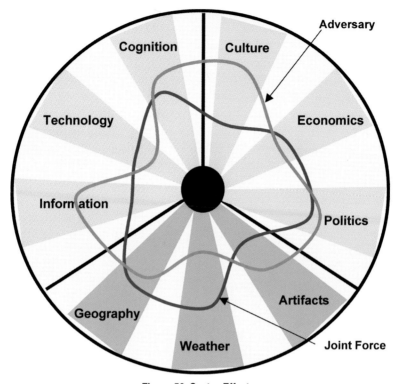

Figure 50. Sector Effects

Source: Author.

Information Effects

Whether dependency and uncertainty exist is a result of the interplay among information, technology, and cognition. In the CT context, information effects warranting further investigation relate to organization, publicity, attacks, and decisionmaking. The information dimension affords opportunities and constraints as a result of the availability and quality of information, the sophistication and reliability of technology, and the limitations of human cognition. We are well aware of the information dependencies for the joint force, but there is also general consensus among terrorism experts that among the various trends in terrorism over the last decade,

[w]hat has been particularly significant has been the logical extension of the profound impact of television and satellite communication through the rapidly developing and expanding use of the Internet and the revolutionary change that characterizes all aspects of computer technology. The terrorists now have at their disposal the medium to disseminate information and increasingly coordinate attacks against a wide range of targets from the relative safety of cyberspace. In addition they will increasingly be able to conduct terrorism against the vulnerable technological infrastructure of industrial and post-industrial societies by targeting critical infrastructure, particularly in reference to computer facilities and networks. Through their actions, they will have the potential to directly and indirectly place large numbers of people in harm's way by degrading an air traffic control network, public health care system, or other complex systems that can profoundly threaten both personal and societal security.[248]

The information dimension is having profound effects on the shape and capabilities of the joint force, and has enabled NGOs, IGOs, terrorists and other stakeholders to extend their reach and increase their effectiveness. Among other *organizational effects*, advances in IT combined with declining costs of processing, are impacting command and control structures. Increasingly, the old hierarchical, cell-based terrorist group is giving way to IT-based networked organizations. According to RAND analysts, many of the newer Islamist extremist groups, such as Hamas, have become more "loosely structured," with activists using chat rooms and email to coordinate activities.[249] IT, and the Internet in particular, enable several other organizational functions, including collecting and sharing information, recruiting, publicizing propaganda, debating agendas, coordinating action, and conducting attacks.[250] Internet-based recruiting is just one powerful example of how IT can dramatically change the nature of terrorism. Terrorist websites routinely post "be all you can be" videos, martyr testimonies, and

---

[248] Stephen Sloan, "The Changing Nature of Terrorism," *The Terrorism Threat and U.S. Government's Response: Operational and Organizational Factors,* eds. James Smith and William Thomas. (US Air Force Academy, CO: USAF Institute for National Security Studies, March 2001), 61-62.

[249] John Arquilla, David Ronfeldt, and Michele Zanini, "Networks, Netwar, and Information-age Terrorism," *Countering the New Terrorism*, eds. Ian O. Lesser and others (Santa Monica, CA: RAND Corporation, 1999), 65.

[250] For a full discussion of each, I recommend Dorthy E. Denning, "Activism, Hacktivism, and Cyberterrorism: The Internet as a Tool for Influencing Foreign Policy," *Networks and Netwars,* eds. John Arquilla and David Ronfeldt (Santa Monica, CA: RAND Corporation, 2001), 239-288. For the overall best discussion of information-age effects, see Gregory J. Rattray, *Strategic Warfare in Cyberspace* (Cambridge, MA: MIT Press, 2001).

interviews.[251] The job of the IPB analyst is to determine the availability of IT, what capabilities it affords, what are its vulnerabilities, and what are the consequences associated with its disruption or failure—and do this for the joint force, terrorist group, and stakeholders having direct influence. If it sounds like hard work replete with "unknowns," it is. At the same time, we must not overestimate the role of IT for organizational purposes. Al-Qaida's famed reliance on satellite phones quickly gave way to an old-school courier service—a reminder that technology is a double-edged sword.

The media establishment is the landlord of the information space. Publicity is central to the violent theater of terrorism, ensuring that *media effects* are part and parcel of CT IPB. There is a natural symbiosis between the terrorist and the media. Terrorist groups exploit media coverage to extend the psychological impact of the act of violence on the target audience. Examples span the history of terrorism, but just during the time of this writing, media coverage of the bombing in Madrid and Riyadh, suicide attacks in Israel and the Palestinian territories, elevated threat levels in U.S., and a video-taped beheading in Iraq have all contributed to increased public anxiety and ensured widest coverage of propaganda by deed. When press coverage is absent, terrorists generate their own through faxes, newspapers, and increasingly, websites. Some of the more popular include www.hizbollah.org, www.palestine-info.net/hamas, and www.alneda.com (a main al-Qaida site).[252] The idea that media coverage provides the terrorist with tactical and operational advantages is supported by terrorism expert Walter Laqueur, who argues that "media coverage has provided constant grist to the terrorist mill; it has magnified the political importance of many terrorist acts out of all proportion."[253] It is not clear, however, whether it always has strategic benefits, as set forth by Hoffman:

---

[251] "Examining the Cyber Capabilities of Islamic Terrorist Groups," presentation by the Technical Analysis Group, Institute for Security Technology Studies, Dartmouth College, November 2003, slide 18. A good example of a bin Laden recruitment video can be found at the Columbia International Affairs On-line website (ciao.net). Cited hereafter as "Cyber Capabilities."

[252] Michele Zanini and Sean J.A. Edwards, "The Networking of Terror in the Information Age," *Networks and Netwars*, 43

[253] Walter Laqueur, *The New Terrorism: Fanaticism and the Arms of Mass Destruction* (New York: Oxford University Press, 1999), 44.

While terrorists certainly crave the attention that the media eagerly provides, the publicity that they receive cuts both ways. On the one hand, terrorists are indeed assured of the notoriety that their actions are designed to achieve; but, on the other, the public attitudes and reaction that they hope to shape by their violent actions are both less predictable and less malleable than either the terrorists or the pundits believe.[254]

Figure 51. Public Affairs

A Combat Camera photographer allows a Somali woman to look through the view finder while documenting the delivery of food to the villagers during Operation Restore Hope.

Source: Joint Pub, 3-61.

In addition to figuring out the impact of the media on terrorist COA, effects on the joint force must also be factored. Key issues to determine overall media effects include reporter access; the media outlet's capacity to communicate locally, regionally or internationally; the likely spin to be put on CT actions; the opportunity to shape the story; and other concerns that shade into public affairs or psychological operations. To be clear,

> psychological operations use specific techniques to influence favorable behavior or beliefs of non-U.S. audiences. In contrast, joint PA [public affairs] operations should not focus on directing or manipulating public actions or opinion. They provide a timely flow of accurate information to both external and internal publics. While they reinforce each other and involve close cooperation and coordination, by law PA and PSYOP [psychological operations] must be separate and distinct.[255]

Strictly on the public affairs side, the media provide advantages for a range of CT missions. A civil-affairs mission to the jungles of the southern Philippines, for example, might leverage media effects to advertise the public benefits of the mission, keep citizens informed of health concerns, and coordinate meetings to increase participation. On the flip side, media presence can undermine surprise,

---

[254] Hoffman, 147.

[255] Joints Chiefs of Staff, Joint Publication 3-61, *Doctrine for Public Affairs in Joint Operations* (Washington, DC: GPO, 14 May 1997), III-18.

expose and fuel terrorist behaviors. The type of media effects desired and realized will depend on the CT mission, but as a general rule for the "hearts and minds" emphasis of CT, the advantages outweigh the risks.

When sophisticated IT is combined with skilled computer technicians, the possibility exists for *cyberterrorism*. There are few pure examples, although the 1998 email bombing against Sri Lankan embassies by the Internet Black Tigers comes closest; the psychological impact of email disruption or server meltdown pales in comparison to the death of innocent people.[256] Evidence suggests terrorist groups do seek cyberterrorism skills, and there is a growing community of hacker groups affiliated with terrorists. The Anti-India Crew, Unix Security Guards, G-Force Pakistan, and the World's Fantabulous Defacers are Islamist hacker groups, apparently trapped in a hip-hop identity crisis, but also committed to defacing Indian and Israeli sites.[257] This may be just the beginning. According to Sheikh Omar Bakri Muhammad, a London-based Islamic cleric with known ties to Osama bin Laden, "in a matter of time you will see attacks on the stock market...I would not be surprised if tomorrow I hear of a big economic collapse because of somebody attacking the main technical systems in big companies."[258] The combination of available technology, skills, and willingness raise the likelihood that cyberterrorism will increasingly be a weapon in the terrorist arsenal. As a corollary, information operations will gain significance within the CT mission, and with it, IPB applications will emerge.

The stress thus far on IT is not meant to diminish the criticality of the brain piece. In fact, the cognitive styles of individuals and groups as well as the attitudes, beliefs and perceptions of other stakeholders, including the public, is probably the most important to CT. Why are people joining Hamas in droves? Why did she become a suicide bomber for Hamas? What are bin Laden and Musab al-Zarqawi planning? Is this community sympathetic to us or to Ansar al-Islam? What are public attitudes toward our presence in Najaf? These are important questions, but very, very difficult to answer. In terms of *cognitive effects*, we should seek answers using HUMINT as we can, but it is more likely that such insight will come from the participants themselves, who give speeches, make martyrdom tapes, give interviews, and participate in public opinion polling. Cognitive inquiry, particularly psychological profiling and opinion analysis, are integral to the analysis of the adversary in phase three. At this point, it is sufficient to note that cognitive effects spring from the individual mind, organiza-

---

[256] Denning, 283.

[257] "Cyber Capabilities," slide 49.

[258] Dan Verton, "Bin Laden Cohort Warns of Cyberattacks," PCWorld On-line, 18 November 2002, URL: http://www.pcworld.com/news/article/0,aid,107052,00.asp, access on 26 May 2004.

tional behaviors, and public attitudes. Cutting across these cognitive domains are several general influences, or factors, that will affect the decisionmaking and perceptions of all stakeholders—bounded rationality, the role of affect, and the importance of narrative.

Cognitive biases have already been introduced as limitations on all decision-making. Our COA must anticipate that other stakeholders will not only suffer from the same biases, but that we must be careful in assuming their actions are the result of a rational calculus. An old idea remains salient here—bounded rationality. Decisionmakers "often lack important information [uncertainty] on the definition of the problem, the relevant criteria," the range of possible outcomes, and other factors.[259] As a result, it is very difficult for us or our adversary to always calculate the optimal choice; instead, we often forego the "best solution in favor of the one that is acceptable or reasonable."[260] Even when we cannot get at the terrorist's calculus, we can appreciate that all stakeholders are affected by limits on ability to choose the best COA. Organizational decisionmaking suffers from the same constraints. There is a lot of room for work on the cognitive front, particularly with regard to how the functioning of the brain affects decisionmaking, and while this research unfolds, the IPB analyst must rely on historical precedent, public statements, and confidential communications to get at the decisionmaking style of the adversary. Getting at public perception is equally difficult, but not impossible. Given its integral relationship with cultural factors, it is picked up in the next section.

Social Effects

The links between terrorism and the sectors of the social dimension are profound. Modern terrorism reflects the cultural influence of religion, the power imbalances of the international system, and the socio-economic conditions of their purported constituents. U.S. counterterrorism, in turn, reflects Western values, the state system, and economic strength among other qualities. For all military operations, but particularly for CT, the range of available COA reflects what this contest affords. The health standards in a local village affect the type of clinic that should be built. Various factors ranging from religious beliefs regarding fasting to norms governing nocturnal habits drive mission timing. Preferences of local leaders impact rules of engagement. Kinship ties open doors to new intelligence. Codes of honor prevent the surrender of a terror suspect. Since it is not possible to address every type of effect in this bucket, the following discussion

---

[259] Bazerman, 5.
[260] Bazerman, 5.

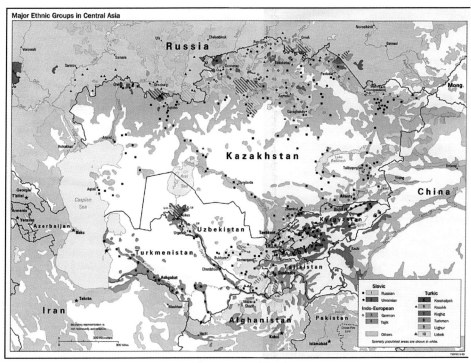

Figure 52. Central Asia Ethnicity, 1993

Source: Perry-Castañeda Library
Map Collection, University of Texas, on-line, URL: http://www.lib.utexas.edu/maps/index.html,
accessed on 25 May 2004.

integrates the cultural, political, and economic features into an analysis of demographic, cultural and perception effects.

Demographic analysis offers a picture of how the population looks on paper based on a host of defining societal characteristics, including religion, ethnicity, language, income levels, type of economic activity, or age. We are most familiar with this type of analysis, which gives us a static picture of population composition as exemplified in the 1993 depiction of ethnic groups in Central Asia just after the collapse of the Soviet Union (Figure 52). The utility of these snapshots is that they offer a graphic representation of the positioning of mission-relevant social features in relation to the physical dimension. Similar types of cross-dimensional mapping can be done in cyberspace. Among other benefits, they highlight possible lines of contention, areas in greatest need of assistance, and a first cut at religious preferences.[261] Of course, this type of analysis must be scalable. Increasingly, precision operations require highly localized, or micro-geographic insight to specific cities, swamps, jungles, mountains and coast lines.[262]

Grasping *demographic effects* requires going beyond the static look by analyzing changes in population composition over time. Central Asia offers a prime example of how such changes can create demographic pressures on communities, ripening individuals for recruitment and fueling terrorist rhetoric. The compositional factor most often associated with demographic pressures in Central Asia is the "youth bulges" (where the population is skewed toward a younger demographic)—most of the developing world is experiencing a similar fate.[263] Assuming net migration is zero, persistent fertility rates above the replacement value of children per family cause the population to expand, while the converse—fertility rates below the replace value—result in a shrinking population. A rapidly increasing population places demands that are beyond the capacity of the local government, reinforcing failures in governance. When high fertility rates are combined with rapidly declining death rates, the result is a population explosion that will persist until the demographic transition is completed by a corresponding decline in fertility.[264] This population explosion has been forestalled in Central Asia due primarily to acute underdevelopment and migration which has kept death rates relatively high. Nonetheless, the relatively high fertility rates and strong growth rates are creating demographic pressures that will be destabilizing soon. These trends can be shown on an overlay that links age to employment to location.

Another approach to understanding how the population looks in practice is cultural intelligence, which "augments demographic analysis by describing how demographic traits and relationships between groups can act, or have already acted, to stabilize or destablize conditions."[265] *Cultural effects* are a function of deep-seated norms and values. With good planning, the IPB analyst should gain

---

[261] Medby, 57.

[262] "Irregular warfare exists in highly specific operational environments, "microclimates," which need to be understood by intelligence analysts, military commanders, and policymakers. This presents several challenges. First, these operational environments consist of a number of elements, including geography, ecology, history, ethnicity, religion, and politics. These are not topics to which the military intelligence community devotes much attention. Second, for irregular warfare, these have to be seen in a detailed and nuanced context. It is specific local geography, history, and politics that are crucial. Arab history is one thing, the history of Christian-Druze conflict in Lebanon is another, and the role of specific families and family members yet another. Collecting, analyzing, and assimilating information at this level of detail is a formidable challenge for intelligence analysts, policymakers, and warfighters alike." Jeffrey B. White, "A Different Threat: Some Thoughts on Irregular Warfare," *Studies in Intelligence* (Washington, DC: Center for the Study of Intelligence, 1996), 2.

[263] Thomas and Kiser, 24.

[264] Thomas, 24.

[265] Medby, 59.

familiarity of the local culture through an inquiry of history, language, and other social studies. The USMC's on-going seminars and reports on cultural intelligence are useful in this regard. Open source literature is particularly useful for gaining solid background information that goes beyond custom and folklore. As we dig through these resources, keep an eye for norms—enacted values—that are likely to characterize interaction with the adversary or another stakeholder. To illustrate, Margaret K. Nydell's book, *Understanding Arabs: A Guide for Westerners*, is a highly regarded study examining Arab values:

(1) A person's dignity, honor, and reputation are of paramount importance and no effort should be spared to protect them, especially one's honor;

(2) It is important to behave at all times in a way which will create a good impression on others;

(3) Loyalty to one's family takes precedence over personal needs; and

(4) Social class and family background are the major determining factors of personal status, followed by individual character and achievement.

Simple, but useful. In four bullets, Nydell provides deep insight into the nature of likely interaction on the Arab street and with other stakeholders. Community leaders, for example, are unlikely to admit failure; they will lie to you before compromising their family; and they are unlikely to challenge poor-performing high-ranking officials. When background research is not possible, boots-on-the-street communication and observation should focus on patterns of behavior that suggest underlying norms.

Graphically describing cultural effects follows from other types of overlays. A recent RAND study on urban warfare suggests several useful products, including: lists and timelines of salient cultural and political events; cultural comparison charts; line of confrontation overlay; culturally significant structures overlay; power templates; and the so-called status quo ante bellum overlay. The last compares the status quo conditions before a significant event with the conditions afterward to understand how the population responds.[266] On the rare occasion that such historical data are available, the resulting insights into changes in population shifts, resource movements, or increased violence will allow COAs to incorporate

---

[266] Medby, 61.

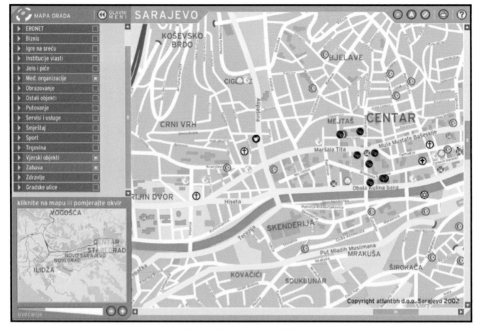

Figure 53. Sarajevo, 2004

Source: The Map Network (Used with Permission)

a more accurate assessment of how the social dimension is likely to change.[267] Figure 53 shows a commercially available example of a cultural structures overlay for Sarajevo with the additional feature of NGO and IGO locations.

Culture drives perception, and *perception effects* determine the temperature of the operational area. A sense of overall attitude proves useful in anticipating effects on a mission. Will there be protests? Will we be welcomed? Will our presence be betrayed? Can we expect to gather street-level intelligence? Doing our cultural homework enables current attitudes to be gauged in relation to a historical benchmark. Getting at current conditions requires aggressive street-level interaction, and if possible, public opinion polling, either formally or informally. Not without precedent, the Coalition Provisional Authority (CPA) in Iraq commissioned a poll by the Gallup Organization in early 2004 that revealed that "80 percent of the Iraqis questioned reported a lack of confidence

---

[267] Medby, 61.

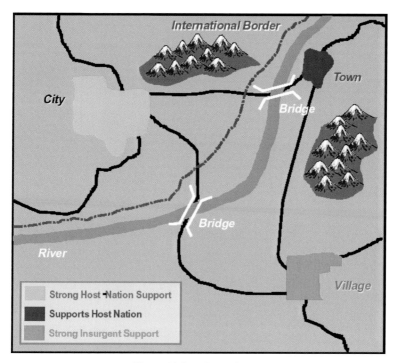

Figure 54. Population Status

Source: Joint Pub, 2-01.3, V-21.

in the Coalition Provisional Authority, and 82 percent said they disapprove of the U.S. and allied militaries in Iraq."[268] No doubt, this affects planning.

When attitudes are known, joint doctrine recommends an overlay showing the disposition of the populace as shown in Figure 54. The RAND study offers the perception assessment matrix as another useful tool. The intent of the matrix is to "measure the disparities between friendly force actions and what population groups perceive."[269] Returning to the urban warfare example, the matrix shown in Figure 55 integrates a social snapshot of the local population with an equally penetrating look at the joint force.

---

[268] Thomas E. Ricks, "80% in Iraq Distrust Occupation Authority," *Washington Post,* 13 May 2004, URL: http://www.washingtonpost.com/ac2/wp-dyn/A22403-2004May12?language=printer, accessed 25 May 2004.

[269] Medby, 65.

Condition	Cultural norm	Alternative proposed by friendly force	Population's perception	Acceptable difference?	Root of difference	Possible to change?	Proposed solution	Possible consequences of not changing
Food	Rice	Meat and potatoes	Inadequate/ inconsiderate	No	Cultural proclivity, no known physically detrimental effects	No; logistically restricted	Just offer potatoes, seek exchange for rice	Starvation, rioting
Use of guns	All men carry weapons	All weapons confiscated	Unfair	No	Culture	No; soldier safety	PSYOP campaign; just weapon search	Armed backlash
Government structure	Tribal	Hierarchical	Tolerable as long as needs are fulfilled by group in charge	Yes	History	No	Bargain	Unknown

Figure 55. Perception Matrix

Source: Medby, *Street Smarts*, 67.

Cumulative Effects

At the end of the day, we pull our analysis together into an integrated whole to enable COA evaluation and prioritization. Essentially, the commander's staff will expect an assessment of cumulative effects: the "aggregate of many direct or indirect effects."[270] Given a specific COA—provide route and clinic construction security from 0800-1500 using a mix of helicopters and light vehicles—the IPB analyst must provide an assessment of what the battlespace affords. Time, skills, and resources permitting, the IPB team will assess each sector and dimension using the highlighted concepts and methodologies to determine dependencies and affordances. Moreover, an overall assessment of uncertainty, stakeholder effects, and nesting should be provided with specific implications for decisionmaking, command and control, and COA planning. Stepping through each COA, an assessment is made as to whether the sector, dimension, and ultimately the OA, AOI and battlespace provide advantages or disadvantages. Once adversary COA are determined and prioritized, an assessment of comparative advantages can be made, which may allow the joint force to actually shape the environment to improve COA options.

---

[270] JFCOM Glossary, under "Cumulative Effects."

PARTING SHOTS

Not all the effects are important all of the time, but effects are present every time. In this chapter, the goal of phase two—describe the battlespace—is achieved by leveraging existing doctrine and TTP. The concept of effects retains its fundamental role in IPB, and it is peeled back here to get at differences between direct, indirect, cascading and cumulative effects. Direct effects grab our attention with their in-your-face immediacy and impact, while indirect effects are often overlooked due to their subtle wear-you-down approach. Effects are only important insofar as they condition specific plans, or COA, for achieving CT missions, terrorist objectives, and stakeholder interests. Turning to our battlespace buckets, the OCOKA methodology for evaluating effects in the physical dimension stands the test of time with the requisite CT adjustment. Joint and service guidance for the information domain has legs, particularly with regard to the impact of information loss, but it does not

Figure 56. Khiva, Uzbekistan

The author pursues cultural insight during three weeks in Central Asia, July 2001.

get us much further. The social dimension is even less developed for CT, but concepts and methods from MOOTW get us underway. Section two brings us home with a pioneering inter-disciplinary approach to assessing total battlespace effects. Degrees of uncertainty, measured by change and complexity, shape decisionmaking styles, organizational structures, and COA planning. Nesting highlights the vertical and horizontal axes of effects—the strategic corporal to the tactical general. Tactical effects, like rules of engagement, can have strategic consequences when violated. The interrelationships among stakeholders present a web of influence that COA must navigate. Reversing directions, the view from the unit's window reveals dependencies on critical and scarce resources, constraining action and exposing vulnerabilities. The battlespace also affords real advantages and disadvantages that may be misconstrued due to a lack of creativity or flawed perception. Complementing these overall effects are new concepts and methods for the information and social dimensions. In a CT context, the information front fosters organizational, media, attack, and cognitive effects. On the social front, demographics, culture, and perceptions work to forge COA options. Taken together, total and dimensional effects enable an initial cut at which COA are most likely to achieve objectives and what comparative advantages or disadvantages the joint force and terrorist can expect. It is an initial cut because effects are not static, and the results of phase three and four will necessitate a return trip. Phase two makes the transition from Orient to Decide in the OODA Loop, and more importantly, enables the joint force's OODA Loop to dominate that of the adversary. In the end, phase two answers the question, "How does it impact us?"

CHAPTER 4

EVALUATING CAPABILITIES

Hezbollah's new game show, "The Mission," reinforces their view of the world by advancing winning contestants toward Jerusalem; bags of liquefied sarin gas are released in the Tokyo underground by the cult/terrorist group Aum Shinrikyo; and a warren of tunnels along the Afghanistan-Pakistan border provides shelter for elusive leftovers of the Taliban regime.[271] These real-world examples demonstrate the critical capabilities enjoyed by our adversaries—attractive packaging of propaganda, an ability to deliver weapons of mass destruction (WMD), and relatively free access to sanctuary, or safe haven. These capabilities also indicate the changing nature of our adversary, reflecting both the low-tech approach of yesterday's isolated cells and the high-tech techniques of today's self-sustaining, clandestine networks. Modern terrorism has become a multi-faceted, global enterprise where violence is no longer the only product, and in fact, it may not be the most important to group survival. In addition to upholding the time-honored tradition of blowing things up, terrorists now run clinics and schools, produce and ship drugs, operate charities, and host game shows.

Combining these commercial and social capabilities with the relentless pursuit of exotic weaponry and a persuasive mythology results in an adversary that is extremely tough to "know." As argued by Bruce Hoffman and others, our challenge is to understand an "enigmatic enemy who fights unconventionally and operates in a highly amenable environment where he typically is indistinguishable from the civilian populace."[272] The distinction between ally and adversary can be murky, and the diversity of counterterrorism missions requires us to know quite a lot about a broad range of stakeholders and their capabilities, including service delivery by NGOs, the rhetorical appeal of religious leaders, and coercive influence of local politicians. Notwithstanding the very real limits of what we can

---

[271] "In 'The Mission' contestants battle for points which enable them to step toward Jerusalem on a virtual map. Questions range from the date of the French Revolution to names of militants who carried out suicide attacks...al-Manar spokesman Ibrahim Musawi told the newspaper that the show—which draws on contestants from across the Arab world—wanted to put its message 'into a form that would appeal to a wider segment of the population.' Contestants compete for prizes of up to $3,000, with each question they answer correctly they move one step closer on a virtual map toward Jerusalem. Should a contestant successfully reach Jerusalem the show plays a favorite Hezbollah song which declares 'Jerusalem is ours and we are coming to it.'" BBC News on-line, "Hezbollah's unconventional quiz," URL: http://news.bbc.co.uk/2/hi/middle_east/3640551.stm, accessed on 2 June 2004.

[272] Bruce Hoffman, "A Nasty Business," in *Terrorism and Counterterrorism*, eds. Russell D. Howard and Reid L. Sawyer (Guilford, CT: McGraw-Hill, 2003), 301

Figure 57. Afghan Tunnels

Soldiers with the 10th Mountain Division secure the opening of a cave in the mountains of Afghanistan after throwing a grenade inside to deny its use by Taliban or Al-Qaida terrorists.

Source: DOD, URL: www.defendamerica.mil/photoessays/apr2004/p041504a6.html, accessed 2 June 2004.

know about the full spectrum of players, phase three of CT IPB offers a set of tools for narrowing the knowledge gap.

Building on the battlespace insights gained in phases one and two, phase three pursues knowledge of adversary capabilities. In addition to relying on this traditional focus on the enemy as addressed above, CT analysis and synthesis demands consideration of all actors (NGOs, IGOs, communal groups, businesses) with a capability to directly influence joint force COA. When successfully performed, the result is a realistic assessment of what the stakeholder is and is not capable of given existing battlespace conditions. We proceed as before by looking at contemporary IPB doctrine to determine enduring concepts and methods. A four-step process for diagnosing the adversary is retained in modified form as are several schoolhouse solutions for analyzing capabilities and activities. The core concept of *center of gravity* is preserved, but is more deeply examined in order to iron out doctrinal inconsistencies and optimize its utility for CT. The existing requirement to model stakeholders is upheld, but is substantially reformed to deal with the complexity of the organizations as they relate to core ideological and environmental factors. *Network* and *systems* models and analytical methods are introduced as state-of-the-art practices for determining organizational strengths and weaknesses. Section two also expands our stakeholder net to ensure we factor in all influential players based on a clearer definition of adversary. To the questions: What are we trying to achieve? (mission analysis); What out there matters most? (define the battlespace); How does it impact us? (describe battlespace effects); we now add "What can they do to us?"

ADVERSARY CAPABILITIES

In the third phase of IPB—evaluate the adversary—we diagnose stakeholders to determine their sources of strength, range of capabilities, and potential vulnerabilities. We do this for the adversary, other influential actors, and the joint force itself—reverse IPB. Phase three provides the commander with a realistic assessment of whether the terrorists and others are able to interfere with the mission and what form that interference might take. Can Abu Sayyaf fight off an attack on its training camp? Can Khalid Sheikh Mohammed elude capture in Karachi's slums? Can the Somalia-based Al-Ittihad al-Islami (AIAI) disrupt NGO activities in Ethiopia? Can the FARC shoot down our reconnaissance aircraft? Equipped with an answer to these questions, the joint force leverages our strengths and that of our allies against the weaknesses of the terrorist group. Knowing our adversary while denying knowledge of us delivers an asymmetric OODA Loop advantage. The knowledge gained in phase three is one half of the traditional threat equation: threat = capabilities + intent. While intent does factor into a capabilities assessment, particularly in terms of motivation and strategy, phase four provides a more explicit examination of intent to include COA.[273] In this section, the four-step process recommended by joint and service doctrine is inspected to determine the concepts and methods applicable to CT IPB:

---

[273] An argument that doctrine should be revised to eliminate confusion regarding the difference between "intent" and "COA" is made by Major Lawrence Brown, who notes "The Enemy we were Fighting was not what we had Predicted," *What is Wrong with IPB at the Dawn of the 21st Century,* monograph, School of Advanced Military Studies (Fort Leavenworth, KS: US Army Command and General Staff College, 2004), 29. He observes, "Today, confusion is caused when Army doctrine states "success requires identifying enemy capabilities (strengths and vulnerabilities), intentions, and courses of action." This statement still implies that the two are mutually exclusive when they are not. Other Army doctrinal manuals differentiate the two actions as well. He asks us to remember that the specific task to "seek enemy intentions" was an imported concept into Army doctrine in 1976, while the task of "determining and prioritizing enemy courses of action" has always been a part of Army doctrine. Instead of combining the two tasks into the same term, official doctrine left both at large. No one has made the effort to restate the requirement as "seek enemy intentions to include enemy courses of action."

Figure 58. Cessna Crash

A Cessna 208 plane shortly after it crashed in southern Colombia on 13 February 2003. FARC terrorists killed the plane's American pilot and a Colombian national on board and kidnapped the three remaining American survivors.

Source: Department of State, *Patterns of Global Terrorism 2003*, URL: http://www.state.gov/s/ct/rls/pgtrpt/2003/31640.htm, accessed 2 June 2004.

(1) Identify adversary centers of gravity;

(2) Update or create adversary threat models;

(3) Determine the current adversary situation; and

(4) Identify adversary capabilities.[274]

This process presumes we have already garnered a basic understanding of how the battlespace influences relevant players; however, it also acknowledges the need to refine phase two analyses based on a higher fidelity look at these groups. Failure to accurately size up our adversary can result in having joint force vulnerabilities exposed, being surprised by adversary operations, wasting effort against capabilities that may not exist, and ultimately, mission failure.

---

[274] Joint Pub 2-01.3, II-46.

Centers of Gravity

What is the key to al-Qaida survival? Is it the narrative appeal of the *jihadist* worldview, its careful personnel selection and intense socialization program, or the leadership of Osama bin Laden? What enables the Provisional IRA to resist over time? Is it a decentralized cell structure, persistent poverty, or political exclusion? What is the United Self-Defense Forces/Group of Colombia (AUC's) source of strength?[275] Is it the lucrative drug trade, well-trained guerrillas, or failures in governance? Or, are they all of the above? The answers to these questions are likely to reveal *centers of gravity* (COG), which is central to achieving operational effects. According to joint doctrine, "COG analysis is conducted after an understanding of the broad operational environment has been obtained [phases one and two] and before a detailed study of the adversary's force occurs."[276] Essentially, we are expected to answer the fundamental questions posed above before we have analyzed actual capabilities in any detail. While it may not always make sense to start

Figure 59. Osama bin Laden Poster

During a search and destroy mission in Afghanistan, Navy SEALs found intelligence information, including this Osama Bin Laden propaganda poster located in an al-Qaeda classroom.

Source: US Navy, URL: http://www.hnn.navy.mil/ archives/020222/terrorism_022202.htm, accessed 2 June 2004.

---

[275] "The AUC—commonly referred to as the paramilitaries—is a loose umbrella organization formed in April 1997 to consolidate most local and regional self-defense groups each with the mission to protect economic interests and combat FARC and ELN insurgents locally. The AUC is supported by economic elites, drug traffickers, and local communities lacking effective government security, and claims its primary objective is to protect its sponsors from insurgents. Some elements under the AUC umbrella, and under the influence of its political leader Carlos Castano, have voluntarily agreed to a unilateral cease-fire, though violations of the ceasefire do occur." *Patterns 2003*, 136

[276] Joint Pub 2-01.3, II-45.

phase three with COG analysis, determining COG for all players is an enduring requirement.

Centers of gravity are fundamental to military theory and practice. A COG is that "characteristic, capability, or locality from which a military force, nation or alliance derives its freedom of action, physical strength, or will to fight."[277] It is the conceptual offspring of the work of Prussian military theorist Carl von Clausewitz, who articulated it in the context of an examination of the nature of war in his seminal work, *On War (von Krieg)*. Reflecting on the revolutionary, citizen-based character of the Napoleonic wars of the late 18th century and the "skulking" tactics of the wild Cossacks of Russia, Clausewitz stated: "One must keep the dominant characteristic of both belligerents in mind. Out of these characteristics a certain center of gravity develops, the hub of all power and movement, on which everything depends. That is the point at which all our energies should be directed."[278] The importance of determining COG is echoed in joint doctrine,

> The COG concept is useful as an analytical tool [in] designing campaigns and major operations to assist JFCs [joint force commanders] and their staffs in analyzing friendly and adversary sources of strength as well as weaknesses and vulnerabilities. Analysis of COG, both friendly and adversary, is a continuous process throughout a major operation or campaign. This process cannot be taken lightly, though; a faulty conclusion as to the adversary COG because of a poor or hasty analysis can have very serious consequences; specifically, the inability to achieve the military objectives at an acceptable cost and the unconscionable expenditure of lives, time, and materiel in efforts that do not produce decisive strategic or operational results. Accordingly, a great deal of thought and analysis must take place before the combatant commander and staff can determine proper COG with any confidence.[279]

COG Ladder

COG are sources of power, not weakness. Although doctrinal inconsistencies confused this issue in the past, more recent guidance has embraced the clarifying work by Joe Strange.[280] Strange's approach retains the original Clausewit-

---

[277] Joint Chiefs of Staff, Joint Publication 1, *Joint Warfare of the Armed Forces of the United States* (Washington, DC: GPO, 14 November 2000), V-3.

[278] Carl von Clausewitz, *On War*, eds. and trans. Michael Howard and Peter Paret (Princeton, NJ: Princeton University Press, 1976), 595-596.

[279] Joint Pub 5.00-1, II-6.

zian meaning of COG as a "primary source of moral or physical strength, power and resistance," and links it to the valuable doctrinal concept of critical vulnerabilities (CV).[281] *Critical vulnerabilities* are "those aspects or components of the adversary's critical capabilities (or components thereof), which are deficient, or vulnerable to neutralization, interdiction, or attack in a manner achieving decisive or significant results, disproportionate to the military resources applied."[282] Strange bridges the gap between COG and CVs by introducing the concepts of *critical capabilities* (CC) and *critical requirements* (CR), which have been embraced in joint and service doctrine as the "critical factors" of our analysis. Critical capabilities are "those adversary capabilities that are considered crucial enablers for the adversary's COG to function as such, and are essential to the accomplishment of the adversary's assumed objective(s)."[283] Critical requirements are those "essential conditions, resources, and means for a critical capability to be fully operational."[284]

Figure 60. Basque Nationalism Graffiti, Vitoria, Spain

Source: William Casebeer (with permission), photo taken while traveling with author, December 2003.

---

[280] Joe Strange, *Centers of Gravity and Critical Vulnerabilities: Building on the Clausewitzian Foundation so that we can all Speak the Same Language*, Perspectives on Warfighting (Quantico, VA: Defense Automated Printing Service Center, 1996).

[281] Strange, 2-3.

[282] Joint Pub 5.00-1, II-7.

[283] Joint Pub 5.00-1, II-7.

[284] Joint Pub 5.00-1, II-7.

Linking the concepts together results in a conceptual ladder for diagnosing stakeholders: COG-CC-CR-CV. For example, it is likely that our analysis of the Basque Fatherland and Liberty (ETA) party in the Basque region of Spain will reveal that a highly secretive cell structure is at least one COG at the operational level. This COG is enabled by their ability to find sanctuary in urban areas like Bilbao and San Sebastian and the ability to maintain internal discipline. These critical capabilities of securing sanctuary and ensuring security require a sympathetic population, restraints on intrusive police action, a bountiful recruiting pool, and effective physical cover and concealment. Over its 45-year history, ETA has been generally able to secure each of these requirements, which reflect dependent relationships between the organization and the battlespace (phase two). The post 9/11, and now 3/11 (2004 al-Qaida attack on trains in Spain), environment has changed in ways to create vulnerabilities where they previously did not exist, or could at least be managed. After 9/11, Spain and France enacted tougher anti-terrorism laws along with many other countries, and improving economic conditions tempered separatist ambitions. Moreover, the 3/11 Madrid train bombings, which initially were blamed on ETA, created a popular backlash against terrorism in general.

During the author's visit to the Basque region in December 2003, however, the recruiting situation appeared to remain favorable. For example, hidden down a narrow alley in the old quarter, or Parte Vieja, of San Sebastian was one of many small bars crammed with young people wearing t-shirts championing Basque nationalism and chain-smoking under a large poster of Che Guevara. The bar, and probably most of the youth, were loosely associated with the banned Herri Batasuna (Popular Unity) political party, which was linked in its 1979 origins with ETA. Several of these youths spent the early hours before daybreak spray-painting "ETA" and other nationalist slogans across the old city—a ritual simultaneously conducted in the region's other major urban centers of Vitoria and Bilbao. From among these rebellious youth, several will one day be approached by ETA recruiters, and if selected, their participation in vandalism will end while their indoctrination in terrorism begins. According to officials of the Basque Nationalist Party, however, recruitment is becoming more difficult for ETA. Improved economic conditions as well as the increased societal rejection of violence have reduced the pool of potential recruits, forcing ETA to make do with fewer than the optimal number of new members. Given the arrests of key ETA leaders over the decades, and most recently in France in 2002 with the arrest of ETA's commando leader, Jon Ibon Fernandez, the rebellious youth of the back alley bar may even rise to the rank of senior military leader in just a few years.[285] A declining recruiting pool, waves of leadership purges, and decreased member discipline are combining with other factors to weaken, or create deficiencies that undermine, critical capabilities and that over time sap the secretive cell structure as a COG.

COG-CC-CR-CV are the targets of our phase three analysis and the backbone of operational planning. We work our way up and down the critical factors ladder to determine whether our adversary has weakness that can be exploited to achieve desired effects. Figuring this out requires rigorous analysis supported by appropriate models and methods. As argued in joint doctrine,

> [t]he importance of identifying the proper COG cannot be overstated. Determining the adversary's strategic COG and critical vulnerabilities is absolutely essential to establish clarity of purpose, to focus efforts and, ultimately, to generate synergistic results in the employment of one's forces. In fact, detailed operational planning should not begin until the adversary's COG have been identified. Identifying COG is an analytical process that involves both art and science.[286]

COG Characteristics

The art and science of COG analysis involves additional considerations. First, although Clausewitz suggested that "the first principle is that the ultimate substance of enemy strength must be traced back to the fewest possible sources, and ideally to one alone," he also recognized that there is no guarantee of only one COG existing.[287] In fact, there may be several COG at each of our levels of analysis and action. For example, a strategic-level COG in the fight against religious terrorist groups is likely to be the *jihadist* ideology itself, while an operational-level COG may be the network of individuals and technology that spread the message, and a tactical-level COG may be a specific media source or messenger. As is often the case, a CC of a higher-level COG (capability to disseminate narrative) is a COG itself at the next level down.[288] Second, as the above examples suggest, COG often exist outside the organization, residing in the environment or as a function of a key relationship between stakeholders. Where terrorism is interlaced with an insurgency, for example, the strategic COG are often popular support or

---

[285] For a discussion of the Basque region, which includes insight into ETA's development, see Mark Kurlansky, *The Basque History of the World* (New York: Penguin Books, 1999). Insights for this vignette were also derived from the author's visit to the Basque province in December 2003, which involved informal discussions with members of the ruling Basque Nationalist Party as well as leaders of several non-governmental social organizations pursuing non-violent solutions to the Basque conflict.

[286] Joint Pub 5.00-1, II-8.

[287] Strange, 14-15.

[288] FPAM 14-118, 177.

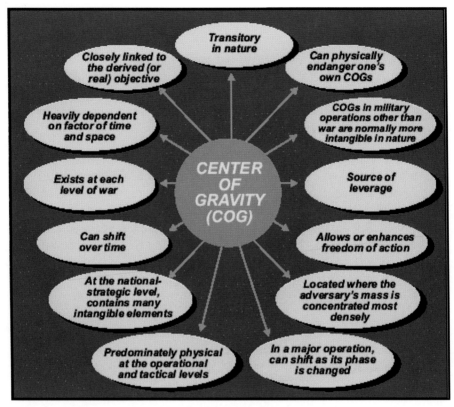

Figure 61. Center of Gravity Characteristics

Source: Joint Pub 5.00-1, II-7.

grievances against the state. Third, COG can dictate courses of action—sources of strength suggest specific activities. For example, a well-trained urban guerrilla force is an operational COG for the AUC. Although the AUC will not always employ urban terrorism as part of a short-term strategy, the fact that it is a source of strength argues for its continued use. Fourth, CV and CR may represent high-value and high-payoff targets, or decisive points, which when targeted by CT missions can have a decisive effect on the COG.[289] Figure 61 highlights additional COG characteristics that apply to all missions, including CT, with two exceptions. First, in CT the adversary COG is more likely to exist in the information or social dimensions than the physical—weapons or training camps are less likely to be a COG than is divine sanction or communications technology. Second, terror-

---

[289] AFPAM 14-118, 176.

ist COG are not necessarily located where the organization is massed; in fact, the organic qualities of the organization, including decentralization and dispersed operations, are sources of power.

Figure 62. Humanitarian Mission

A soldier from the 25th Infantry Division talks with Tora Ray village locals during a humanitarian assistance mission in Afghanistan

Source: DOD, URL: http://www.defendamerica.mil/photoessays/ apr2004/p041504a8.html, accessed 3 June 2004

COG analysis is not only relevant to the adversary, but it should be applied to the joint force and other stakeholders. In the case of the former, reverse IPB offers insight into what we need to defend, what the terrorist is likely to target, and what capabilities we can draw on to gain an asymmetric advantage. Red teaming is a useful technique for this and particularly for COA development in phase four; therefore, a full discussion of this method is reserved for the next chapter. NGOs, religious leaders, businesses and other stakeholders can also be diagnosed using COG analysis. Take, for example, the Islamist cleric Abdessalam Yassine, who heads the Justice and Charity party and is under house arrest in Sale, Morocco.[290] Yassine's survival is rooted in his popular appeal and status, which depend on several non-traditional critical capabilities, including religious credentials, effective rhetorical style, and a party organization that can sustain grassroots appeal. These CC not only require individual skills, but depend on his ability to access an audience—preaching at Friday prayers or disseminating audio tapes—and the freedom of his party to operate in the suburbs of Morocco's major cities. Each of these requirements has proven vulnerable: the state controls access through house arrest and

---

[290] Sale sits across an estuary from Rabat, the capital, and was visited by the author in May 2004.

banning the party. Of course, these actions change the battlespace, creating disaffection elsewhere and generating new sources of support.

Given the broad range of CT missions, the joint force's goal will not always be to exploit weakness on the path to achieving the "paralysis" of an adversary COG. In fact, CT missions to diminish underlying conditions or improve ally CT capabilities will focus instead on strengthening an allied COG by building capabilities, creating more reliable and secure dependencies, and minimizing vulnerability. Using an NGO illustration, the delivery of medical aid (CC) to a remote Afghan village requires a secure operating environment (CR). As recently as 3 June 2004, Doctors without Borders (*Medecins Sans Frontieres*) suspended operations in Afghanistan after five of its workers were killed in an ambush, reflecting their vulnerability to attack (CV).[291] A likely CT mission is to remove the NGO vulnerability, which in turn requires finding and exploiting Taliban vulnerabilities. The interrelationships among stakeholder COG are an important part of the puzzle.

Where to Start

The examples provided thus far reflect an initial cut at COG-CC-CR-CV without looking behind the scenes at the model and methods available for deriving such key conclusions. According to existing joint doctrine, "a proper analysis must be based on a detailed knowledge of how opponents organize, fight, make decisions, and their physical and psychological strengths and weaknesses." This requirement begs the question of whether phase three should begin or end with COG analysis. Beginning with COG identification means theory leads fact. This risks a bias toward selecting evidence that confirms our first look, or it provides "the basis for ignoring evidence that is truly indicative of future events" and capabilities.[292] On the other hand, starting with theory has the advantage of economizing thought and overcoming the inevitably anemic data. The other tack is to allow the results of step two to reveal COG-CC-CR-CV; however, this data immersion or situational logic approach carries its own costs. In addition to the potential time cost of wading through vast amounts of data absent a theoretical framework, situational logic suffers from three weaknesses. First, the clandestine nature of the adversary makes it unlikely that robust intelligence will be available, resulting in only partially informed speculation on our part.[293] Second, it fails to "exploit

---

[291] According to press reporting, Taliban rulers claimed responsibility for the attack in the northwest of the country. BBC News on-line, URL: http://news.bbc.co.uk/2/hi/south_asia/3773217.stm, accessed on 4 June 2004.

[292] Heuer, Chapter 4, np.

[293] Heuer, Chapter 4, np.

the theoretical knowledge derived from study of similar phenomena" elsewhere and in other time periods.[294] Third,

> [t]o think of analysis in this way overlooks the fact that information cannot speak for itself. The significance of information is always a joint function of the nature of the information and the context in which it is interpreted. The context is provided by the analyst in the form of a set of assumptions and expectations concerning human and organizational behavior. These preconceptions are critical determinants of which information is considered relevant and how it is interpreted.[295]

In reality, we are obliged as elsewhere with CT IPB to go at our problem from both directions. We cannot afford to neglect existing terrorism theory, nor can we allow theoretical constructs to become a self-fulfilling prophecy that blinds us to changes in adversary capabilities and intentions. For example, recent conventional wisdom that religious groups do not collaborate with drug syndicates has been shattered. When time is of the essence and evidence is unavailable, theory reigns. Prior to the crisis, we should do our homework and test theories about COG against the evidence. COG analysis, modified only slightly here for CT, generates the "big picture" of stakeholder capabilities. Figuring out critical factors as well as the supporting details of operations requires the use of models and methods introduced below and in the next section.

Old Models

Step two models the adversary, depicting preferred modes of operation under ideal conditions.[296] Absent battlespace effects, what does the adversary look like, how does he behave, and what targets will he attack? The models and associated methods offered by current doctrine are a good start for CT, but do not provide the optimal theoretical framework and tools for examining terrorist groups—they are suited to state actors relying on conventional forces. That said, several of the concepts described below remain valid, setting up the introduction of more appropriate models in section two of this chapter. Although current doctrine does not so indicate, we must remember that step two is a means to an end—figuring out COG-CC-CR-CV either by substantiating our initial assessment or changing it based on the more detailed results of steps two through four.

---

[294] Heuer, Chapter 4, np.
[295] Heuer, Chapter 4, np.
[296] FM 34-130, Chapter 2, 34.

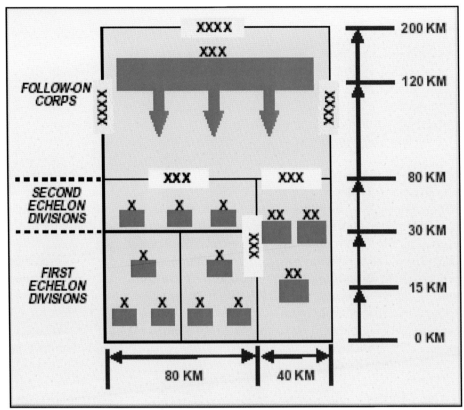

Figure 63. Ground Doctrine Template

Source: Joint Pub 2-01.3, II-47.

Standard Practice

Models consist of three elements: (1) doctrinal templates; (2) description of preferred tactics, techniques and procedures (TTP) and options; and (3) identification of high-value targets (HVT).[297] Taking each in turn, doctrinal templates "illustrate the employment patterns and dispositions preferred by an adversary when not constrained by the effects of the battlespace environment."[298] Typically, they offer a scaled, graphic depiction (Figure 63) for each component of the state's military force—air, ground, sea, space. Templates are also produced for each broad type of COA, such as attack, defend, reinforce, and retrograde.[299] In

---

[297] Joint Pub 2-01.3, II-46.
[298] Joint Pub 2-01.3, II-46.
[299] Joint Pub 2-01.3, II-46.

addition to the basic factors of organization and disposition of forces, current doctrine recommends the following be incorporated for all threats: information, composition, tactics, training, logistics and command and control.[300] Adding MOOTW to the mix, which includes CT, these factors are added: propaganda themes, agents of influence, personality types, ISR capabilities, perception, deception, WMD capabilities, weather, local grievances, internal discord in groups, and motivation.[301] It is an impressive list; however, little guidance is offered for how to integrate these diverse factors into one threat model, let alone graphically display them.

Activities

Once our template is molded, our next task is to describe "the types of activities and supporting operations that various adversary units portrayed on the doctrinal template are expected to perform."[302] Types of activities refer to operations and their associated tactics. For example, the U.S. Air Force performs close air support operations using a range of combat platforms based on a push/pull command and control construct. Tactics depend on a host of variables, including the platform, commander, and skills of operators to name a few. For example, a B-52 will circle at high altitude using both precision-guided munitions and "dumb bombs," while an A-10 will close at low-to-medium altitude, using a combination of its 30mm cannon and precision weapons to rip up the enemy. Similar breakdowns are applied to adversary forces to determine preferred operating locations, phasing, timing, distances, weapons systems, tactics, and approach to the OCOKA factors presented by the battlespace. Additionally, this second element of our model describes the options (branches and sequels) available to the adversary depending on the outcome of the operation. For example, the Iraqi regular army chose to disband in the face of a superior U.S. adversary in March and April 2003 rather than regroup in defensive positions around Baghdad. One tool for capturing how the adversary prefers to sequence operations is the time-event matrix shown in Figure 64. If possible, we are also encouraged to "identify and list any decision criteria known to cause the adversary to prefer one option over another."[303]

---

[300] AFPAM 14-118, 40.
[301] List derived from content analysis of joint and service IPB doctrine for MOOTW.
[302] Joint Pub 2-01.3, II-46.
[303] Joint Pub 2-01.3, II-48.

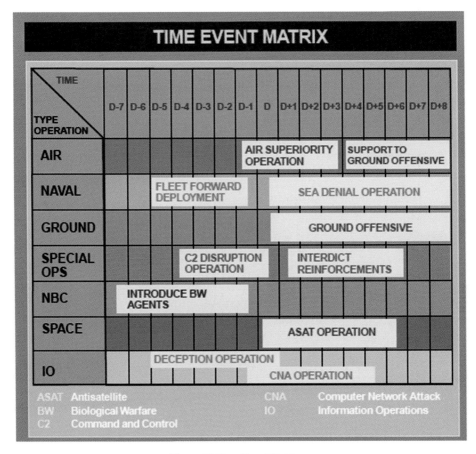

Figure 64. Time Event Matrix

Source: Joint Pub 2-01.3, II-50.

High-Value Targets

High value targets are the third piece of the model and include assets that the adversary requires to perform the desired operations (critical requirements). HVT are evaluated by a four-step method: (1) identify HVT by mentally war-gaming adversary operations to determine how assets are used; (2) determine the impact of losing any of the HVT; (3) evaluate and rank-order the HVT based on relative worth; and (4) construct a target-value matrix (Figure 65) by grouping HVT according to function (FM 34-130 suggests thirteen: command, control and communications; fire support; maneuver; air defense; engineer;

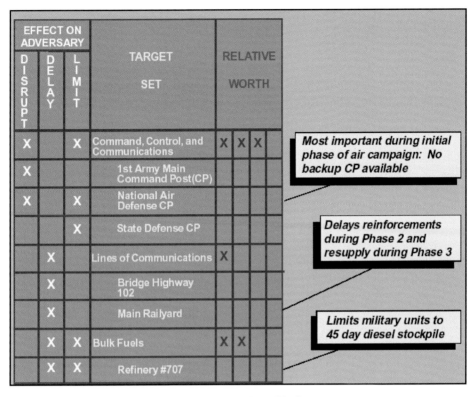

DISRUPT	DELAY	LIMIT	TARGET SET	RELATIVE WORTH					
X		X	Command, Control, and Communications	X	X	X			Most important during initial phase of air campaign: No backup CP available
X			1st Army Main Command Post(CP)						
X		X	National Air Defense CP						
		X	State Defense CP						Delays reinforcements during Phase 2 and resupply during Phase 3
	X		Lines of Communications	X					
	X		Bridge Highway 102						
	X		Main Railyard						Limits military units to 45 day diesel stockpile
	X	X	Bulk Fuels	X	X				
	X	X	Refinery #707						

Figure 65. Target Value Matrix

Source: Joint Pub 2-01.3, II-51.

reconnaissance, intelligence, surveillance and target acquisition (RISTA); radio electronic combat; bulk fuels; ammunition storage and distribution; maintenance and repair; lift; and lines of communication).[304]

Five Rings

Pulling these three ingredients—template, activities and HVT—into one model is rare in joint and service doctrine with the exception of the Air Force Five-Ring model based on the work of former Air Force Colonel John Warden. The Five-Ring model is embraced in Air Force warfighting doctrine and has served as a guiding construct for air campaigns against several nation-states, including Iraq and Serbia. The model views the "adversary from the top down, with infrastructures linked as a "system of systems" with mutual dependen-

---

[304] FM 34-130, Chapter 2, 35-38.

cies."[305] Systems thinking has been applied to CT IPB previously in this work, so it comes as no surprise to us that a terrorist group, the joint force, and other stakeholders might be best thought of as systems, consisting of interlocking subsystems, where the focus is on critical relationships rather than as isolated parts.

According to Warden, the systems model offers a "comprehensible picture of a complex phenomenon so that we can do something with it."[306] Based on his reading of systems theory, all systems consist of five subsystems: leadership, organic essentials, infrastructure, population, and fighting mechanism.

War is a contest of wills, reminding us that at the core of every system is a human(s) who gives direction and meaning.[307] The Five-Ring model has leadership at its center:

> A strategic entity—a state, a business organization, a terrorist organization—has elements of both the physical and the biological, but at the center of these whole systems and of every subsystem is a human being who gives direction and meaning. The ones who provide this direction are leaders, either of the whole country or some part of it. They are the ones

Table 1

Systems

	Body	State	Drug Cartel	Electric Grid
Leadership	Brain • eyes • nerves	Government • communication • security	Leader • communication • security	Central control
Organic Essentials	Food and oxygen (conversion via vital orgrans)	Energy (electricity, oil, food) and money	Coca source plus conversion	Input (heat, hydro) and output (electricity)
Infra-structure	Vessels, bones, muscles	Roads, airfields, factories	Roads, airways, sea lanes	Transmission lines
Population	Cells	People	Growers, distributors, processors	Workers
Fighting Mechanism	Leukocytes	Military, police, firemen	Street soldiers	Repairmen

Figure 66. Five-Ring Model

Source: John Warden, "The Enemy as a System," Airpower Journal 9, no 1 (Spring 1995), 44, URL: http://www.airpower.maxwell.af.mil/airchronicles/apj/warden.html, accessed 10 April 2004.

---

[305] AFPAM 14-118, 37.

[306] John A. Warden III, "The Enemy as a System," *Airpower Journal 9*, no 1 (Spring 1995), 40-55, URL: http://www.airpower.maxwell.af.mil/airchronicles/apj/warden.html, accessed on 10 April 2004.

[307] Warden, 44.

on which depends the functioning of every subsystem, and they are the ones who decide when they want their strategic entity to adopt or not to adopt a different set of objectives. They, the leaders, are at the strategic center, and in strategic warfare must be the figurative, and sometimes the literal, target of our every action.[308]

From this perspective, the center ring of leadership is always the COG. When possible, we must attack it directly; however, if the COG lacks discernable vulnerabilities, we go at it indirectly by attacking the other rings. Figure 66 shows elements of each of these subsystems for four types of systems. Organic essentials are energy inputs (resource dependencies if you will) that are converted to enable the system to function.[309] Infrastructure is the skeleton, which enables mobility, but is usually sufficiently redundant to allow workarounds when parts of it are disrupted or destroyed.[310] The fourth ring directs our attention to the social dimension and the web of relationships in which the organization is caught. Finally, the forces that protect the system—fielded forces, police, spies, politicians—are its fighting mechanism. Each ring has capabilities that may be critical as well as key nodes (HVT) that represent systems-threatening vulnerabilities.

Salvage Yard

What is salvageable for CT? First, the requirement to "model" stakeholders is an enduring concept. Models represent theories as a set of concepts and relationships, which serve to make abstract understanding more tangible.[311] Models provide a generalized abstraction of the phenomenon in question—organizations in the case of CT—that has descriptive attributes and properties.[312] A model is a framework for organizing and relating intelligence evidence based on a theory of how the organization looks and works in practice. Figure 62 models a conventional ground force engaged in a linear battle. Not only is the model inadequate for today's non-linear conventional battlespace, but it falls well short of what is required for CT where non-linearity, adaptability, innovation, dynamism, and asymmetry describe the players and battlespace. The Five-Ring Model is a major step in the right direction; however, it suffers from three key shortcomings when applied to CT: (1) it assumes the primary COG to be the leadership, which may not be supported by evidence or is secondary to other candidates as COG: ideology, network structure, sanctuary; (2) it is does not sufficiently account for battlespace effects (it is a closed system, not allowing for feedback effects); and (3)

---

[308] Warden, 44.
[309] Warden, 45.
[310] Warden, 45.
[311] Hatch, 14.
[312] Waltz, 181.

it does not adequately address the social (cultural) and information (ideology) dimensions of organizations. Therefore, better models are needed that capitalize on current doctrinal strengths while incorporating factors relating to the social and information dimensions. Doctrinal templates remain useful if adapted to portray more fluid structures and operations. Moreover, the need to describe activities and options remains valuable as a way of putting flesh on the template skeleton and providing greater fidelity into CC, CR, and CV. Finally, HVT can be retained if recast in terms of decisive points or key nodes associated with a COA, CV or CR—it is good to remember that a CR may have a decisive point, or HVT, that is not, for the moment, vulnerable.

The Real World

Step two evaluates stakeholders as they would look and behave in an unconstrained, idealized world; step three brings us back to earth by balancing the ideal against the reality of what the battlespace affords. The value of this sanity check is echoed in Air Force doctrine:

> The pressures and uncertainties imposed by the battlespace environment will place constraints on adversary actions or provide opportunities to exploit. An analysis of the current situation provides a link between what the adversary believes he can accomplish according to his doctrine and what he is actually capable of doing given the constraints imposed by the environment.[313]

---

[313] AFPAM 14-118, 43.

By first evaluating an unconstrained adversary capable of optimizing battlespace advantages, we avoid overlooking and being surprised by capabilities. Having grounded this analysis as a result of phase two—describe battlespace effects—we place previously performed analysis into the current operational context.[314] This approach remains equally valid for CT. Our step one analysis of the AUC, for example, notionally reveals a doctrinal capability for generating income that

Figure 67. Poppy Field, Colombia

Source: Department of State, URL: http://usembassy.state.gov/colombia/wwwsnasc.shtml, accessed on 17 May 2004.

depends on "sponsors" for 40 percent and obtains the other 60 percent by taxing peasants and running drugs. In reality, AUC leaders, as Carlos Castaño indicated in a televised interview in 2000, actually generate 70 percent of their funds through drug trafficking and taxation.[315] The reasons for this difference between "ideal" and "real" are likely to be found in the environment (internal government crackdowns, increasing profit margins on drugs) and in the organization itself (strategy change, cultural shift related to demographics). In addition to evaluating how the adversary, joint force, and other stakeholders look in the light of day, this step requires us to figure out how specific COA, developed in phase four, are impacted. A hypothetical Jemaah Islamiya (JI) COA to disrupt the electrical grid in Singapore may have been within the group's capabilities; however, by passing "strict new legislation to protect the country's computer systems" from attack in 2003, Singapore has changed the battlespace and rendered the COA less attractive even if the capability remains.[316]

---

[314] AFPAM 14-118, 43.

[315] Angel Rabasa and Peter Chalk, *Colombian Labyrinth: The Synergy of Drugs and Insurgency and it's Implications for Regional Stability* (Santa Monica, CA: RAND Corporation, 2001), 59

[316] The Singapore government "has said the measures are necessary because of rising cases of successful hacking—there were just 10 in 2000, but that had risen to 41 last year." The laws allow the monitoring of all computer activity and pre-emptive action. BBC News, "Singapore tackles' cyber terror,'" 11 November 2003, URL: http://news.bbc.co.uk/2/hi/asia-pacific/3259601.stm, accessed 4 June 2004.

Can Do

With the ideal balanced against the real, step four closes out this third phase by identifying the set of "broad COAs and supporting operations that the adversary can take to interfere with the accomplishment of the friendly mission."[317] More simply, what are the stakeholders capable of doing? The capabilities are determined by comparing the results of step three with the models of step two. When the terrorist or NGO is capable of meeting or exceeding the doctrinal standards of step two, the capability should be considered a strength.[318] If the al-Qaida template calls for unobstructed access to an economic target, such as an oil terminal in Saudi Arabia, with at least two trucks loaded with explosives, and it is able to get three trucks to the desired engagement area, this COA (attack terminal) and supporting capability (move and ignite explosives) is a strength. More likely, the stakeholder will fall short of the doctrinal ideal due to battlespace constraints, revealing a deficiency.[319]

The results of step four analysis can take the form of specific statements of capabilities tied to specific COA such as these apt examples from the Army Field Manual:

(1) The enemy has the capability to attack with up to 8 divisions supported by 170 daily sorties of fixed-wing aircraft.

(2) The enemy can establish a prepared defense by 14 May.

(3) The enemy has the ability to insert up to 2 battalions of infantry in a single lift operation.

(4) The drug smugglers have the capability to detect the radars used at our observation posts.

(5) The threat can conduct up to three separate smuggling operations simultaneously.

(6) The protesters can effectively block traffic at no more than 7 different intersections.[320]

Similar statements can be made for other stakeholders, including the ability of an NGO to deliver aid, an IGO to negotiate a settlement, an allied security force to

---

[317] Joint Pub, 2-01.3, II-52
[318] Joint Pub, 2-10, II-52
[319] Joint Pub, 2-10, II-52
[320] FM 34-130, Chapter 2, 40.

learn new CT skills, a civil-affairs team to build relationships with village leaders, a religious cleric to recruit potential terrorists, or a terrorist group to survey a target. An important, but often overlooked aspect of stating capabilities is to incorporate **time**. When possible, add a timing factor to each statement, such as "within three hours," "continuously," "every two or three days," and the like.

FULL SPECTRUM CAPABILITIES

Intelligence is in service to the mission. Our responsibility in phase three of CT IPB is to provide an accurate and timely diagnosis of mission-relevant capabilities. The goal is not a static display of the adversary, rich in historical vignette and packed with organizational charts and tables of equipment. Rather, intelligence is charged with providing a motion picture of what the terrorist, joint force and other stakeholders are capable of over time. We must emphasize functions over inventories and relationships over hierarchies. We still want to know what the adversary possesses, but such intelligence is subordinate to how people, things, and information interact to carry out a particular course of action. What are the capabilities of all the players in the CT battlespace? How do they match up? Who has the advantage? What deficiencies can be exploited, need to be protected, or require healing? What dependencies are open to exploitation? Current doctrine and TTPs provide a foundation for answering these questions, but they only take us part way down the road to a fluid, operational capabilities assessment. To this end, new ideas and methods are introduced here.

We begin by returning to our familiar "stakeholders first" approach by further clarifying and expanding the framework for characterizing and relating key players for the CT mission. The intent is to make sure we are accurately capturing the range and priority of potential actors before embarking on a capabilities assessment. We want to be straight on who the threat is and what we can expect out of other players. Second, we build on the four-step process as modified in the last section. Centers of gravity and the other critical factors of capabilities, requirements and vulnerabilities are enduring concepts that serve operational requirements. Figuring them out for CT missions requires a new approach in step two— model the adversary—based on more appropriate templates. Expressly, CT templates must integrate (1) battlespace effects, (2) ideology and/or culture, and (3) organizational performance. Concepts and analytical methods are provided for integrating these elements, including the introduction of network and systems models as state-of-the-art practices.

Agents of Influence

We previously addressed the difficulty of accurately identifying the adversary; a challenge compounded by the diversity of stakeholders to CT missions. Legitimate NGOs turn out to be front organizations for terrorist financing, and once-favored political leaders betray our capabilities to a hostile state. And as has been the case in Iraq since the fall of Baghdad on 9 April 2003, even the basics of defining the enemy can be elusive. As argued by Bruce Hoffman in a July/August 2004 issue of *The Atlantic Monthly*, "the Iraqi insurgency today appears to have no clear leader (or leadership), no ambition to seize and actually hold territory (except ephemerally, as in the recent cases of Fallujah and Najaf), no unifying ideology, and most importantly, no identifiable organization."[321] While the identity swamp is not *always* so murky for modern terrorism, it often is. Therefore, the issue of sorting out stakeholders is revived here as a precursor to assessing capabilities. A summary of the general types of links, hard and soft, that most often exist between groups is also introduced.

In phase one, we developed an inventory of stakeholders—individuals and groups with an interest in the outcome of the CT mission. In phase two, we mapped the stakeholders as a web of influence to get a general sense of their ability to affect CT missions directly or indirectly. In phase three, we seek greater fidelity as we assess their ability to impact COA by clarifying the very meaning of adversary and by implementing a RAND concept, *the continuum of relative interests*. The aim is to:

(1) Determine a stakeholder's potential utility in meeting mission demands;

(2) Determine a stakeholder's potential for manipulation; and

(3) Provide a basis for detecting and monitoring shifts in relevant relationships.[322]

The first, and most basic question to ask about the stakeholders inventoried in phase one is whether they are currently an adversary (stressing the present tense recognizes that today's ally may be tomorrow's enemy). In the absence of an accepted DOD definition, the RAND study *Street Smarts: Intelligence Preparation of the Battlespace for Urban Operations*, offers one with CT utility: an **adversary** has some current *capability* and intention to negatively influence our mission accomplishment by exploiting a friendly *vulnerability*.[323] This definition

---

[321] Bruce Hoffman, "Plan of Attack," *The Atlantic Monthly* (July/August 2004), 42.

[322] Medby, 96.

[323] Medby, 97.

incorporates and is consistent with key concepts (italics) developed throughout this work. Underlying the definition is a recognition that stakeholder *interests* (the underlying motivation for the pursuit of an activity) drive *intention* (mode chosen to fulfill the corresponding interest).[324] This is a critical insight for two reasons. First, intentions are notoriously hard to determine, particularly when the stakeholder actively works to keep its intentions secret. Interests, however, are normally more open to examination and are often stated explicitly. We may not be clear on how the Eastern Turkistan Islamic Movement (ETIM) in China's western Xinjiang Province intends to use terrorism, but we do know that its interests include group survival and the establishment of an Islamic state.[325] Even if intentions are elusive, knowing interests helps scope the range of likely intentions. Second, interests are more durable than intentions. That is, interests are less prone to change, particularly when backed by a persuasive or coercive ideology; however, the mode chosen to secure the interest, or intention, is often open to change. This difference between interest and intention is a sound basis for negotiation, manipulation, and influence.

---

[324] Medby, 98.

[325] ETIM "is the most militant of the ethnic Uighur separatist groups pursuing an independent "Eastern Turkistan," an area that would include Turkey, Kazakhstan, Kyrgyzstan, Uzbekistan, Pakistan, Afghanistan, and Xinjiang. ETIM is linked to al-Qaida and the international mujahidin movement. ETIM militants fought alongside al-Qaida and Taliban forces in Afghanistan during Operation ENDURING FREEDOM. In October 2003, Pakistani soldiers killed ETIM leader Hassan Makhsum during raids on al-Qaida–associated compounds in western Pakistan. U.S. and Chinese Government information suggests ETIM is responsible for various terrorist acts inside and outside China. In May 2002, two ETIM members were deported to China from Kyrgyzstan for plotting to attack the U.S. Embassy in Kyrgyzstan as well as other US interests abroad. *Patterns 2003*, 144.

Using the definition and distinctions as a guide, we can further nuance the categories of stakeholders introduced in phase two (ally, neutral, adversary) into the five types:

Adversary: A population element with the capability, interest, and intent to exploit a friendly vulnerability.

Hindrance: A population element with an active capability to exploit a friendly vulnerability. Current interests may or may not be compatible with friendly force goals, but there is no intention to interfere with friendly force activities.

Neutral: A population element whose interests do not conflict with either the friendly or the adversarial force. Capability to affect the friendly force mission may exist, but it is currently inert.

Accomplice: A population element with the capability to capitalize on a friendly or adversary vulnerability whose intentions are compatible with friendly force objectives.

Figure 68. Bangladesh Bombing

A member of the Bangladesh Army inspects a movie theater in Mymensingh after a bomb blast that killed 15 persons on 7 December 2002 (AP).

Source: State, *Patterns 2002,* URL: http://www.state.gov/s/ct/rls/pgtrpt/2002/html/19982.htm, accessed on 6 June 2004.

Ally: A population element whose interest and intent is to assist in accomplishing friendly force objectives.[326]

To this list, we should retain the category of **unknown** to avoid forcing the application of a label that is not supported by the evidence. Moreover, we note that these categories are relative to not just the joint force, but to the terrorist group and other players. Depending on the time of day, our accomplice may also an obstacle. The *continuum of relative interests* is a useful guide, which has the benefit of (1) taking us out of the "us" versus "them" mentality of traditional IPB; (2) providing a framework for recognizing, shaping and possibly anticipating stakeholder shifts along the continuum based on changing battlespace conditions and

---

[326] Medby, 97. "Hindrance" replaces RAND's "Obstacle" to avoid confusion with the use of "Obstacle" for the OCOKA methodology.

COA; and (3) reminding us of the need for reverse IPB to relate stakeholder intentions and capabilities to joint force vulnerabilities.

The web of terrorist influence is an important sub-set of the overall set of linkages among all stakeholders. As argued in the *National Strategy for Combating Terrorism,*

> [t]errorist groups with objectives in one country or region can draw strength and support from groups in other countries or regions. For example, in 2001, three members of the Irish Republican Army were arrested in Colombia, suspected of training the FARC in how to conduct an urban bombing campaign. The connections between al-Qaida and terrorist groups throughout Southeast Asia further highlight this reality.[327]

Globalization has made transnational coordination easier for friend and foe alike. In the 1970s and 1980s, our focus was on the linkages between secular and nationalist groups, such as the open cooperation between ETA and the IRA. Now we are witnessing the diffusion of religious extremist terrorists, consisting of regionally-based groups and globally-nomadic operatives and cells. The linkages between groups take two general forms. *Hard links* reflect direct influence and involve concrete transactions.[328] Hard links include: financial support, sharing intelligence, coordinating action,

Figure 69. IRA Suspects

Suspected IRA members captured in Bogota for suspected collaboration
with the FARC in 2001 (AP).

Source: State, Patterns 2001, URL: http://www.state.gov/s/ct/rls/pgtrpt/2001/,
accessed 7 June 2004.

---

[327] *National Strategy,* 8.

[328] The hard and soft links concepts are taken from *Combating Terrorism in a Globalized World,* Report by the National War College (NWC) Student Task Force on Combating Terrorism (Washington, DC: National War College, November 2002), np, URL: www.ndu.edu/nwc/writing/AY02/ combating_terrorism/index.htm, accessed on 17 February 2004. Cited hereafter as NWC.

sharing safe havens, sharing materials and resources, and sharing personnel.[329] *Soft links* refer to indirect influence involving the exchange of intangible social and information capital: sharing opportunities, sharing responsibility, public diplomacy, sharing ideological values.[330] Of the two, hard links are more susceptible to collection, analysis, and CT effects; however, soft links are more critical to groups pursuing a transcendent agenda.

At this point in our stakeholder analysis, we are equipped with (1) the inventory of stakeholders from phase one, (2) an initial cut at direct or indirect influence by each from phase two, (3) a typecasting of each based on relative interest from phase three, and (4) an initial cut at the type of linkages. Thus equipped, we are able to prioritize stakeholders for collection, analysis and incorporation into COA development. In this light, information on an adversary stakeholder with direct influence (such as Harakat ul-Jihad-i-Islami) on an foreign internal defense mission to Bangladesh should be at the top of our "to do" list, while a neutral stakeholder with indirect influence is near the bottom, and only earns our attention if time and resources are available or if a consequential shift is likely in mission or interest.[331] For example, the Bangladesh-based NGO, Proshika, is one of the world's largest NGOs and plays a major role in poverty reduction in Bangladesh.[332] Its neutral position and indirect influence on a short-term mission to train Bangladesh soldiers in CT skills make it a low priority; however, in the longer-term mission to diminish underlying conditions, Proshika has the potential to move from accomplice to ally with direct influence. These stakeholder analysis methods set up an evaluation of stakeholder-specific capabilities and contribute to COA forecasting in phase four.

Supermodels

The complexity of terrorism requires a superhero model, able to organize and relate the full spectrum of variables that animate the battlespace and its CT partic-

---

[329] NWC, Chapter 2, np.

[330] NWC, Chapter 2, np.

[331] *Harakat ul-Jihad-i-Islami/* Bangladesh (HUJI-B), Movement of Islamic Holy War, is led by Shauqat Osman and has a mission "to establish Islamic rule in Bangladesh. HUJI-B has connections to the Pakistani militant groups Harakat ul-Jihadi-Islami (HUJI) and Harakat ul-Mujahidin (HUM), who advocate similar objectives in Pakistan and Jammu and Kashmir. Funding of the HUJI-B comes primarily from madrassahs in Bangladesh. The group also has ties to militants in Pakistan that may provide another funding source." *Patterns 2003*, 146.

[332] See the Proshika website at http://www.proshika.org/ for more information or recent reporting on the arrest of Proshika's president Qazi Faruque Ahmed and deputy, David William Biswas, by the BBC. "Calls for release of aid workers," 25 May 2004, URL: http://news.bbc.co.uk/2/hi/south_asia/3746801.stm, accessed on 4 June 2004.

ipants without overwhelming its user. It must be scalable, allowing the analyst to transition among levels of analysis and action while allowing for varying degrees of magnification and detail, all without sacrificing utility. The absence of consensus over the "right" approach to the study of terrorism complicates the matter. While the two complementary models presented here—networks and systems—do not save us entirely, they are a marked improvement over existing state-focused models. Moreover, their value is gaining recognition in CT circles, resulting in their adaptation and use throughout the U.S. inter-agency system and by foreign governments and agencies.[333]

The network and systems models are able to capture the intricacies of CT because they reflect a multicausal approach that draws on the most persuasive elements of existing theories. From the *political approach*, we take an appreciation for the importance of battlespace effects as both a cause and shaper of terrorism. Particularly at the strategic level, the political approach suggests that the root causes of terrorism, and therefore the keys to diminishing terrorism, can be found in the environment.[334] In fact, strategic-level COG are often outside the terrorist organization—socio-economic deprivation, systemic crime and corruption, resource scarcity, failures in governance, intractable conflict, identity cleavages, and demographic pressures.[335] As analysts, we are responsible for understanding the range of environmental causes even if their operational value is not initially obvious. Until strategic-level COG in the battlespace are dealt with, success against terrorist groups will be short-lived. From the *physiological approach*, we

---

[333] Both are directly incorporated into national CT strategy and planning documents, being used throughout the Intelligence Community, employed by operational joint forces, and making the rounds of foreign governments. The author has directly participated in several working groups, projects and operations that employ network and systems analysis methods, including the Partnership for Peace CT Working Group, Joint Intelligence Task Force for CT (JITF-CT), Joint Warfare and Analysis Center (JWAC), Joint Forces Intelligence Center (JFIC), Northern Command, New Mexico Department of Homeland Security, Foreign Service Institute, and others.

[334] Rex A. Hudson, *The Sociology and Psychology of Terrorism: Who Becomes a Terrorist and Why?* (Washington, DC: Federal Research Division, Library of Congress, September 1999), 15.

[335] Troy Thomas and Stephen Kiser examine the relationship between these environmental factors and prosperity of terrorist groups in *Lords of the Silk Route: Violent Non-State Actors in Central Asia*, Occasional Paper #43 (USAF Academy, CO: Institute for National Security Studies, May 2002), URL: http://www.usafa.af.mil/inss/OCP/OCP43f.pdf, accessed on 7 June 2004. According to our analysis, "these system elements interact in a highly dynamic, causative manner to spawn the VNSAs of the developing world. This framework [open systems model] effectively captures the disparate actors that are too often examined in isolation, and draws needed attention to the relationships that enable the cycle of violent collective action to thrive. As an open system, our framework allows for environmental factors, which is particularly important given the transnational character of many VNSAs. It allows us to consider the influence of such international dynamics as globalization and the role of external powers," 5-6.

recognize the role of the information dimension in creating a physical, adrenalin-based response to acts of terrorism as transmitted through the media and other sources.[336] From the psychological approach, we incorporate cognition and motivation at the individual and group level, which is shaped by ideology, religion, personal needs, and in some cases, abnormal pathology.[337] Finally, from the organizational approach we understand terrorism to be either (1) an instrumental means to achieve a political goal as well as (2) the result of organizational processes concerned primarily with group survival.[338] Religious extremism is often an example of the latter, where "[v]iolence has a personal meaning for the individual. It is a path to individual salvation, regardless of the political outcome for the collectivity in the real world. The motivation for terrorism may be to transcend reality as much as to transform it."[339] Each of these approaches is reflected in our IPB work thus far, particularly as part of battlespace effects.

In this section, the network and systems models bring it all together in a way that allows us to climb the COG ladder. Both focus our analysis on the most relevant capabilities, address the asymmetries among CT players, and allow the analyst to use a similar set of analytical methods: timelines, pattern analysis, association matrices, and link diagrams, for example.[340] Bear in mind that this discussion presents only their key attributes, resulting in an operational-level overview of how to structure our thinking. Getting beyond the basics for field use requires (1) homework, including training if possible, on methodology and (2) reachback to organizations and subject matter experts who develop and employ these techniques regularly.[341] Deciding which to use is a decision that is not supported by clear-cut criteria, leaving it up to the commander and staff to determine the most appropriate approach based on its operational utility. The network model

---

[336] Hudson, 17.

[337] Hudson, 18. Mark Kauppi highlights several personal needs met by participation in terrorism: money, family ties, peer pressure, rebellion, and thrill. He continues by stating "the individual with an inner sense of worthlessness, confusion or rage may seek refuge and validation through rebirth within a charismatic mass movement. Young persons with few life prospects may choose to join a terrorist organization for such a simple reason as the expected thrill of life in the underground organization or a way to enhance one's self-esteem and status by becoming a "defender of the community." On-line course material, *Counterterrorism Analysis*, Joint Military Intelligence Training Center. Author completed the course in April 2004.

[338] Martha Crenshaw, "Theories of Terrorism: Instrumental and Organizational Approaches," *Inside Terrorist Organizations*, ed. David C. Rapoport (London: Frank Cass, 2001), 13-27.

[339] Crenshaw, 20.

[340] Methods are introduced as part of the model explanation; they are not repeated for each model even though they can be used to analyze systems and networks.

[341] Advanced analytical methods for systems and network analysis are being developed and employed by a host of organizations with which the author collaborated, including JWAC, JITF-CT, NSA, CTC, JFIC, and the National Air and Space Intelligence Center (NASIC) to name a few.

proves useful if we seek to disrupt performance or influence decisions by engaging a key node. The systems model is appropriate if we seek to leverage deficiencies in resource dependencies in order to disrupt a critical capability. In the absence of certainty, either will serve the joint force better than existing models.

Network Model

Of the two, the network model is the most widely embraced, reinforced in the *U.S. National Strategy for Combating Terrorism:*

> The terrorist threat is a flexible, transnational network structure, enabled by modern technology and characterized by loose interconnectivity both within and between groups. In this environment, terrorists work together in funding, sharing intelligence, training, logistics, planning, and executing attacks... The terrorist threat today is both resilient and diffuse because of this mutually reinforcing, dynamic network structure.[342]

---

[342] *National Strategy*, 8.

Figure 70. Saddam Hussein

Picture taken following his capture as part of
Operation Red Dawn,
14 December 2003.

Source: CENTCOM, URL: http://
www.centcom.mil/operations/iraqi_Freedom/
reddawn/OperationRedDawn_files/
frame.htm,
accessed 7 June 2004.

The sketch that follows includes an overview of guiding principles, key concepts, fields of analysis, and the model's connection to COG-CC-CR-CV. Its proponents are correct in asserting that it remains in the early stages of development for CT application; however, its widespread adoption, particularly by the joint force, has already contributed to the capture of al-Qaida leaders and operatives, and in a notable public advertisement for its front-line utility, Saddam Hussein. The process of finding Hussein began with four names that morphed into a network of three hundred names, and ultimately, the single "source" who led the Army to the famous spider hole.[343] According to one of the intelligence analysts involved, it was "like we are detectives suddenly."[344] CT IPB is detective work with an operational imperative.

While more varied than the following discussion suggests, the network approach is unified in its emphasis on the relationships between nodes, which inform organizational design, strategy, operational modes, technology use, decisionmaking, and other CT-relevant capabilities. Like the systems approach described later, dynamic relationships within the organization, with other stakeholders, and with the battlespace are central. The network has properties that are more than the sum of its parts—adaptive, fluid, and resilient to name a few. The network as a whole is worthy of our analysis as are the specific actors and relational ties that make it up. In addition to an emphasis on hard and soft linkages, the network perspective embraces familiar guiding principles:

(1) Actors and their action are interdependent rather than independent, autonomous units;

---

[343] Farnaz Fassihi, "Two Novice Gumshoes Charted the Capture of Saddam," *Wall Street Journal* 18 December 2003, A1, A6.

(2) Relational ties (linkages) between actors are channels for transfer (flow) of resources;

(3) Network models view the environment as providing opportunities or constraints for action; and

(4) Network models conceptualize structures [battlespace dimensions] as lasting patterns of relations.[345]

Embedded in these principles are several key concepts requiring up-front definition. The **nodes** of a network can be most anything (people, organizations, computers, ideas) as long as they are hooked up in a meaningful way.[346] That said, network analysis tends to focus on social linkages among **actors**, or social entities.[347] As in our stakeholder analysis, nodes are linked by **relational** ties taking

---

[344] Quote attributed to Lieutenant Angela Santana, Fassihi, A1. The story continues: "By mid-September, after many sleepless nights spent sifting through tens of thousands of pages of information" Lieutenant Angela Santana and Corporal Harold Engstrom narrowed a list of 9,000 to 300 names. "The duo read through sheaves of interrogation reports from detainees and interviews with local Iraqis. They plumbed a huge database provided by central military intelligence. Eventually, they created what they nicknamed 'Mongo Link,' a four-page, 46-by-42-inch color-coded chart with their 300 names on it. It was basically a family tree, with Mr. Hussein's picture at the center, and lines connecting his tribal and blood ties to the six main tribes of the Sunni triangle: the Husseins, al-Douris, Hadouthis, Masliyats, Hassans and Harimyths. The military believed members of these clans shielded Saddam for eight months, financed the resistance, and planned assassinations and attacks against Iraqis and coalition forces. Next to each of the names, Lt. Santana and Cpl. Engstrom scribbled down bits of information they were able to gather about individuals: their ages, home village, spouses and children, where the names came from, whether people on the list were in custody and how they got there... As the chart grew, the pair started to see patterns. They realized the resistance was multilayered, as they pieced together who was related to whom among the tribes. The tribal leadership was tightly linked through a web of marriages and intensely loyal to Mr. Hussein, the analysts concluded. Below that level were a number of other people clearly part of the insurgency. These fighters were likely in it for the money. The two sleuths noticed how few of the resistance fighters who had been caught planting bombs or carrying out raids were relatives of the tribal principals. They concluded that the bosses were distancing themselves from the rank and file...Next to every name on the chart is a physical description—hair and eye color, height, facial features that stand out—as well as details about where they were last seen or any other information that might lead to their arrest. Several dozen of the names are already in custody of the coalition forces and color-coded with red ink. The main people around Hussein are then linked to dozens of others, many of whom the military believes to be ringleaders for resistance cells plotting attacks against Americans in Tikrit, Samarra, Fallujah, Ramadi and Baghdad." Fassihi, A1, A6.
[345] Stanley Wasserman and Katherine Faust, *Social Network Analysis: Methods and Applications* (Cambridge: Cambridge University Press, 1996), 4. Another useful resource is John Scott, *Social Network Analysis: A Handbook* (London: Sage Publications, 2000).
[346] Phil Williams, "Transnational Criminal Networks," in John Arquilla and David Ronfeldt, *Networks and Netwars* (Santa Monica, CA: RAND Corporation, 2001), 66.
[347] Wasserman, 17.

many forms simultaneously: evaluative (friendship, respect); transactional (resource exchanges); association (membership, attendance); behavioral (talking, fighting); mobility (migration, transport); physical (road, bridge); formal (authority, chain of command); and biological (kinship).[348] A set of linkages of a specific kind among actors is a relation—the hard and soft linkages of diplomatic relations, intelligence sharing, financial transfers. Putting it all together, a network "consists of a finite set or sets of actors and the relation or relations defined on them."[349] How we define the network depends on the mission and the level of analysis and action. A disrupt-CT mission at the strategic level will demand analysis of the global al-Qaida network, whereas the same mission at the tactical level requires analysis of the specific, mission-relevant cell. Of course, even regional cells have links to strategic level players; Jamal Ahmidan, for example, is thought to have been one of the 3/11 cell commanders in Spain with al-Qaida ties.

Terrorist, joint force, and stakeholder capabilities are assessed through organizational network analysis (ONA). ONA views networks as "a distinct form of organization, one that is gaining strength as a result of advances in communications."[350] Network organizations are more organic than the mechanistic organizations discussed in previous chapters: (1) organizational design reflects horizontal over vertical relationships; (2) communication and coordination emerge based on task as opposed to being formalized by rules and procedures; (3) internal nodes connect to external nodes in the battlespace; and (4) "internal and external ties are enabled not by bureaucratic fiat, but rather by shared norms and values."[351] This last quality is particularly important for transnational groups as it enables "members to be 'all of one mind' even though these are dispersed and devoted to different tasks. It can provide a central ideational and operational coherence that allows for tactical centralization."[352] There is no standard methodology for analyzing the organizational network, as stated by its RAND sponsors; however, the current state-of-the-art argues for directing efforts at five reinforcing "fields of analysis": organization; narrative; doctrine; technology; and social.[353] Each field represents a set of capabilities and characteristics that lend themselves to COG analysis.

---

[348] Wasserman, 19.

[349] Wasserman, 20. For an excellent summary in the changing forms of organization over time, see David Ronfeldt and John Arquilla, *The Advent of Netwar* (Santa Monica, CA: RAND Corporation, 1996), URL: http://www.rand.org/publications/MR/MR789/, accessed on 8 June 2004.

[350] David Ronfeldt and John Arquilla, "What Next for Networks and Netwars," Arquilla, 319.

[351] Michele Zanini and Sean J.A. Edwards, "The Networking of Terror in the Information Age," Arquilla, 31-32.

[352] John Arquilla and David Ronfeldt, "The Advent of Netwar," Arquilla, 9

[353] "Field" replaces "level" found in Ronfeldt and Arquilla to avoid confusion with our levels of analysis and action—strategic, operational, tactical. Ronfeldt, 324.

One of the key takeaways from the network model is the idea that the organization itself is a capability.[354] Recalling our analysis of overall battlespace uncertainty in phase two, the organizational structure, or **design**, can be optimized for the mission and environment. A network with a small number of critical nodes (mechanistic), for example, is more susceptible to disruption and information overload, while one that is highly decentralized is able to resist, adapt, re-route flows, and repair itself. On the other hand, communication and coordination are more difficult in spider webs. Generally, the organization will at least be a critical capability if not a COG itself. To get a sense of whether the organization is a strength or weakness, what its vulnerabilities are, and how it might be affected directly or indirectly, we need to assess its design, the independence of its units, the location of leadership, and "how hierarchical dynamics may be mixed with the network dynamics."[355]

The three basic forms of networks (Figure 71) are chain, hub, and all-channel as described in *Networks and Netwars:*

The **chain** or line network, as in a smuggling chain where people, goods, or information move along a line of separated contacts, and where end-to-end communication must travel through the intermediate nodes.

The **hub**, star, or wheel network, as in a franchise or a cartel where a set of actors are tied to a central (but not hierarchical) node or actor, and must go through that node to communicate and coordinate with each other.

The **all-channel** or full-matrix network, as in a collaborative network of militant peace groups where everybody is connected to everybody else.[356]

These pure forms are not resident in the real world. Rather, most stakeholder organizations will consist of a combination of these and more traditional hierarchal forms. Hybrids are likely, such as a terrorist group with an "all-channel council or directorate at its core," but using hubs and chains for tactical operations.[357] Terrorism expert Rohan Gunaratna describes al-Qaida's design prior to Operation ENDURING FREEDOM along similar lines:

Al-Qaida's structure enables it to wield direct and indirect control over a potent, far-flung force. By issuing periodic pronouncements,

---

[354] This recognition is reflected in the joint force's structure as well. The Air Force, for example, treats the Air Operation Center as a weapon system—it represents a command and control capability for employing air and space power.

[355] Rondfeldt and Arquilla, 325

[356] Arquilla and Ronfeldt, 7.

[357] Arquilla and Ronfeldt, 9.

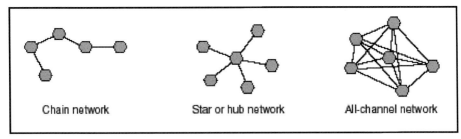

Figure 71. Network Designs

Source: Arquilla and Ronfeldt, *Networks and Netwars,* 8, URL: http://www.rand.org/ publications/MR/MR1382/MR1382.ch1.pdf, accessed 7 June 2004.

speeches and writings, Osama indoctrinates, trains and controls a core inner group as well as inspiring and supporting peripheral cadres...in 1998 al-Qaida was reorganized into four distinct but interlinked entities. The first was a pyramidal structure to facilitate strategic and tactical direction; the second was a globalist terrorist network; the third was a base force for guerilla warfare inside Afghanistan; and the fourth was a loose coalition of transnational terrorist and guerrilla groups.[358]

NGOs, the joint force, and commercial stakeholders are likely to embrace greater hierarchy than crime syndicates, insurgencies and many of the terrorist groups we face. Leadership may be at the end of the chain, the center of the star, or diffused across several channels. As these simple examples make clear, the chain is easier to disrupt than the all-channel, while exercising command and control is more demanding for the all-channel than the others. A simple network can afford to be more reliant on a single charismatic leader and fewer communication channels, while a multi-link network demands a cohesion that can only come from a shared culture. We are only scratching the surface of design implications; however, the rules-of-thumb suggested here highlight the importance of deepening our knowledge of organizational theory and practices for CT. Moreover, the design implications have to be balanced against battlespace effects and other stakeholder capabilities to determine whether vulnerabilities exist.

All CT missions involve competitive **story-telling**. Whether seeking to alter perceptions, shrink the pool of recruits, entice defection, or discredit a group, a narrative is involved. The narrative is variously called public diplomacy, propa-

---

[358] Gunaratna, 56-57.

ganda, strategic communications, and the "truth." It is delivered through a variety of means, including speeches, sermons, *fatwas*, policy documents (*National Strategy*), web postings, posters, graffiti and many others. The narrative is both a function of rhetoric and actions, and in many cases, actions tell a different story than the public pronouncements suggest. The narrative answers important questions for CT participants: who we are (identity), where we are (location), how we are (rules for living), when we are (sense of history), and why we are (meaning of existence).[359] A compelling story provides cohesion and works against defection, enables relations with other groups, and generates a "perception that a movement has winning momentum."[360] The story is shaped by the battlespace, which in turn shapes attitudes in the social and information dimensions.

Al-Qaida has proven most adept at competitive story-telling, evidenced by the highly influential fatwas issued on behalf of Osama bin Laden and Ayman al-Zawahiri. One of the earliest appeared on 22 February 1996 wherein bin Laden announced the formation of the *World Islamic Front for the Jihad against the Jews and the Crusaders*, delivering a story that remains a core element of the global jihadist insurgency:

> [b]ased upon this and in order to obey the Almighty, we hereby give all Muslims the following judgment: The judgment to kill and fight Americans and their allies, whether civilians or military, is an obligation for every Muslim who is able to do so in any country... In the name of Allah, we call upon every Muslim, who believed in Allah and ask for forgiveness, to abide by Allah's order by killing Americans and stealing their money anywhere, anytime, and whenever possible.[361]

William Casebeer provides further insight into myth creation in *Violent Systems: Defeating Terrorists, Insurgents, and other Violent Non-State Actors*,

> [t]he fanatical devotion shown by al-Qaida operatives stems in large part not from any rational deliberative process but rather from the success Osama bin Laden and others have had in fashioning a coherent and appealing foundational myth. The events of 11 September 2001 can be thought of as the punch line of a chapter in an epic that sets "the warriors of God" against an "infidel West." This myth did not propagate itself via rational actor channels, but instead was indoctri-

---

[359] Michael Vlahos, "Terror's Mask: Insurgency within Islam," Occasional Paper (Laurel, MD: Joint Warfare Analysis Department of the Applied Physics Laboratory, Johns Hopkins University, May 2002), 8

[360] Ronfeldt and Arquilla, 328.

[361]Bergen, 95-96.

nated via a multi-pronged effort on the part of fundamentalist strains of Islam.[362]

According to Michael Vlahos, former Director of the State Department's Center for the Study of Foreign Affairs, the al-Qaida narrative draws heavily on the symbolism of the Prophet Mohammed's life. He points to four elements reflected in the current *jihadist* story and strategy: (1) heroic journey of mythic figure; (2) history as an epic struggle; (3) commanding charge of renewal; and (4) history revealed through mystic literary form.[363] The symbolic framework embraced by Salafist, Wahhabi, Ikhwani, Deobani and other Islamic subcultures leads to a fierce conviction of the cause's righteousness, a willingness to embrace hardship and death, and a belief that "the act of the struggle itself is triumph."[364]

Figure 72. Two Sheiks

A Frame from an Osama bin Laden videotape released by the DOD on 13 December 2001.

Source: DOD, URL: http://www.defenselink.mil/photos/ Dec2001/011213-D-0000X-003.html, accessed 7 June 2004.

For IPB, our task is to understand the narrative and its role in the organization. The former requires some basic knowledge of rhetoric as well as the elements of a good story. Effective rhetoric involves credibility (ethos), appeal to reason (logos), and appeal to emotion, or affect (pathos).[365] When CT-related messages are presented by an official who lacks credibility, or the message fails to anticipate emotional responses, it is likely to fall on deaf ears, or actually generate frustration or rage. This is not only a clarion call for the joint force to gain allies through the investment of social capital, but to guard against mirror-imaging by assuming that our penchant for fact-

[362] Thomas and Casebeer, 65.

[363] Vlahos, 8.

[364] Vlahos, 10.

[365] Based on the ideas of Thomas Coakley, "The Argument against Terror: Globalization, the Peruvian Experience, and the Necessity of US Military Transformation," paper presented at the Institute for National Security Studies Annual Research Results Conference, USAF Academy, CO, 13 November 2003. Interview with author on 14 November 2003.

based reasoning appeals to everyone. As an example, bin Laden's video-taped dinner conversation with another sheikh shortly after 9/11 (Figure 72) included the rhetorical device of mystical revelation through dreams:

He [Abd Rahman al-Ghamri] told me a year ago: "I saw a dream we were playing a soccer game against the Americans. When our team showed up in the field, there were all pilots!' He didn't know anything about the operations until he heard it on the radio. He said the game went on and we defeated them. That was a good omen for us.[366]

By dissecting the narrative, we gain insight into the questions asked above and how the story shapes the organization and the battlespace. For CT, the narrative is almost always a COG, and the ability to develop and disseminate it is a critical capability. Whether the critical requirements of speaker, rhetoric, story elements, and distribution means are vulnerable to CT missions depends on the audience's orientation, the availability of alternative storytellers, and the existence of a more compelling narrative.

The principles and practices that guide organizational behavior are its doctrine and TTPs, explaining why and how individual members and the organization as a whole operate as they do. Principles and practices make clear how groups "operate strategically and tactically, without necessarily having to resort to a central command or leader."[367] In this sense, it not only explains role behaviors, but provides insight into the types of behaviors we can expect—setting up COA analysis in phase four. The concept of **operational code** captures what we are trying to achieve in this field: (1) perception of the political world and 2) boundaries on responses to the political world.[368] The former reflects the philosophical beliefs discussed as narrative above, and the latter deals with instrumental issues: "norms, standards, and guidelines that influence the actor's choice of strategy and tactics, his structuring and weighing of alternative courses of action"[369] Operational codes are not just about weapons and tactics, but rather focus on the more fundamental character of an organization's modus operandi. Are certain targets off-limits? Are certain types of weapons (WMD, cyber, explosives) preferred over others? Is deception acceptable, or is it considered dishonorable? Are attacks announced? Does the terrorist take credit for attacks, or not, and why? What is the risk thresh-

---

[366] Vlahos, 10.

[367] Ronfeldt and Arquilla, 333.

[368] Stephen Benedict Dyson, "Drawing policy implications from the 'Operational Code' of a 'new' political actor: Russian President Vladimir Putin," *Policy Sciences* 34, nos. 3-4 (December 2001), 330.

[369] Dyson, 331.

old of the NGO? Where do the media draw the line? Answers to these questions require a level of analysis that goes beyond inventories of equipment and a list of preferred tactics—it requires analysis of the organization's over-arching strategy, relationships across all sectors, and existing and planned operational capabilities.

As an example, Brian Jenkins of the RAND Corporation is among the first to have broken-out the operational code for al-Qaida based in part on a red teaming project with the Defense Advanced Research Programs Agency (DARPA). Keeping in mind that operational codes change over time, this analysis revealed the following key elements of al-Qaida planning:

(1) Long planning horizons, patient;

(2) Persistence—a preferred target not easily abandoned (World Trade Center);

(3) Al-Qaida learns, perfects (boat bombs [USS *Cole*]);

(4) Stick to familiar playbooks, core competencies, centers of excellence;

(5) Imaginative low-tech over challenging high-tech (box-cutters, ricin);

(6) Operations planning is de-centralized, and therefore entrepreneurial; and

(7) Proposals start big, then back off (can't do the American embassy, can't do the Brooklyn Bridge).[370]

One key take-away from this analysis is that al-Qaida is less concerned with how it attacks than with sustaining attacks to maintain the momentum of the organization. In the same briefing to the Army Science Board, Jenkins covers the sources of the operational code: Islam, patterns of pre-Islamic warfare, tribal warfare, selected history and myth, current circumstances, terrorist tactics observed and discussed, and their own playbook.[371] In fact, al-Qaida produces a regular magazine, *Camp al-Battar,* which trains and shapes behaviors with guidance on everything from physical fitness to small arms tactics.[372]

---

[370] Brian Jenkins, "The Operational Code of the *Jihadists*," brief to the Army Science Board, 1 April 2004, Slide 32.

[371] Jenkins, Slide 36.

[372] One open source for translated copies of *Camp al-Battar* is the Intel Center, Alexandria, VA, URL: www.intelcenter.com.

Technological infrastructure is the fourth field of network analysis. Two broad types of technology are most important to CT: information and weapons. As discussed in phase two, information technology serves organizational and operational purposes. Weapons technology sets limits to operations, but not necessarily to destructive and disruptive potential. Crude car bombs, execution-style assassination with a knife, and box cutters are often sufficient. Rather than repeating past discussion, our goal in phase three is to answer several basic technology-related questions. Is the organization high-tech, low-tech, or more likely, a combination of both? Does it have low-tech back-up to its high-tech capabilities? What technology is possessed? What is sought? Do they have the knowledge, skills, and abilities to use the technology? Is there infrastructure to support it? How is it used? Is it critical to other capabilities? Does it have any vulnerability? Can it be used to attack or defend? These questions and others apply to all stakeholders; reverse IPB is vital in this field due to the joint force's reliance on an asymmetric technology advantage over our adversaries.

The final field of analysis views the relations among individuals as a capability with its own strengths and weaknesses—it is the agent-level complement to stakeholder analysis. The study of social relations, known as **social network analysis** (SNA), is the forerunner to ONA and remains a core analytical approach. SNA sees networks in all social exchanges ranging from businesses to families to international relations. SNA's analytical focus is on underlying formal and informal relational ties and the roles of actors in making the organization work.[373] Actor importance derives more from social capital (interpersonal or relational skills) than human capital (personal characteristics).[374] Actors are further qualified in terms of their centrality, access, and roles. This has implications for CT missions; the actor with the most linkages of a highly prioritized type is often a lucrative HVT for capture or influence. On the other hand, an actor with only a few linkages but extensive social capital (Ayman al-Zawahiri) may represent cognitive leaders that either are COG or represent a critical capability supporting a COG.[375]

Figure 73 is an example of SNA performed on Iranian senior leadership using open-source material. In his analysis, Robert Renfro is showing degree of social closeness (1-3), direction of influence, and number of agents per group based on a list of 384 individuals and openly available reporting on their roles and activities.[376] While more detailed than what is feasible on the front lines, it is similar in

---

[373] Williams, 66.

[374] Ronfeldt, 318.

[375] This line of argument runs counter to the conclusion of some that "networks are often thought to lack a center of gravity as an organization." Ronfeldt, 343.

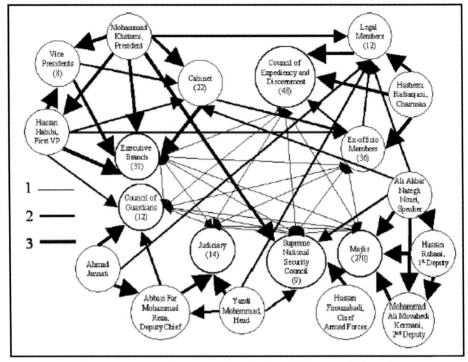

Figure 73. Iranian Network, with degree of social closeness indicated.

Source: Renfro, 143.

concept to the Saddam Hussein example. At operational and strategic levels, intelligence agencies are able to draw on advanced modeling and simulation tools to build elaborate network models that can be tested to determine effects of removing nodes, altering relations, and affecting overall performance through battlespace effects.

In the field, SNA methods are more likely to involve basic association matrices, link diagrams, time lines and pattern analysis. Each is well-developed in doctrine and expertly taught at several schools including the Joint Military Intelligence Training Center (JMITC). As a review, matrices show relationships between people and people, events, time, and locations (Figure 74). The associations identified in the matrix can be visually depicted using link diagrams (Figure

---

[376] Robert Renfro, "Modeling and Analysis of Social Networks," Ph.D. Dissertation, Graduate School of Engineering and Management, Air Force Institute of Technology, Air University, Air Education and Training Command, December 2001, 142-143, URL: https://research.au.af.mil/papers/ay2002/afit/afit-ds-ens-01-03.pdf, accessed 7 June 2004. Renfro reminds his readers that the source of the names is an Iranian opposition group of questionable reliability.

74), which are coded to reflect the various types of relationship discussed here and tailored to the CT mission. The activities matrix of Figure 75 relates individuals to specific roles played in the network; it too can inform a link diagram. Finally, time-pattern analysis is useful to determine the periods of highest violence, illegal activity, and movement. Pattern analysis builds capability-specific knowledge that shape COA, such as knowing when is the best time to deliver supplies, enter a neighborhood, or meet with key leadership. Figure 76 is an example from joint doctrine that shows key activity in an urban area over a 24-hour period during the course of a week.[377]

---

[377] Joint Pub 2-01.3, V-13.

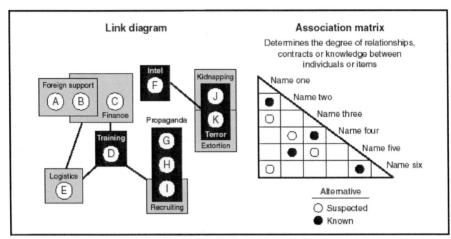

Figure 74. Relationship Mapping

Source: U.S. Army Intelligence Center, *MOOTW Instructional Materials for the Military Officer Transition Course*, Fort Huachuca, AZ: United States Army Intelligence Center and Fort Huachuca, 1999. Reprinted in Medby, 110.

Remarks	Death Squads	Drug Trafficking	Arms Smuggling	Supports Terrorism	Politician	Name of Individual
Ambitious. Wants to become president	●				☆	Argubright
		☆				Boaz
Constantly persecuted Possible inside ally	☆		☆			Brehany
Crafty and very diplomatic	☆			●	☆	Copeland
	☆			☆	☆	Grim
Warrant — Known to have conducted executions	☆			☆		James
			☆	☆	☆	Kanakis
					☆	Manning
Warrant			☆	☆		Norvell
	●					Riley
Tactical genius	☆				●	Swansburg
	☆				☆	Williams

Legend: ☆ CONFIRMED ● SUSPECTED

Figure 75. Activities Matrix

Source: Joint Pub 2-01.3, V-26.

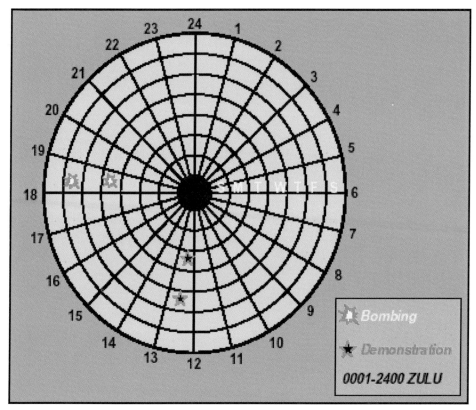

Figure 76. Pattern Analysis

Source: Joint Pub 2-01.3, V-15.

OPEN SYSTEMS MODEL

There is growing recognition of the value in treating organizations as open systems, interacting in a dynamic battlespace. In doctrinal terms, the USMC made the case to shift our thinking as far back as 1997:

> The attempt to apply a scientific approach can result in some misleading ideas. For example, some political scientists treat political entities as unitary rational actors, the social equivalents of Newton's solid bodies hurtling through space. Real political units, however, are not unitary. Rather, they are collections of intertwined but fundamentally distinct actors and systems. Their behavior derives from the internal interplay of both rational and irrational forces as well as from the peculiarities of their own histories and of chance. Strategists who

accept the unitary rational actor model as a description of adversaries at war will have difficulty understanding either side's motivations or actual behavior. Such strategists ignore their own side's greatest potential vulnerabilities and deny themselves potential levers and targets—the fault lines that exist within any human political construct. Fortunately, the physical sciences have begun to embrace the class of problems posed by social interactions like politics and war. The appropriate imagery, however, is not that of Newtonian physics. Rather, we need to think in terms of biology and particularly ecology.[378]

The open systems framework developed and applied here is guided by modern organization theory, which is rooted in the interdisciplinary approach recommended by the USMC and others. As a way of thinking about organizations of all types, organization theory has evolved beyond a rigid emphasis on scientific management and bureaucratic structures, which characterize mechanistic organizations, to an organic view based on natural and biological systems.[379] That is, structural theory does not reveal the inner workings of the organizations to include the complex informal interactions that constitute the "real" group. Our analysis must go beyond formal structural theory to appreciate these complexities as an aspect of the dynamic, even organic, character of CT players. Organization theory as intended for businesses, non-profits and legitimate political organizations guides their diagnosis for the purpose of solving problems to improve performance. We turn this on its head for CT—solving threat assessment problems in order to decrease and deny performance.

---

[378] Marine Corps Doctrinal Publication (MCDP) 1-1, *Strategy* (Washington, DC: Department of the Navy, 1997), 16-18. Continuing, "[t]o survive over time, the various members of any ecosystem must adapt—not only to the external environment, but to each other. These agents compete or cooperate, consume and are consumed, join and divide, and so on. A system created by such interaction is called a complex adaptive system. Such systems are inherently dynamic. Although they may sometimes appear stable for lengthy periods, their components constantly adapt or fail. No species evolves alone; rather, each species "co-evolves" with the other species that make up its environment. The mutation or extinction of one species in any ecosystem has a domino or ripple effect throughout the system, threatening damage to some species and creating opportunities for others. Slight changes are sometimes absorbed without unbalancing the system. Other slight changes—an alteration in the external environment or a local mutation—can send the system into convulsions of growth or collapse. One of the most interesting things about complex systems is that they are inherently unpredictable. It is impossible, for example, to know in advance which slight perturbations in an ecological system will settle out unnoticed and which will spark catastrophic change. This is so not because of any flaw in our understanding of such systems, but because the system's behavior is generated according to rules the system itself develops and is able to alter. In other words, a system's behavior may be constrained by external factors or laws but is not determined by them."

[379] Daft, 25-27.

Violent Systems

At its most basic, this model shares the Five-Ring approach of viewing all organizations as *systems*. In the words of our old friend von Bertalanffy, it conceptualizes a system as an "organized cohesive complex of elements standing in interaction."[380] The interaction refers to two main patterns of behavior: (1) the relationship between the organization and the battlespace; and (2) the relationships among functions (capabilities). Regarding the former, organizations are too often analyzed in isolation from the environment with excess emphasis on internal structures, including organization charts, leadership, rules, and formal communications. While a useful aspect of organizational diagnosis, this closed system approach neglects the simple realities of IPB in general and our phase two analysis specifically; an organization "must interact with the environment to survive; it both consumes resources and exports resources to the environment."[381]

Figure 77. Ricin

Castor beans can be processed by terrorist groups with crude equipment and basic knowledge to produce the deadly toxin ricin.

Source: CIA, "Terrorist CBRN: Material and Methods," URL: http://www.cia.gov/cia/reports/terrorist_cbrn/terrorist_CBRN.htm, accessed on 6 June 2004.

It is an understatement to say that systems are highly complex. As put by noted organization theorist and practitioner, Richard Daft, "the organization has to find and obtain needed resources, interpret and act on environmental changes, dispose of outputs, and control and coordinate internal activities in the face of environmental disturbances and uncertainty."[382] To simplify, all organizations share the following basic components: (1) importation of resources; (2) conversion of these

---

[380] Thomas G. Cummings, quoting von Bertalanffy in *Systems Theory for Organization Development* (New York, NY: John Wiley and Sons, 1980), 6.

[381] Daft, 14.

[382] Daft, 14.

resources; (3) export of a product to the environment; and (4) feedback-based pattern of activities. Organizational inputs are many, but generally include raw materials, money, people, equipment and information.[383] Some of these inputs will represent the resource dependencies introduced in phase three, and a subset of these resource dependencies will qualify as the critical requirements our COG analysis seeks. Outputs can be objective and subjective, but generally include products, services, ideas and in the case of terrorists, violence. The conversions—the ways it transforms inputs into outputs—are often the most difficult to diagnose, particularly given the elusive character of terrorists—it is hard to penetrate the black box. Finally, all relationships inside and outside the system are dynamic; they involve feedback. As put by Daniel Katz and Robert Kahn in their seminal work on organizations, *The Social Psychology of Organizations*, "inputs are also informative in character and furnish signals to the structure about the environment and about its own functioning in relation to the environment."[384]

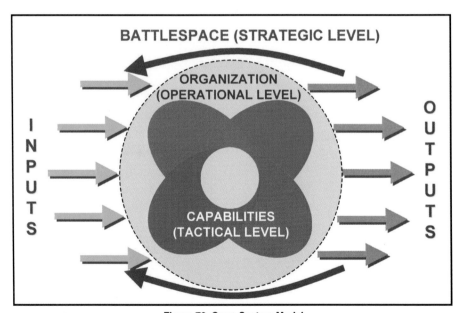

Figure 78. Open System Model

Source: Author.

---

[383] Michael I. Harrison and Arie Shirom, *Organizational Diagnosis and Assessment: Bridging Theory and Practice* (Thousand Oaks, CA: Sage Publications, 1999), 44.

If we can see inside the organization, we will confront a dizzying array of activities and behaviors. The open systems model helps by structuring these activities for us. Patterns of activity in all organizations are both formal and informal, and they reflect the most basic level of analysis. By examining how people interact with information and tools to accomplish tasks, we discern functions. *Functions* are patterns of activity with a specific purpose that contribute to the whole. Synching this up with COG analysis, *functions that can be performed are a capability*. The function of a flashlight is to shine light. If the flashlight works, it has the capability to shine light. In CT terms, the function of the suicide bomber is to die in an act of violent destruction. If Hamas can successfully deploy suicide bombers, it has this capability. All social organizations have a similar set of capabilities that fall into one of four general categories: support, maintenance, cognitive, and conversion. The specific patterns of activities that characterize the capability and its overall contribution to performance (strength or weakness) are unique to each group. Figure 78 is a model of an organization as a system, consisting of capabilities embedded in the organization, which are exchanging resources and information with the battlespace. The following paragraphs look at these capabilities in turn with one or two specific examples each.

---

[384] Daniel Katz and Robert L. Kahn, "Organizations and the System Concept," *The Social Psychology of Organizations* (New York, NY: John Wiley and Sons, 1966). Reprinted in *Classics of Organization Theory*, eds. Jay M. Shafritz and J. Steven Ott (Fort Worth, TX: Harcourt College Publishers, 2001), 262.

Figure 79. Human Shields

Terrorists use Filipino hostages as human shields after seizing them in Zamboanga, Philippines, in late November 2001 (Reuters).

Source: State, *Patterns 2001,* URL: http://www.state.gov/s/ct/rls/pgtrpt/2001/, accessed 7 June 2004.

Religious students in Islamic schools, or *madrassahs*, are identified and recruited for *jihad*, money is collected and laundered through a front charity, small arms are purchased on the black market, and communiqués are faxed to media outlets around the world.[385] These are just a few of the routine activities that constitute support capabilities, which manage resource dependencies, attend to stakeholder associations, and provide logistics (shelter, food, transport). *Recruiting* is an important, if not critical support capability that involves linking needs and expectations within a community to an agenda. Terrorists, the joint force, and others rely on a menu of incentives including the tangible benefits of a salary, training or shelter (transactional) and the more persuasive intangible incentives of ideology, sense of belonging, power, greed and possibly the promise of eternal life (transcendental).[386] Religious extremist groups recruit through mosques and *madrassahs* to support a radical theology; warlords with private militias recruit through family and clan associations to support predatory wealth accumulation; Maoist insurgents recruit students through universities to support a proletariat revolution.[387] And as evidenced on the streets of Baghdad and Tikrit during 2003-2004, Sunni groups hired one-shot terrorists using hard cash payments of over $2500.[388] Selection is an important aspect of

---

[385] Thomas and Casebeer, 23, available at URL: http://www.usafa.af.mil/inss/OCP/OCP52.pdf, or Thomas and Casebeer, "Violent Non-State Actors: Countering Dynamic Systems, *Strategic Insights,* (March 2004), URL: http://www.ccc.nps.navy.mil/si/2004/mar/casebeerMar04.asp, accessed 6 June 2004.

[386] Thomas and Casebeer, 25.

[387] Thomas and Casebeer, 25.

[388] According to NPR reporter Emily Harris, "Some 90 U.S. troops have been killed by hostile fire since May 1 (2003), when President Bush announced an end to major combat. Many of the attacks on American forces appear to be coming from Iraqis loyal to Saddam Hussein's regime." From "US Troop Toll Mounts in Iraq," *NPR Morning Edition,* 2 October 2003

recruitment that preserves stability by weeding out risky, low performing recruits or those that might prove difficult to socialize—it is tailored to the organization and what the battlespace affords.

Acquiring resources and attending to stakeholders are key support capabilities that have been developed throughout, requiring only modest elaboration now. The *resource acquisition* capability involves manipulation of the battlespace in order to obtain requirements for system performance (similar to organic essentials).[389] Like organisms, the resources required to sustain a group or carry out other capabilities become increasingly elaborated as the group moves through its life cycle (see below). As a reminder for phases one and two, resource dependency theory requires us to inventory resources of all types and assess their criticality and scarcity. *Attending to stakeholders* is an important capability for any organization, but particularly terrorist groups trying to survive in a state system. A useful method for evaluating this capability is to determine the actual and perceived value of a given association by looking at the group's strategy for dealing with them. *Proaction* involves extensive effort to maintain relations, address stakeholder interests and anticipate future requirements—Hezbollah's relationship with Iran in the 1980s.[390] *Accommodation* is a less active strategy that might entail infrequent interface, or only partial efforts to satisfy interests-suggestive of Hezbollah's relationship to Tehran in the 1990s.[391] The *defense* strategy involves doing the minimum required to keep the relationship alive, while *reaction* typically entails ignoring or rejecting the relationship—the "LTTE must be proactive in dealing with donor organizations in the Tamil Diaspora, whereas it takes a defensive, or even reactive approach to dealing with moderates and scholars in Tamil society who do not share their agenda."[392]

Jihadists are groomed through training camps and battlefield experience, a Maoist insurgent is executed by a comrade for collaboration with the state, and an AUC assassin is promoted for successfully killing a justice minister.[393] These

---

[389] Katz and Kahn, 84.

[390] Approaches for dealing with stakeholders are adopted from research by several organizational theorists into understanding stakeholder value to a given company throughout its development. Stakeholder dependency theory is admirably discussed in I.M. Jawahar and Gary L. McLaughlin, "Toward a Descriptive Stakeholder Theory: An Organizational Life Cycle Approach," *The Academy of Management Review* 16, no. 3 (July 2001), np, ProQuest.

[391] Thomas and Casebeer, 30.

[392] Thomas and Casebeer, 30. During the 1990s, the LTTE assassinated leading moderates and scholars in Sri Lanka. Daniel Byman and others, *Trends in Outside Support for Insurgent Movements* (Santa Monica, Ca: RAND, 2001), 47.

[393] Thomas and Casebeer, 30.

maintenance capabilities work on the people in the organization by socializing them to a set of values (culture) and enforcing role behaviors through a schedule of rewards and sanctions. Recruitment brings in members; *socialization* weds them to a set of norms and values, which as discussed in phase two, combine as culture. In phase two, it is the culture of the battlespace; here it is the culture of the stakeholder that is of interest. For an organizational value to be operationalized as a norm, three criteria must be met: (1) there is evidence of beliefs by individual members that certain behaviors are expected; (2) a majority of group members share the belief; and (3) there is general awareness that the norm is supported by most of the group's members, not just the leadership.[394] Norms, reflective of values, constitute the group's ideology and provide a more "elaborate and generalized justification both for appropriate behavior and for the activities and functions of the system."[395] *Rewards and sanctions* reinforce culture, generating the discipline required for groups to survive member defection. For CT, members who "display cowardice, reveal operational secrets to the government, or betray the organization in any way are often killed."[396] On the other hand, increased pay, promotion, prestige and even promises of a martyr's paradise are used to reward a job well done.[397] Tracking who gets what and for what reason provides insight to this capability as well as specific individuals who are more highly valued—suggestive of HVT.

---

[394]Katz and Kahn, 386.
[395] Katz and Kahn, 385.
[396] Thomas and Casebeer, 33.
[397] Thomas and Casebeer, 34.

Figure 80. Ahmed Omar Sheik

Pakistani police escort Ahmed Omar Sheik from the police station to the high court in Karachi, Pakistan, on 25 February 2002. The British-born Islamic radical was accused of masterminding the kidnapping of murdered *Wall Street Journal* reporter Daniel Pearl (Reuters).

Source: State, *Patterns 2002*, URL: http://www.state.gov/s/ct/rls/pgtrpt/2002/, accessed 7 June 2004.

A spy gathers intelligence, key leaders meet to plan a series of urban bombings, a cell structure is implemented to ensure secrecy, and directions are issued for acquiring nuclear materials. Cognitive capabilities are responsible for ideology and strategy development, decision-making, learning, and exercising control over the organization. The development and dissemination of *ideology*, or the core narrative, is among the most important cognitive capabilities whether using the system or network model. Ideology shapes strategy development. An optimal strategy matches capabilities to the demands of the battlespace and against the vulnerabilities, and ultimately the COG, of the opponent. Assessing "strategy is analytically challenging because you cannot simply rely on the statements of leadership or members—strategy is emergent, not directed."[398] Since organizations are organic, it is more appropriate to think of strategy as the direction the organization takes, regardless of whether it is intentional.[399] Diagnosing strategy begins by comparing the publicly disclosed strategy as reflected primarily in leadership statements and communiqués with the observed strategy based on pattern analysis of past activities and operations.[400] An explanation for the difference between "stated" and "observed" most often lies in battlespace conditions, a critical vulnerability, rhetorical excess, or intentional deception.

---

[398] Thomas and Casebeer, 38.
[399] Hatch, 113.
[400] Thomas and Casebeer, 38.

Strategy is implemented by the *control* capability, which attempts to align individuals and capabilities with the strategy. Control is implemented through formal and informal social structures. If a formal organizational structure exists, it is most often hierarchal, functional, matrix, or cellular. The informal structure is more important to actual performance, but more difficult to figure out. Social network analysis provides the best method for figuring out the linkages among agents, resources, and information. *Communication*—"the exchange of information and the transmission of meaning"—is a core capability for disseminating strategy and exercising control.[401] As the terrorist group grows and replicates, communication becomes increasingly complex, necessitating restrictions to prevent system "noise," or information that distracts and misleads.[402] As argued earlier, even though terrorists continue to rely on couriers and face-to-face interaction to ensure security, sophisticated information technologies have improved communication in three ways: reduced transmission time, reduced costs, and increased scope and complexity of information.[403] To avoid detection, al-Qaida and others have adapted common web-based communication systems with increased cleverness. For example, Microsoft Network's Hotmail email system is used to communicate, not by sending messages, but by preparing messages and saving them in the "draft" folder, where they sit until another operative logs on using the same account name—the message is never actually sent and is thus less susceptible to interception.

Terrorist associations, like all organizations, are cybernetic systems; they have a reflexive feedback capability that enables correction and in some cases, self-awareness.[404] CT players can survive without learning when the battlespace is simple and stable. Conversely, a high degree of uncertainty necessitates at least simple *learning* for survival—reflecting back on the relationship between information and battlespace uncertainty. *Single-loop* learning is the most basic, involving learning from the consequences of previous behavior, resulting in changes in "strategies of action or assumptions underlying strategies in ways that leave the values of a theory of action unchanged."[405] More simply, we adjust behaviors based on mistakes or new information, but do not question underlying norms and values. The Islamic Army of Aden (IAA) in Yemen offers an example of behavior adjustment without letting go of its *jihadist* values:

---

[401]Katz and Kahn, 428.

[402] Katz and Kahn, 430.

[403] Zanini, 35-36.

[404] Hatch, 371.

[405] Chris Argyris and Donald Schon, *Organizational Learning II: Theory, Method and Practice* (Reading, MA: Addison Wesley Publishing Company, 1996), 20.

In 1998, the IAA kidnapped sixteen western tourists, including twelve Britons, two Australians and two Americans. Led by Abu Hassan, the group's purposes included protesting the 1998 US military operation in Iraq known as Desert Fox and seeking the release of three colleagues being held by the Yemeni government on bombing charges. A rare attempt by Yemeni security forces to rescue the hostages initiated a two-hour fire-fight, leaving four hostages and three kidnappers dead. No prisoners were released, and Abu Hassan went to prison with two henchmen. Having failed to secure their objectives through kidnapping, the IAA changed tactics. In January 2000, an attempt to bomb a US warship failed when the explosive-laden raft sank immediately after being launched. This feedback did not cause a change in tactics, but a re-engineering of explosives on the raft. On 12 October 2000, a second raft blew a massive hole in the USS *Cole*.[406]

Single-loop learning is sufficient when operational and tactical change is all that is necessary to achieve goals. As uncertainty increases, decisionmakers must question and possibly adjust underlying norms and values—drive cultural change—or risk stagnation, irrelevancy, and defeat. The ability not only to correct behavior, but determine what behavior is correct, is essential for surviving crises—this is *double-loop learning*.[407] We learn to learn. Back to our IAA example, the value of attacking Westerners was never abandoned even though tactics changed; adopting non-violent protest or shifting strategy against apostate Muslim regimes instead of against the U.S. are examples of double-loop learning. Pattern analysis, status quo ante bellum overlays, timelines, and content analysis of strategy documents are methods for analyzing learning. Investigation of the mechanisms for collecting, analyzing and processing intelligence throughout the system is also required—all capabilities provide information through interaction with the battlespace, and "every individual, whether trained to collect intelligence or not, is a sensor."[408]

Child soldiers learn to shoot an AK-47, health services are delivered to a community, a suicide bomber records a martyr's video, underground bunkers are built, a politician is kidnapped, or aircraft are used as missiles to attack landmarks.[409] These examples of conversion capabilities prepare resources brought into the organization for export back into the battlespace. The terrorist *attack* is an important capability that anti-terrorism focuses on defending against; however,

---

[406] Thomas and Casebeer, 36 based on Bergen's reporting, 167-181.
[407] Hatch, 372.
[408] Thomas and Casebeer, 37.
[409] Thomas and Casebeer, 43.

CT IPB cannot afford to overlook other capabilities that may be more important to sustaining the group or a particular COA. For example, *training* converts recruits into terrorists, criminals, logisticians, accountants, or propagandists, while *production* converts resources into useful materials, including drugs (cocaine, heroin), weapons (vehicle-born improvised explosive devices, suicide vests), or social services.[410] Although conversion capabilities are often the main focus of combating terrorism, it is important to note that terrorist groups can survive an extended period of dormancy in their conversion capabilities as long as other capabilities remain active. Hezbollah, for example, can restrict kidnappings and suicide bombings for a year as long as it continues to recruit, socialize, sustain stakeholder relations, and propagate its ideology.[411]

System Properties

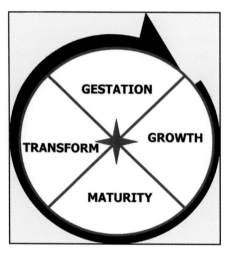

Figure 81. Life Cycle

Source: Author.

In addition to decomposing the organization into a core set of capabilities, systems analysis introduces three organizational-level properties too often neglected in the study of terrorist groups—life cycle, negative entropy and congruence. Terrorist groups do not spontaneously appear as rational organizations with well-ordered structures and patterns of activities. Rather, they pass through a distinct series of *life cycle* phases in form and function (Figure 81). As one example, when the conditions of violence meet a weak state and a charismatic leader with resources, incubation occurs and a terrorist group may be born—gestation. As the organization takes initial form, it will grow, adapting to its environment and becoming increasingly complex and differentiated by adding layers, cells, and capabilities. If allowed to prosper uncontested, or if highly adaptive even in an uncertain battlespace, the terrorist group may reach maturity where growth plateaus, but increased efficiencies and the birthing of terrorist progeny may occur—witness al-Qaida's transformation into a movement and the emergence of regional offspring. The life cycle is not necessarily

---

[410] Thomas and Casebeer, 45.

[411] Thomas and Casebeer, 47.

linear, since even mature organizations continue to experience growth in some areas. Maybe as a result of conscious strategy, but more likely due to battlespace conditions, organizations revert back to another phase.

Knowing where an organization is within its life cycle has implications for COG analysis as certain capabilities tend to be more critical than others at the various stages.[412] As a general rule, support capabilities are the most critical during gestation and early growth, whereas maintenance and cognitive capabilities are more important in late growth. Groups with transcendental goals, such as religious extremist groups, will value maintenance capabilities more than transactional groups like narco-terrorists who value conversion capabilities such as production and delivery of cocaine.

---

[412] For a summary of life cycle vulnerabilities see Thomas and Casebeer, 47-52.

Unlike organisms, organizations can live forever. Of course, their ability to do so is contingent on many factors, not the least of which is an ability to avert the natural entropic process. The tendency toward disorder and decline—information is lost, people fail to uphold role behaviors, conditions worsen—is forestalled by building negative entropy. *Negative entropy* is the "stock of energy," the "store of fuel," and the "winter fat" on which the terrorist draws during periods of crisis. It is common and often appropriate to think of cash reserves, abundant recruits and backup sanctuaries as the forms of negative entropy. Through application of the systems approach, however, other more potent and less appreciated forms emerge, including culture, socialization, social services, intelligence gathering, and command and control structures. In particular, adherence to designated roles due to an emphasis on maintenance capabilities can ensure a group survives a loss of a leader or sanctuary, financial interdiction, or seizure of weap-

Figure 82. ETA Bombing

Spanish police officers inspect the remains of a passenger bus set ablaze after a car bomb, blamed on the ETA, exploded near Madrid on 30 October 2000. The attack killed three persons, including a Spanish Supreme Court judge, injured more than 60 others, and destroyed dozens of cars.

Source: State, Patterns 2000, URL: http://www.state.gov/s/ct/rls/pgtrpt/2000/2434.htm/, accessed 7 June 2004.

ons. Figuring out how to cause defection, or deviation from role behaviors, may be the most powerful means of undermining performance. The source of negative entropy is a COG—CT strategy must deplete the stores of negative entropy in order to keep the terrorist from reemerging down the road.

The third property, *congruence*, deals with the "fit" or "alignment" among capabilities in the context of the battlespace. A terrorist organization is most likely to prosper when it achieves reinforcing working relationships among its parts, and importantly, between it and the battlespace. Good "fit" or congruence works against entropy, optimizes performance, and propels the group along its life cycle path. Al-Qaida demonstrated good fit with changing battlespace conditions by shifting to soft targets in Africa when the hardening of targets in the U.S.

and Europe made operational success less likely.[413] Misfit, or bad congruence, can disrupt organizational performance, ultimately leading to defeat—ETA shows poor congruence when it recruits undisciplined youth to carry out detailed attacks that demand strict adherence to operational secrecy.[414] Congruence analysis requires us to determine the factors that contribute most to harmonizing capabilities with the battlespace.

A clarifying example comes from an examination of the Colombian FARC.[415] The FARC imports recruits as well as guns, training (this includes training from outside groups, such as the urban tactics training provided by the Provisional IRA since 1998) and drug monies (resource dependencies). The FARC converts, or transforms the recruit input into a trained guerrilla. The reorganized input is exported to the battlespace; the FARC recruit joins a unit and conducts attacks on Colombian armed forces. This pattern of activity is cyclic; the attacks generate new resource inputs—recruits, resources, governmental responses. In a clear rejection of the closed-system approach, the FARC seeks to avoid inevitable disorganization and death by importing more energy (recruits, guns, funds) than it expends. Indeed, it is this adaptive characteristic that has enabled the FARC to survive CT efforts—suggestive of a CC. The energy inputs are also informative, providing intelligence about the battlespace. The quality of available recruits provides insight into changes in the social dimension and a change in the payments schedule by the drug cartels provides intelligence on the current profitability of the drug market. In more obvious feedback cases, the FARC conducts covert surveillance against a police station to determine vulnerabilities, which in turn impacts operational planning. Defeat in combat also provides the negative feedback required to drive a fundamental shift in tactics.

Universal Model

To summarize, the open systems approach asks us to analyze all organizations, including terrorists, on three levels: environment (battlespace), organization (system), and internal elements (functions). In addition to stressing the importance of conducting analysis on relationships within and across levels, systems analysis leaves us with these key ideas:

(1) An organization's effectiveness and success depends heavily on its ability to adapt to its environment, shape the environment, or find a favor-

---

[413] Thomas and Casebeer, 16.
[414] Thomas and Casebeer, 16.
[415] Adapted from Thomas and Casebeer, 14-15.

able environment in which to operate;

(2) Organizations will use their products, services and ideas as inputs to organizational maintenance and growth;

(3) An organization's effectiveness depends substantially on its ability to meet internal system needs—including tying people to their roles in the organization, conducting transformative processes and managing operations—as well as on adaptation to the environment; and

(4) Developments in and outside of organizations create pressures for change as well as forces for inertia and stability.[416]

It also directs analysis at four generic and several specific capabilities that are candidate critical capabilities for COG in the environment, ideology or organization itself. Insight into life cycle, negative entropy and congruence also help zero us in on the right steps in the COG ladder. Prioritization and focus is the key; USMC doctrine argues:

> We should try to understand the enemy system in terms of a relatively few centers of gravity or critical vulnerabilities because this allows us to focus our own efforts. The more we can narrow it down, the more easily we can focus. However, we should recognize that most enemy systems will not have a single center of gravity on which everything else depends, or if they do, that center of gravity will be well protected. It will often be necessary to attack several lesser centers of gravity or critical vulnerabilities simultaneously or in sequence to have the desired effect... We should try to understand the unique characteristics that make the enemy system function so that we can penetrate the system, tear it apart, and, if necessary, destroy the isolated components. We should seek to identify and attack critical vulnerabilities and those centers of gravity without which the enemy cannot function effectively. This means focusing outward on the particular characteristics of the enemy rather than inward on the mechanical execution of predetermined procedures. [417]

The open systems model is a universal framework for a global problem set. As a transportable tool, it allows for structured analysis across regions, which is increasingly important given the transnational character of terrorism. Recognizing the uniqueness of groups, it also provides common scaffolding on which to

---

[416] Harrison and Shirom, 47-48.
[417] MCDP 1-1, 47, 76.

build the signatures of specific organizations ranging from the IRA to JI to Earth First!

PARTING SHOTS

On its worst counterterrorism day, the joint force engages determined enemies, cautious communities, stressed security forces, raging identity entrepreneurs, and conflicted NGOs. These stakeholders and others form a web of influence that the joint force and its allies must negotiate to accomplish the mission. Our understanding of this web gains fidelity in phase three by incorporating the *continuum of relative interest* concept, which tags stakeholders based on interest and utility to the CT mission. Even when intentions are not known, a range of potential COA and the opportunity for influencing them can be gauged by a clear assessment of interest. The prospects for operational success are further improved by an "actionable" evaluation of capabilities that enables us to (1) affect centers of gravity and (2) bound the set of potential COA.

Phase three of joint IPB doctrine prescribes four steps for evaluating capabilities that are retained for CT IPB with modifications. Step one is the alpha and the omega of capabilities evaluation—COG analysis. Centers of gravity are the hubs of power, the sources of strengths, and the ultimate focus of CT efforts to undermine or bolster stakeholder performance and mindset. Despite arguments to the contrary, there are no "magic lists" of COG for CT, although there are prime candidates depending on the level. At the strategic level, battlespace conditions (poverty, exclusion from power), ideology (extremist theology, revolutionary Marxism), and global networks are prime candidates. Cutting across levels, leadership (Osama, Abimael Guzman) is a perennial favorite; however, experts caution against such optimism, particularly in networked forms of organizations where leadership is decentralized.[418] Other operational-level "A-list" COG include intelligence gathering, finances, sanctuary, command and control, culture, skilled operatives with weapons, and alliances.

COG are enabled by critical capabilities, which may themselves be COG lower on the ladder. The network and system models suggest several CC, many overlooked by traditional analysis, including: resource acquisition, socializa-

---

[418] In an 18 August 2003 interview, four leading RAND CT experts (Brian Jenkins, Bruce Hoffman, John Parachini, William Rosenau) agreed that the capture of bin Laden would change the Al-Qaida organization, but would not bring it down. According to Rosenau, "Although enormously important to the movement, bin Laden's death or capture would not mean the end of Al-Qaida. Al-Qaida isn't like Peru's Shining Path, where the arrest of its leader, 'Presidente Gonzalo,' led to the group's virtual collapse." *Symposium: Diagnosing Al-Qaida*, reprinted from *Front Page Magazine*, 18 August 2003, URL: www.rand.org/news/newslinks/fp.html, accessed on 7 April 2004.

tion, narrative construction, organizational learning, communications, and service delivery. Good sense also suggests that our analysis look into the less sexy, but equally important tactical-level capabilities of eating, sleeping, moving, sheltering. CC have resource requirements (information, money, people, objects, space) that may reflect dependencies on the battlespace. To the extent that these dependencies are critical and susceptible to disruption, manipulation, or strengthening, they represent critical vulnerabilities. Key nodes, decisive points, or HVT are most likely to be found in CC and CR, and where they can be accessed, they are CV.

An initial cut at COG-CC-CR-CV gives focus to step two: update threat models. Traditional threat models are insufficient for CT, leading to the introduction of network and systems models as cutting-edge approaches. Both require us to evaluate the stakeholder in relationship to the battlespace and as a whole. Breaking the organization down, analysis is directed at relationships and core functions. Moreover, these models capture several capabilities that are often more relevant to CT missions, including ideology dissemination, strategy development, social service delivery, and others mentioned above. Importantly, CT IPB does not dismiss the need to develop inventories of equipment, chart authority structures, or analyze tactics. Instead, it subsumes these basics of conventional analysis into an overall *operational code*. Models display stakeholder capabilities under ideal conditions, necessitating the reality test of step three—what the battlespace affords. In step four, sanity-checked capabilities are translated into a set of potential COA stated as capabilities—Abu Sayyaf can kidnap three people a week; Hezbollah can fund twelve clinics a year; NetAid can open and support three alternative *madrassahs* a year. Once the set of available COA and supporting capabilities are identified, we update our COG analysis to (1) determine which represent critical capabilities and (2) how CC link up to COG. Working back down the ladder, we figure out (3) what CR exist for each and (4) whether any of the CR have critical vulnerabilities. Time and resources depending, this process is conducted for every stakeholder in prioritized order. At a minimum, it is done for the terrorist and reversed against the joint force. We are cautioned against engaging the enemy without first having figured out our own COG ladder. When successfully performed, phase three not only answers the question, What can they do to us?, but What can we do to them?

CHAPTER 5

ANTICIPATING ACTIONS

Forty-one armed Chechens, including several female suicide bombers, seize the Dubrovka Theater in Moscow; the al-Jihad organization merges with al-Qaida and begins operations outside of Egypt; and in Iraq and Afghanistan we see increased targeting of non-governmental (NGO) and inter-governmental (IGO) organizations.[419] These real-world examples are indicative of terrorist group courses of action (COA) in response to changing battlespace conditions and efforts to combat terrorism by the U.S. and others. The first represents dramatic tactical action in October 2002 by a Chechen group, calling itself the Islamic Suicide Squad, to achieve strategic effects in the heart of Russia. The second reflects a major change in stakeholder association intended to leverage a shared ideology and operational code against their declared enemies, including the U.S., Saudi Arabia and Egypt. The third example suggests an operational-level trend in targeting with strategic and tactical consequences. Anticipating these and other terrorist actions is not only difficult; it is often impossible. While our analysis may reveal interests, it can rarely penetrate the veil of secrecy, deception, misperception and uncertainty that shrouds intentions. Mark Kauppi, director of counterterrorism analysis for the Joint Military Intelligence Training Center (JMITC), clarifies our challenge:

> Trying to determine if a military conflict or invasion is about to occur is challenging enough—the intelligence community has been given a failing grade for not anticipating Pearl Harbor, the Korean War, China's entry into that war, the 1973 Arab-Israeli War, and the Iraqi invasion of

---

[419] On 23 October 2002, 41 Chechen separatists took 800+ Moscow theatergoers hostage. The 57-hour crisis ended in the death of 129 hostages and 41 terrorists due primarily to the use of the aerosol opiate, fentanyl by Moscow authorities. Before being knocked out by the green gas pouring through the vents, one of the female bombers reported told a hostage, "We have come here to die, we all want to go to Allah, and you will be going with us." John Donahoe, "The Moscow Hostage Crisis: An Analysis of Chechen Terrorist Goals," *Strategic Insights,* May 2003, URL: http://www.ccc.nps.navy.mil/ rsepResources/si/may03/russia.asp, accessed 10 June 2004. Also see: "Hostages speak of storming terror," BBC News, 26 October 2002, URL: http://news.bbc.co.uk/2/hi/europe/2363679.stm, accessed on 10 June 2004. Al-Jihad, or Egyptian Islamic Jihad, reportedly merged with Al-Qaida in 2001 after at least a decade of cooperation, and increased its presence in Yemen, Afghanistan, Pakistan, Lebanon, the United Kingdom, and possibly elsewhere. Audrey Kurth Cronin, "Foreign Terrorist Organizations," Report to Congress (Washington, DC: Congressional Research Service, 6 February 2004), 49. The United Nations, International Committee for the Red Cross, Catholic Relief Services and Save the Children were all bombed during 2003. *Patterns 2003,* iii.

Kuwait. This was despite the fact that intelligence collection assets were directed on such "observables" as tanks, ships, planes, and foreign military and diplomatic facilities.

Anticipating terrorist action is an even more daunting task... The analogy of putting together pieces of the puzzle is apt. But for the terrorism analyst there is no box cover to assess progress, no piece has a straight edge, and hundreds of pieces from other puzzles are part of the mix.[420]

Despite the inherent difficulties, it remains our responsibility to assess possible stakeholder actions in relation to CT missions. Wide-eyed to the reality of not knowing what we do not know, phase four of CT IPB recommends methods for reducing surprise and developing a plausible set of COA available to the terrorist and other influential stakeholders.

Phase four ties together threads from previous phases, building on concepts and methods introduced thus far to go beyond battlespace awareness to battlespace knowledge.[421] It evaluates and anticipates the "Decide" and "Action" elements of the adversary's OODA Loop, enabling the joint force to leverage its knowledge advantage to decide on optimum COA while preparing for a range of

Figure 83. Chechen Terrorists

Source: Donahoe, URL: http://www.ccc.nps.navy.mil/ rsepResources/ si/may03/russia.asp, accessed 10 June 2004.

---

[420] Mark V. Kauppi, "Counterterrorism Analysis 101," *Defense Intelligence Journal* 11, no. 1 (Winter 2002), 42, 44.
[421] Joint Pub 2-01.3, II-53.

potential behaviors that may inhibit or enhance the CT mission. CT requires us to consider COA for all stakeholders with direct, and time permitting, indirect influence on mission accomplishment. Moreover, the emphasis of CT missions on diminish, disrupt, and defeat as opposed to defending against terrorist attack (anti-terrorism) necessitates preparing for a larger menu of possible COA. Predicting the what, where, when, why and how of the next big attack is certainly an important responsibility of the Intelligence Community; however, phase three's capabilities assessment indicates that stakeholders take a greater spectrum of actions relevant to their agenda (achieve goals/survive) and the joint force's mission. Will the pro-independence Kashmir Liberation Front (KLF) embrace the extremist Islamist agenda of Hizb ul-Mujahidin (HM) in an effort to reassert its influence?[422] Will Jemaah Islamiah (JI) try to establish training camps in the Philippines, or will it collaborate with pirates to move operatives and establish new revenue streams? How will the Algerian Salafist Group for Preaching (Call) and Combat (GSPC) respond to the Pan-Sahel Initiative (PSI) and increased Malian security capabilities? These are just a handful of the types of questions that can only be answered with insight into intentions and the specific plans to carry them out. Determining which questions to ask, identifying the set of possible options available, and evaluating each COA in sufficient detail to determine its likelihood and associated risks is the manual labor of phase three.

In this chapter, a multi-step process recommended by joint and service doctrine is introduced and modified to serve CT. The process has enduring value because it reflects an awareness of our knowledge gaps (holes really), takes into account adversary perceptions, and scopes the set of possible COA based on sound criteria. It begins by identifying stakeholder objectives, which guides the generation of all possible COA in step two. Step three evaluates and prioritizes the COA based on what the battlespace affords, the stakeholder perceives, and capabilities allow. Steps four and five increase fidelity and identify targets for collection, monitoring, and achieving effects. Rather than changing the process, the concepts and methods introduced here focus on how to achieve each step with

---

[422] According to Patterns *2003*, 147, "Hizb ul-Mujahidin, the largest Kashmiri militant group, was founded in 1989 and officially supports the liberation of Jammu and Kashmir and its accession to Pakistan, although some cadres are pro-independence. The group is the militant wing of Pakistan's largest Islamic political party, the Jamaat-i-Islami. It currently is focused on Indian security forces and politicians in Jammu and Kashmir and has conducted operations jointly with other Kashmiri militants." Further (136), "The Salafist Group for Call and Combat (GSPC), an outgrowth of the GIA [Armed Islamic Group], appears to have eclipsed the GIA since approximately 1998 and is currently the most effective armed group inside Algeria. In contrast to the GIA, the GSPC has gained some popular support through its pledge to avoid civilian attacks inside Algeria. Its adherents abroad appear to have largely co-opted the external networks of the GIA and are particularly active throughout Europe, Africa, and the Middle East.

Figure 84. Bali Bombing

Flags of Australia, Indonesia, and the U.S. hang at the explosion site in Kuta, Bali, Indonesia, 17 October 2002. More than 180 people, most of them foreign tourists, were killed and hundreds injured when a car bomb exploded at the nightclub. (AP)

Source: Department of State, URL:
http://www.state.gov/r/pa/ei/pix/events/b/eap/id/events/14470.htm/,
accessed 10 June 2004.

tools that have applicability beyond CT. Stakeholder analysis, which has been integral to every phase, is advanced by the introduction of an effects-based methodology for determining an adversary's desired end-state. Time-tested, but often overlooked methods are introduced for use in identifying and evaluating possible COA, including analysis of competing hypotheses, scenario analysis, and red teaming. Overall, this chapter argues for the adoption of *hypothesis* as an accurate and useful concept and hypothesis generation and evaluation as more valid methods. Success in phase four depends on knowing what we are trying to achieve over what time period and at what level of focus. Are we interested in anticipating the movement of a specific shipment of weapons into Somalia, or are we concerned with the changing role of communications technology in the al-Qaida network? But even as we focus our analysis, we are reminded that these actions have nested effects—tactical developments have strategic consequences. To the questions: What are we trying to achieve? (mission analysis); What out there matters most? (define the battlespace); How does it impact us? (describe battlespace effects); What can they do to us? (evaluate capabilities); we now add, "What will they do?"

BAD INTENTIONS

Phase four of IPB—determine adversary courses of action—attempts to figure out what plans are being devised and which are most likely to be implemented. The universe of possible COA is limited by the effects of the battlespace (phase two), the extent of stakeholder capabilities (phase three), and perceptions of both. Importantly, the only plans worthy of our time and effort are those that can influence the mission. For example, the GSPC might publish a new anti-U.S. website with no direct impact on a short-term CT mission of training Malian security forces—we would ignore it based on the methods offered here. Building on the *continuum of relative interests* from phase three, a complementary phase-four goal is to exploit adversary plans through disruption and manipulation to enhance the prospects for joint force success. Where other stakeholders are concerned, phase four guides us in influencing their actions to improve their contribution, persuade them with respect to key decisions, and influence their behaviors. These reinforcing objectives are achieved through five steps:

(1) Identify the adversary's likely objectives and desired end-state;

(2) Identify the full set of courses of action available to the adversary;

(3) Evaluate and prioritize each course of action;

(4) Develop each course of action in the amount of detail time allows; and

(5) Identify initial collection requirements.[423]

Air Force doctrine offers the only divergence from this "standard" approach, recommending steps to explicitly identify assumptions, conduct reverse IPB to consider adversary perceptions, and identify targets valuable to COA execution.[424] These recommendations appear to add value and are incorporated into the five-step process. "Perceptions" and its sister concept of "affordances" are integral to steps one through three, while assessing high-value and payoff targets are wrapped into step four. Before applying each step to CT, we pause to review key definitions and address a persistent debate regarding the evaluation of intentions.

---

[423] Joint Pub 2-01.3, II-54, and FM 34-130, Chapter 2, 44.
[424] AFPAM 14-118, 46.

First, intentions spring from interests, which are the underlying motivation for the pursuit of an activity.[425] Thus, the first step of phase four is focused on determining interests as they relate to desired objectives and end-states. Intentions are the mode for achieving an interest, and when translated into plans and actions, intentions become COA. For the joint force, a COA is a specific plan for achieving the mission. It details forces, time-phasing, schemes of maneuver, and other operational details, providing the basis for an operational order. For the terrorist, COA are plans to achieve a desired end-state, which can be conceived as a political goal and/or group survival (organizational goal). For other stakeholders, COA are the plans to deliver a service, achieve a political objective, or earn a profit. Whether a potential plan is relevant to the mission is a function of direct/indirect effects and the level of action—strategic, operational, and tactical. For example, a joint force COA to seize and destroy a weapons cache in Afghanistan is less concerned with the indirect, strategic COA of the Taliban to re-establish an Islamist regime than it is with a direct, operational plan by the militants to reinforce the position and defend the assets at all costs.[426] The key to assessing relevant COA lies in addressing the question: Can it influence mission success?

Second, determining intent is so difficult, so fraught with uncertainty, that many argue we should not even try "predicting the future." Rather, our focus should be squarely on capabilities. Cynthia Grabo, in *Anticipating Surprise: Analysis for Strategic Warning*, makes a case echoed by military commanders throughout history:

> Confronted with military forces which may attack him or which he is preparing to attack, it is essential that the commander have the most accurate possible assessment of the capabilities of enemy forces and that he prepare his defense or plan his offense against what the enemy is capable of doing rather than attempting to guess what he might do. There is no doubt that battles and probably even wars have been lost for failure to have followed this principle and that the commander who permits his judgment of what the adversary intends to do override an assessment of what he can do is on a path to potential disaster.[427]

---

[425] Medby, 98.

[426] During Operation Anaconda in March 2002, al-Qaida and Taliban forces put up a tough fight to defend a cave complex despite the most likely COA identified by the joint force being "escape." Brown, "The Enemy We Were Fighting Was Not What We Had Predicted," 21. Referencing an after-action report, Brown states, "Slide #54 graphically portrays the most likely enemy course of action titled 'ECOA 1 (Most Likely) Escape;' and slide #55 graphically portrays the least likely enemy course of action titled 'ECOA 2 (Least Likely) Defend/Attack."

[427] Cynthia Grabo, *Anticipating Surprise: Analysis for Strategic Warning* (Washington, DC: Joint Military Intelligence College, December 2002), 17.

Military historian John Keegan derives a similar conclusion in his assessment of the contribution of intelligence to victory in war through history: "[F]oreknowledge is no protection against disaster. Even real-time intelligence is never real enough. Only force finally counts."[428] The reality is that accurate assessments of capabilities and intentions are both difficult—there is an iceberg below the surface of our knowledge that is even bigger when terrorists are involved. Moreover, there are cases in which estimating capabilities has proven thornier than intentions. Grabo highlights the case of Vietnam, where "there was little doubt that North Vietnam intended to move supplies through the Laotian panhandle" to units in the South, yet it "proved very difficult to estimate the actual so-called throughput to the South, let alone the supplies which might reach any given unit."[429] If you are forced to choose between making an assessment of capabilities and intentions, go with capabilities. That said, judging both is inherent in all command decision-making whether we are cognizant of it or not. A simplified model of appropriate weighting based on the decision level is shown in Figure 85. According to Brown, at the strategic level, insight into intentions has historically proven more valuable to avoiding surprise, while at the tactical level, the range of possible intentions is sufficiently narrowed to allow capabilities-based planning.

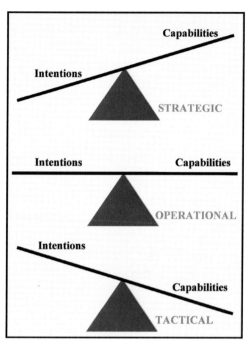

Figure 85. Intentions vs. Capabilities

Source: Brown, 27

End States

Step one begins with the rationalist assumption that plans flow from objectives, which seek to achieve a specific end-state. Objectives are either goal- or target-based. For the former, objectives are "clearly defined, decisive, and attainable."[430]

---

[428] John Keegan, *Intelligence in War: Knowledge of the Enemy from Napoleon to Al-Qaeda* (New York: Alfred P. Knopf, 2003), 349.

[429] Grabo, 20.

[430] DOD Dictionary, under "objective."

An objective can also be "the specific target of the action taken," such as a terrain feature or adversary capability.[431] End-states are "the set of required conditions that defines achievement of the commander's objectives."[432] Under existing doctrine, we determine these by analyzing the current "military and political situation, strategic and operational capabilities, and the country characteristics."[433] Getting only slightly more specific than this requirement to "know everything," doctrine recommends starting by identifying the overall strategic-level objective of the adversary—defend borders—before working out objectives at the operational and tactical levels. Objectives are further broken out for each of the forces involved, and when dealing with military operations other than war (MOOTW), for political and economic goals.[434] For all objectives, we are reminded by joint and service doctrine to state assumptions explicitly when the facts are unknown.[435]

For CT, the first step is even more demanding because we must consider a broader range of stakeholders, end-states, and objectives. Moreover, our dynamic view of the battlespace and organizations in it implies that objectives shift over time and are not always the result of rational calculation. Although changing a desired end-state may be the result of conscious decisionmaking, spurred by double-loop learning, it is also the result of life-cycle phasing, battlespace effects, and joint force coercion—it is emergent. Consider, for example, the case of Chechen rebel groups seeking sanctuary in the Pankisi Gorge of northern Georgia where it borders the Russian Federation republic of Chechnya. Among the groups using the area, the Islamic International Peacekeeping Brigade (IIPB), led by the notorious Shamil Basayev, probably envisioned using the mountainous area outside Tbilisi's control for staging operations, storing weapons, and shielding militants among local inhabitants. The IIPB's departure from Pankisi in 2002 was likely the result of multiple factors, including Russian pressure and U.S. support to the Georgian military through a Train and Equip Program, which gained momentum as reports of IIPB ties to al-Qaida surfaced.[436] There may have been a

---

[431] DOD Dictionary, under "objective."

[432] DOD Dictionary, under "end state."

[433] Joint Pub 2-01.3, II-53.

[434] FM 34-130, Chapter 2, 45.

[435] "There will often be gaps in what is known about the adversary. It may be necessary to develop assumptions to fill the gap(s) between what is known and unknown. Assumptions are educated guesses made when facts are not known... It is important they are recorded and communicated to planners and decisionmakers. At the same time, collection requirements should be [articulated and] submitted to confirm or deny the assumption. In all cases, be sure to distinguish assumptions from facts since assumptions involve some form of risk for planners." AFPAM 14-118, 46.

Figure 86. Georgian Commandos

Members of a Georgian Commando Battalion perform a combat off
load at a training range at Krtsanisi, Georgia. 10th Special Forces
Group (Airborne) participated in the Train and Equip Program.

Source: EUCOM, URL:
http://www.eucom.mil/Directorates/ECPA/Operations/main.htm&2,
accessed on 12 June 2004.

conscious decision to relocate, but it is also possible that it just happened without
much debate—migration often happens this way. As in this example, recognizing
a shift in objectives and if possible, the underlying causes, is just as important as
figuring out the objective itself.

Several concepts and methods have been introduced to help on this front,
including basic insight to group identity (ethnic separatist, religious extremists,
and similar), all of which provides a fix on whether the group is pursuing a transactional or transcendental agenda. The building-block approach taken to stakeholder analysis delivers insight based on a continuum of interests and a set of
relationships. We can learn much about a terrorist group by the crowd it hangs out
with. By using the models in chapter four we assess rhetoric, decisionmaking,
and learn to figure out narratives, strategies, and operational codes. Trend and pattern analysis are also available since many terrorist groups forecast shifts in strat-

---

[436] According to *Patterns 2002*, 136, "The IIPB and its Arab leaders appear to be a primary con-
duit for Islamic funding for the Chechen guerrillas, in part through links to al-Qaida-related financiers on the Arabian Peninsula."

egy and other plans, such as the opening of a new *madrassah*, using faxed communiqués, website posting, and other tip-offs. Friday sermons in mosques are sometimes a good way to harvest intentions for Islamist groups, while changing recruiting and group membership can suggest a new operational direction. Moreover, our approach takes into account end-states that link together objectives for each of the dimensions, going beyond terrain and forces to goals linked to public opinion, resource acquisition, and service delivery. In part two of this chapter, the functional analysis systems technique (FAST) debuts as one more tool for clarifying objectives when intentions are not advertised.

Full Set

Step two places a premium on creativity matched with solid work in earlier phases to develop a complete, consolidated list of all available COA. At a minimum, we must identify plans that: (1) the stakeholder's doctrine (narrative, operational code, charter, business model) considers appropriate for the situation and accomplishment of objectives; (2) could significantly influence the mission even if they are not optimal, according to doctrinal guidance; and (3) are indicated by recent activities or events.[437] The full set of COA is then evaluated in terms of perception, criteria, capabilities, and effects.

Reflecting on affordance theory from phase two, we are reminded that stakeholder perceptions of what the battlespace allows and what the joint force can and will do is often more important than what is really possible or will actually happen. Of course, knowledge of perceptions requires getting inside the adversary's head, which presents the same difficulties as analysis of intentions. As demonstrated later in the chapter, reverse IPB through the use of red teaming is one possible means of discerning what the terrorist thinks we will do so that we can figure out what he will do—it is a causal loop of action, reaction, and counteraction that demands an iterative, circular thinking process. Even with the use of structured methods, it remains unlikely that we can paint an entirely accurate picture of adversary perceptions, let alone our own.

By current doctrine, the list of COA is now to be tested against five criteria: suitability, feasibility, acceptability, uniqueness, and consistency. A COA is *suitable* if its execution can contribute to achieving the objective. A plan to announce a change in leadership, as Hamas did in 2004, is not suitable to achieving the objective of keeping leadership alive when Israel conducts targeted assassinations. A COA is *feasible* if sufficient time, space, and resources are available to carry it out.[438] Keep in mind that terrorist groups, including al-Qaida, operate

---

[437] Joint Pub 2-01.3, II-53.

under long time horizons and with limited or unexpected resources, exemplified by the first (1993) and second (2001) World Trade Center attacks in New York City. *Acceptability* refers to the amount of risk that is tolerable to the organization. Contrary to conventional wisdom, the use of suicide bombers does not indicate a willingness to accept greater risk. Rather, it is reflective of a willingness to sacrifice, and if a martyr's death is believed to herald paradise, it may not even be perceived as sacrifice. Moreover, the originality, or at least surprising nature of many terrorist acts suggests a risk-taking mentality when in fact it is their surprising quality that make them less risky. Terrorist groups perceive risk as well—they need their operations to succeed to publicize their cause, build support, and garner resources. The *unique* criterion is simply a filter to ensure each of the COA is sufficiently distinct from the others to warrant independent analysis. A COA is unique if it has <u>significant</u> differences in terms of effects, resources, location, participants, or operational plans.[439] The final criterion requires COA to be *consistent* with doctrine, or in the case of CT, the operational code. We are cautioned, however, that an adversary may deviate from doctrine to achieve surprise or due to other factors, including desperation, past failures, and changes in leadership.

Criteria screening results in a consolidated list of COA that are next tested against our analysis from phase three—can they do it? Since our evaluation of stakeholder capabilities is certain to be only partially accurate, we should avoid eliminating COA that are just outside the assessed range of capabilities. The Japanese cult and terrorist group, Aum Shinrikyo, for example, surprised everyone with the extent of its chemical (sarin) and biological (botulism toxin) programs as well as efforts to acquire conventional munitions, develop laser weapons, and possibly acquire a nuclear capability.[440] The bottom line is that we "must have a high degree of confidence that the adversary truly lacks the means of adopting such COAs, and is incapable of innovation or change in TTP that may make such a COA feasible" before we drop it.[441] Having narrowed the COA by perceptions,

---

[438] Joint Pub 2-01.3, II-54.

[439] Joint Pub 2-01.3, II-54.

[440] "Documents recovered by Japanese police in the investigation of Aum Shinrikyo involvement in the Tokyo subway sarin gas attack reportedly indicated that the terrorists were collecting information on uranium enrichment and laser beam technologies. A spokesman for Russia's prestigious nuclear physics laboratory, [the] Kurchatov Institute, acknowledged that at least one Aum Shinrikyo follower was working at the institute." Central Intelligence Agency, "The Continuing Threat from Weapons of Mass Destruction, Appendix A: Chronology of Nuclear Smuggling Incidents," 27 March 1996, URL: http://www.cia.gov/cia/public_affairs/speeches/1996/go_appendixa_032796.html, accessed on 10 June 2004.

[441] Joint Pub 2-01.3, II-55.

Figure 87. Aum Shinrikyo Headquarters, 1993

Source: Department of Health and Human Services, URL: http://
www.hhs.gov/asphep/presentation/diagnosticestacio.html, accessed on 12
June 2004.

criteria, and capabilities, we are left with screening based on the results of phase two—Does the battlespace allow it? In this final test, look at the battlespace effects over the period of COA execution to determine whether conditions can significantly shape, disrupt, support, or limit the plan.

With our consolidated list in hand, we are encouraged to review it one more time, looking for any opportunity to refine it with available intelligence on timing, phasing, sequencing, synchronizing, locations, participants, and any other factor that might clarify the COA and hint at plausibility. In doing so, three key requirements surface: (1) consider the possibility that the stakeholder may have objectives and choose COA that do not interfere with the mission; (2) remember that surprise befalls those who predict only one COA, so be certain to have several; and (3) incorporate consideration of *wildcards*.[442] Wildcard COA are less likely, but nonetheless have the potential to directly impede mission success if executed. Unexpected and unorthodox COA may be the result of creative, adaptive thinking by stakeholders, but they are also likely to occur as a result of desperation, misunderstanding, misperception, immature decisionmaking, ignorance, uncertainty, audacity, or a superior understanding of the battlespace.[443] It is worth noting that among all the potential adversaries the U.S. might face, terrorist groups are the most likely

---

[442] FM 34-130, Chapter 2, 48.
[443] FM 34-130, Chapter 2, 49.

to adopt surprising, asymmetric COA because "novelty" is what the battlespace affords, group capabilities permit, and stakeholder actions demand.

Current doctrine offers a solid, comprehensive approach to developing, testing, and filtering COA that requires only modest refinement in principle. In terms of methodology, doctrine says little about how to generate a good list up front, foregoing any explanation of even the most basic brainstorming techniques. Other shortcomings are less a function of the process than they are of imagination and cognitive bias. Perception errors and mirror-imaging are persistent problems that are more acute when trying to forecast another's planned actions. On the perception front alone, Heuer points to these common biases.

(1) We tend to perceive what we expect to perceive;

(2) Mind-sets tend to be quick to form but resistant to change;

(3) New information is assimilated to existing images; and

(4) Initial exposure to blurred or ambiguous stimuli interferes with accurate perception even after more and better information becomes available.[444]

Even the criteria offered by doctrine reflect Western mindsets as to when, why and how something might be done. This does not mean we should discard them, but rather it is a clarion call to greater appreciation of the value of cultural intelligence and the analysis of non-traditional dimensions of social and information transactions.[445] Techniques for helping with creativity and reducing mirror-imaging are introduced in the next section, and the pitfalls of bias must be dealt with always and often through a combination of awareness, collaboration with others, and the structured methods introduced in this book.

Priorities

The COA identified in step two are hypotheses (explanations under investigation) about what stakeholders will do—they are not facts.[446] That is, they offer the

---

[444] Richards J. Heuer, Jr., *Psychology of Intelligence Analysis* (Washington, DC: Center for the Study of Intelligence, 1999), 8-13.

[445] The concept of cultural intelligence naturally applies across several areas of human interaction in a globalizing world. A recent book about the concept as it applies to international business transactions is P. Christopher Early and Soon Ang, *Cultural Intelligence* (Stanford, CA: Stanford University Press, 2003). It seems clear that tactical and operational collection and use of cultural intelligence will be in proportion to the openness and astuteness of our operational forces, as well as of any forward-deployed intelligence professionals.

best estimation of expected behaviors until a better one can be identified; or the hypothesis can be refuted by evidence to the contrary. Hypotheses reflect our most informed impressions of what we can anticipate the adversary and others to do in light of current conditions. Inherent in this process is the recognition that these plans, like the results of all our analysis, are dynamic and will change based on joint force actions, shifting positions of other players across the dimensions, and organizational learning. To render the COA set more useful to operational planning and command decisionmaking, step three evaluates and prioritizes them as follows:

> (1) Analyze each COA to identify its strengths and weaknesses, COG, and decisive points;

> (2) Evaluate how well each meets the criteria of suitability, feasibility, acceptability, uniqueness, and consistency with doctrine;

> (3) Evaluate how well each COA takes advantage of the battlespace environment;

> (4) Compare each COA and determine which one offers the greatest advantages while minimizing risk;

> (5) Consider the possibility that the adversary may choose the second or third most likely COA while attempting a deception operation by evidencing adoption of the best COA;

> (6) Analyze the adversary's current dispositions and recent activity to determine if there are indications that one COA has already been adopted; and

> (7) Guard against being "psychologically conditioned" to accept abnormal levels and types of adversary activity as normal.

These procedures leverage concepts and methods developed here, requiring modification in terms of mindset only. For example, our development of COG analysis argues that decisive points are most likely to represent targets associated with vulnerabilities of critical requirements. While working it out, it is incumbent upon us to situate each procedure and COA within the context of the system of value and norms, or culture, of the stakeholder.[447] We need to adjust,

---

[446] Brown makes a similar argument, stating "a hypothesis is a universal scientific principle used to help explain possible enemy events based on analysis," 43.

[447] Joint Pub 2-01.3, II-56.

for example, our "risk management" model to account for the meaning of action by religious and/or ideological extremists as opposed to the meaning of outcomes. Westerners tend to be goal-driven, while others are often motivated by the symbolism of the act itself. We should not underestimate the potential for deception, but at the same time be blind to the obvious—sometimes terrorists do what they say they will do.

How the results of step three are presented should be the result of a dialogue with the commander and staff. A traditional, probability-based presentation may be sufficient. This type of presentation rates each COA in terms of likelihood relative to the joint force's plan. In its simplest form, we might state that COA #1 is most likely and COA #5 is least likely. For example, COA #1 is: that the Moroccan Islamist Combatant Group (GCIM) is most likely to use suicide bombers to kill tourists in the Djemaa el-Fna square in Marrakech during the month of August.[448] Even when using verbal descriptors of likelihood, some effort should be made to discuss these qualifying words to ensure standardized conceptualization of their meaning. Returning to the work of Heuer, he argues that

> Verbal expressions of uncertainty—such as "possible," "probable," "unlikely," "may," and "could"—are a form of subjective probability judgment, but they have long been recognized as sources of ambiguity and misunderstanding. To say that something could happen or is possible may refer to anything from a 1-percent to a 99-percent probability. To express themselves clearly, analysts must learn to routinely communicate uncertainty using the language of numerical probability or odds ratios.[449]

Figure 88 shows the result of one study involving NATO officers where qualifying words were assigned probabilities based on interpretation of their meaning.[450] Given the variance of perceived meaning, the need to formally assign it is evident. Sherman Kent, the first director of CIA's Office of National Estimates, recognized this problem and proposed the assigned probabilities shown by the gray bar in Figure 88.[451] Probability estimates will not be embraced by

---

[448] Moroccans associated with the GICM are part of the support network of the broader international *jihadist* movement. GICM is one of the groups believed to be involved in planning the Casablanca suicide bombings in May 2003. Members work with other North African extremists engaging in trafficking falsified documents and possibly arms smuggling. The group in the past has issued communiqués and statements against the Moroccan Government." *Patterns 2003*, 153.

[449] Heuer, 154.

[450] Heuer, 154.

[451] Heuer, 154.

everyone, and caution must be taken to avoid representing hypotheses in quantitative terms when they are really subjective creatures. Other options include identifying COA that are the most dangerous to joint force mission success, or most promising to achieve adversary objectives, or highest risk, most destructive, most complex, and any other qualifier that fits with the CT mission, time horizon, and forces involved.

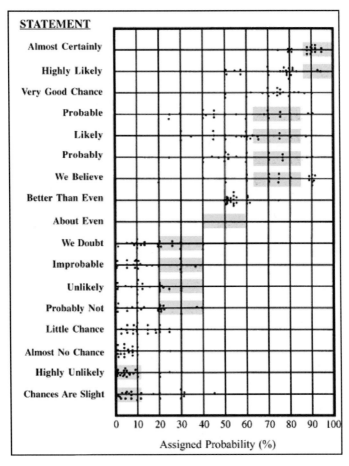

Figure 88. Measures of Probability

Source: Heuer, 155, URL:
http://www.cia.gov/csi/books/19104/art15.html,
accessed on 12 June 2004.

Detailing

Fleshing out and translating the consolidated list into a decision-quality, operational format is next. Working in prioritized order, step four answers five basic questions about each COA:

What—the type of operation: bomb, kidnap, smuggle, hide, recruit, and train (capabilities-based).

When—the timing, usually stated in terms of the earliest time the stakeholder can adopt the COA and its expected duration.

Where—the location (geography, cyberspace, cognitive) where the COA is carried out (positioning across sectors and dimensions)

How—the methods by which the stakeholder employs resources, skills and other assets to execute the COA (informed by an operational code).

Why—the objective or end-state that the COA intends to accomplish (effects-based).[452]

Answers to these questions are related and presented in three parts: situation template, narrative description, and targets. The answers also serve as indicators that can be employed to monitor COA selection and implementation.

The *situation template* is a graphic depiction, whenever possible, of the stakeholder's disposition and actions at key points in time for each COA. Ideally, the situation template captures the situation before the joint force plan is implemented and at critical junctures during the execution of both joint force and terrorist COA. These "snapshots" are strung together to provide a sense of how the situation will develop, including deviations (branches and sequels) to the main COA as events unfold. Several templates are usually required to capture the complexity of the COA and the array of capabilities and/or assets involved.[453] The situation template relates the description of the battlespace from phase one to the stakeholder's doctrinal template (operational code) from phase three and adjusts it based on the reality check of battlespace effects. The examples in Figures 89

---

[452] Adopted from FM 34-130, Chapter 2, np.
[453] Joint Pub 2-01.3, II-57.

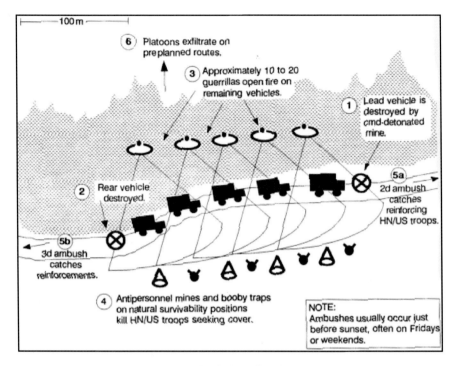

Figure 89. Ambush Template

Source: FM 34-130, URL: http://www.adtdl.army.mil/cgi-bin/atdl.dll/fm/34-130/
Ch3.htm#s3, accessed on 12 June 2004.

and 90 from Army Field Manual 34-130 are for insurgent COA; however, they may be equally applicable to a terrorist group. When an operation or capability does not lend itself to a drawing, or schematic representation, a matrix with discrete cells is superior to words alone as a tool for referencing a set of separate actions against locations, time, and agents.

These examples are suggestive of the types of products that can be created for a host of terrorist actions, including smuggling operations, communication networks, target surveillance operations, and training activities. At the tactical level, a terrorist COA to conduct surveillance against a potential target might involve a map of the urban area marked with options for terrorist transit in and out of the area (foot, mass transit, bicycle), positions for unobstructed observation depending on the equipment used (telescope, camera, eyeball), and optimal times to minimize risk. A *surveillance* template can be combined with a *sanctuary* template to capture another COA centered on the cover and concealment activities of a terrorist cell. At the strategic level, there is value in mapping situation templates for the

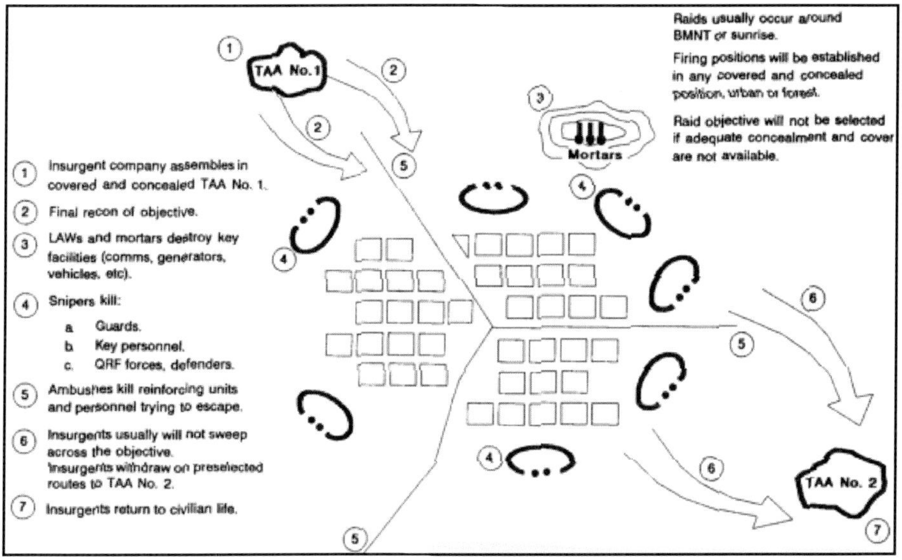
Raids usually occur around BMNT or sunrise.
Firing positions will be established in any covered and concealed position, urban or forest.
Raid objective will not be selected if adequate concealment and cover are not available.
TAA No. 1
Mortars
TAA No. 2
1 Insurgent company assembles in covered and concealed TAA No. 1.
2 Final recon of objective.
3 LAWs and mortars destroy key facilities (comms, generators, vehicles, etc).
4 Snipers kill:
a. Guards.
b. Key personnel.
c. QRF forces, defenders.
5 Ambushes kill reinforcing units and personnel trying to escape.
6 Insurgents usually will not sweep across the objective. Insurgents withdraw on preselected routes to TAA No. 2.
7 Insurgents return to civilian life.

Figure 90. Raid Template

Source: FM 34-130, URL: http://www.adtdl.army.mil/cgi-bin/atdl.dll/fm/34-130/Ch3.htm#s3, accessed on 12 June 2004.

overall al-Qaida recruitment, training, and socialization plan. One can quickly envision a graphic involving physical locations, timelines, organizations, individuals, and instrumental items or events (blood oath, completion of training, combat) involved in the "processing" of names like Jose Padilla, John Walker Lindh, Abu Zubaida, and in the following example, Mohammad Rashed al'Owhali:

> He was born in 1977 in Liverpool, England....Al'Owhali was brought up in a religious manner, in his teens devouring magazines and books about jihad, such as *The Love and Hour of the Martyers* and the *Jihad* magazine published by bin Laden's Services Office. He attended a religious university in Riyadh and considered going to fight in Bosnia or Chechnya in 1996, finally opting for training in Afghanistan. When al'Owhali reached the Khaladan training camp in Afghanistan, he was told that he should adopt an alias like everyone else. At a certain point he was granted an audience with bin Laden, who told him to train some more. He was instructed in the black arts of hijacking and kidnappings, with priority given to planning for attacks against American military bases and embassies and the kidnapping of ambassadors. He also learned how to organize security and gather intelligence. Al'Owhali then volunteered to fight alongside the Taliban, who were at war with Afghanistan's former rulers

in the north of the country. Distinguishing himself on the battlefield, he then moved to a month of specialized instruction "in the operation and management of the cell." The cell, he was taught, was divided into sections—intelligence, administration, planning, and finally execution. He was also taught how to do a site survey of a target using stills and video. Al'Owhali was now judged ready for a big job.[454]

Al'Owhali's "big job" turned out to be the Nairobi embassy bombing. When the massive bomb exploded on 7 August 1998, al'Owhali fled the scene when the plan to kill the gate guard failed—he had forgotten his gun. His case offers insight into capabilities and COA at the strategic level, which shape operational and tactical level COA—nested effects exist for COA as well. That is, COA development must include consideration of how higher- or lower-level COA influence each other.

The graphic situation template is supported by a clear, concise *narrative description*. At a minimum, COA description should address the "earliest time the COA can be executed, location of the main effort, supporting operations, and time and phase lines."[455] CT parallels exist, requiring time, resources, information, agents, and space (location) to be incorporated into a verbal description of activating cells or specific linkages, transferring money, posting to a website, indoctrinating a recruit, and conducting surveillance. The narrative also identifies critical decision points (event, time, or location when a command decision is required to engage the adversary), and if possible high-value targets (HVT) and high-payoff targets (HPT). As a reminder, a HVT is a resource, information, agent, or space that can disrupt or defeat a critical capability and thus indirectly affect the COG. A HVT is often a vulnerability associated with a critical requirement. Although not addressed as such in joint or service doctrine, time can also be a HVT when it can be controlled or manipulated in a way that undermines a terrorist plan. A HPT is a target that must be acquired and engaged (disrupted, defeated, or strengthened for allies) for the success of the joint force mission.[456] For example, a HPT for a COA to intercept an illegal sea-transfer of anthrax might be the ship itself and/or the crew.

In most cases, the details connecting an initial point to the objective are not known, requiring us to mentally wargame, or play out the actions to determine how it is likely to unfold and what its critical junctures, or decisive points are. *Wargaming* involves an action-reaction-counteraction sequence that seeks to

---

[454] Bergen, 107.
[455] Joint Pub 2-01.3, II-59.
[456] AFPAM 14-118, 52.

"visualize the flow of a military operation, given friendly strengths and dispositions, adversary assets and possible COA, and a specific battlespace environment."[457] It is a structured process that brings to bear all the results of our IPB work to test out joint force plans against the most likely or dangerous actions of other stakeholders. Each COA is played out on its own merits with a net assessment of all COA being held off until the end.[458] As the plans are mentally enacted, key decision points, high-value and -payoff targets, and named areas of interest are identified and recorded. Wargaming also helps identify knowledge gaps for collection.

Collection

In the final step, intelligence requirements are derived from the detailed development of COA in steps one through four. Each COA, when sufficiently specified, will suggest areas and activities that when observed will reveal which COA the adversary has adopted.[459] If a known terrorist operative is observed conducting reconnaissance of a housing complex for foreign nationals in Riyadh, Saudi Arabia, the activity serves as an indicator of a COA to target it for bombing. If a new *jihadist* website appears bearing rhetoric suggestive of JI, and it is linked to a server in Saigon, the activity suggests the establishment of a cell in Vietnam. The area where each of these activities is expected to take place is called a *named area of interest* (NAI). The word "area" is used loosely, not just in the traditional geographic sense, and can be a time, event, movement, statement, or any other development that indicates a specific capability is being performed, a plan is being implemented, or a decision has been reached. Importantly, NAI can also be applied to the sectors of the battlespace, serving as markers to assess changing conditions. NAI are only useful if they are sufficiently distinct to allow one COA to be distinguished from another. If all COA under consideration involve a wire transfer of funds as a precursor to any of several options, it should be used only to indicate initiation of a plan, but not to determine a specific one—"concentrate on the differences that will provide the most reliable indications of adoption of each unique COA."[460] Other clues to NAI include knowing the life cycle of an activity.

Named areas of interest are depicted on the event template and matrix. The former is a graphic depiction of where or when the NAI comes into play—it is added to the situation template as in the example for an insurgency of Figure 91.

---

[457] Joint Pub 2-01.3, III-3.
[458] Joint Pub 2-01.3, III-4.
[459] Joint Pub 2-01.3, II-59.
[460] FM 34-130, Chapter 2, 56.

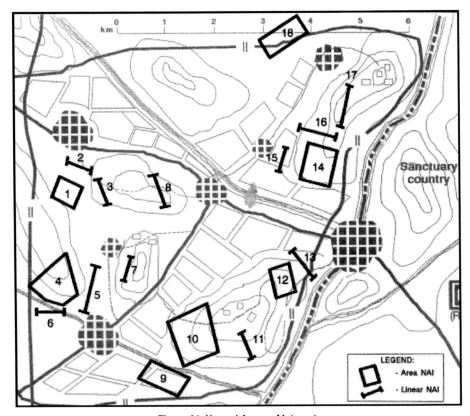

Figure 91. Named Areas of Interest

Source: FM 34-130, URL: http://www.adtdl.army.mil/cgi-bin/atdl.dll/fm/34-130/Ch3.htm#s3, accessed on 12 June 2004.

The insurgency example uses physical locations; however, NAI can also be mapped against a cyber-network, social network, or even time. An indicator that an NGO is preparing to move into the joint force operational area, for example, might be trigged by a phone call to a local activist, or a change in target selection by a terrorist cell might be evidenced by a coded email. The matrix offers a tool for capturing the specific activity expected for each NAI and COA. Figure 92 uses a conventional example to demonstrate how the NAI on the event template are referenced against time to build the matrix. Each NAI gets a full description of the key indicators for collection and monitoring. The integration of time allows for the entire life cycle of a COA to be depicted and used to develop a collection plan. These tools are integrated with the alternative competing hypothesis approach in the next section to maximize our chances of developing and monitoring the COA that are most likely to influence the mission.

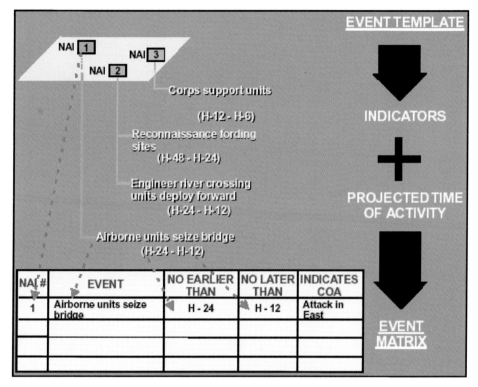

Figure 92. Event Matrix Formation

Source: Joint Pub 2-01.3, II-64.

GOOD PROSPECTS

We cannot allow the rigor of the five procedures developed thus far, or the proliferation of the word "predictive" to seduce us into greater certainty than our analysis allows. The consolidated and prioritized list is at best a set of hypotheses subject to continuous investigation. If we remain fully aware of its inherent limitations, the five-step process is nonetheless practical for anticipating actions that can influence joint force plans—its prospects are improved with the tools introduced here. In the previous section, concepts and methods from prior IPB phases were incorporated to improve the usefulness of each step for CT. Step one's requirement to determine end-states and objectives, for example, is supported by prior stakeholder analysis (web of influence, continuum of relative interests) and an evaluation of the narratives, operational codes, and strategy development capability of the group. In this section, the functional analysis systems technique picks up the stakeholder analysis thread by adding a method for

Figure 93. Mogadishu, Somalia

Source: U.S. Army Quartermaster Museum, URL: http://www.qmmuseum.lee.army.mil/
mout/somalia.html, accessed 7 June 2004.

assessing objectives when the adversary's interests and intent are shrouded. This
section adds new tools to improve our ability to generate a full set of COA without being limited by a lack of imagination or bias. Furthermore, they allow us to
evaluate and monitor COA in a more effective, accountable manner. Specifically, hypothesis generation is improved through pre-mortems, red teaming, and
scenario analysis. Each employs related concepts in a unique manner to avoid
thinking traps, such as mirror-imaging or satisficing, and generates an optimal
set of COA. When it comes to hypothesis evaluation, ACH is always the right
tool to use because it offers a simple, time-tested method for structuring evidence and monitoring COA implementation. In the end, all these techniques will
only take us part way to understanding how the adversary thinks. In the words of
Cynthia Grabo,

The path to understanding the objectives, rationale, and decisionmaking processes of foreign powers clearly is fraught with peril. Nonetheless it is important to try. The analyst, the Intelligence Community, the policymaker or military planner may have to make a conscientious and imaginative effort to see the problem or the situation from the other side's point of view. Fantastic errors in judgment, and the most calamitous misassessments of what the adversary was up to have been attributable to such a lack of perception and understanding.[461]

We must try. In the end, we will not get it exactly right, but the joint force is better off and our mission more likely to succeed if we at least know our adversaries have taken a decision to act and we have a sense of what actions are possible. Indeed, this may be enough. Once the adversary is met, on the streets of Mogadishu or the Internet servers of cyberspace, all COA are certain to change.

Fasting

When rhetoric is vague or inconsistent, when terrorist leadership is reclusive, or when deception and misrepresentation characterize policy, how do we unveil the objectives and desired end-state of the state or terrorist group? In tough cases, such as North Korea or Jemaah Islamiya, we can infer objectives by observing the behavior of the organization. Of course, even this is subject to intense collection difficulties. This approach, informed by systems theory, requires us to decompose the functions of the target organization. In phase three, for example, we used the systems model to identify a core set of terrorist system functions (verb noun pairs: climb mountain, recruit people, acquire resources, communicate guidance, produce weapons, and others.) These functions are the building blocks of a method known as Functional Analysis Systems Technique (FAST). Jason Bartolomei and William Casebeer, in their report to the Defense Threat Reduction Agency (DTRA), argue that systems engineers have long used FAST to "clearly identify the functions of the parts of a physical system."[462] The functions are then arranged in a hierarchal manner, which allows us to infer the objectives of the system "even in the absence of specific knowledge about the intention of the designers."[463]

---

[461] Grabo, 47.

[462] Jason Bartolomei and William Casebeer, "Using Systems Engineering Tools to Rethink US Policy on North Korea," unpublished report to the Defense Threat Reduction Agency, March 2004, 4.

[463] Bartolomei, 4.

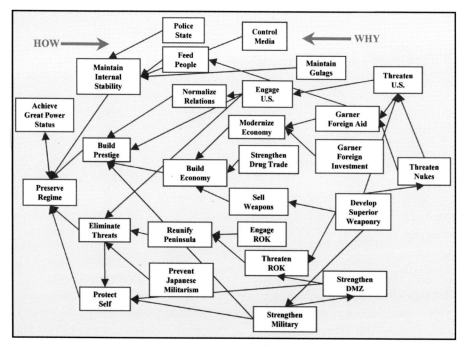

Figure 94. North Korean FAST

Source: Bartolomei, 5.

Bartolomei and Casebeer used this methodology to identify the objectives for all the stakeholders involved in negotiations with North Korea (Democratic Peoples Republic of Korea (DPRK)): U.S., Japan, South Korea (Republic of Korea (ROK)), China, and Russia. By observing the actions of each stakeholder, functions were defined. Their focus on North Korea, which shares some characteristics with terrorist groups in terms of secrecy and deception, offers a practical example that can be readily adapted to CT. The observed activity, for example, of increasing the density of artillery in the demilitarized zone (DMZ) is translated into a *strengthen DMZ* function.[464] In another example, the U.S. decision to introduce Patriot missile batteries along the DMZ served multiple functions, including *threaten DPRK* and *protect ROK*. Subject matter experts are brought on board to help identify all the functions as shown in Figure 94. Once all the observed functions are identified and consolidated, the FAST method organizes them into a hierarchical structure of "How" and "Why."[465] The diagram is read from right to

---

[464] Bartolomei, 4.
[465] Bartolomei, 4.

left to answer "Why" questions and left to right to answer "How" questions. According to their analysis, the DPRK is strengthening its military to protect itself, and

> [it] protects itself in order to preserve Korean Worker Party's (KWP) rule, which in turn helps it achieve great power status. Conversely, how does North Korea achieve great power status? By preserving KWP rule. How does it do this? By focusing on maintaining internal stability. Internal stability is maintained via a police state apparatus.[466]

The "Why" functions define the desired end-state and supporting objectives, and the "How" functions reveal the means by which objectives are achieved. This analysis tags *preserve regime* and *achieve great power status* as highest order objectives for the DPRK. From these, second order objectives to *maintain internal stability, build prestige, eliminate threats*, and *protect self* are readily identified. Working across the diagram, the other functions support these and so it continues until all the observed functions are mapped. If we applied the FAST to a terrorist group, we would likely find interesting higher-order explanations for the observed functions, particularly if we factor in culturally or ideologically-informed functions. For example, the function of *detonate self* links to several higher-order functions such as *access paradise, preserve group,* and *disrupt commerce*. That terrorist functions can simultaneously serve several higher-order functions is what makes it particularly dangerous and difficult to defeat. In its application, FAST is most useful when complementing more direct analysis of rhetoric, psychology, and trends in group behavior as part of phase three.

Hypothesis Generation

Hypothesis generation, or identifying the full set of possible COA, is the linchpin of phase four. Failure to identify the correct hypothesis as one of the initial options guarantees the right one is never evaluated. Canadian hockey legend Wayne Gretzky got it right when he said, "you miss 100% of the shots you never take." In a similar vein, we will miss 100% of the COA we fail to identify up front. A classic method for identifying options is brainstorming, which involves the freewheeling exchange of ideas without constraints of practicality or judgment until all the ideas are on the table. In practice, brainstorming more often turns into discussions over pre-conceived ideas. Brainstorming is inherent to the ideas presented here—pre-mortems, red teaming, and scenario analysis. These more structured methods champion creativity and adjust for the hard truth that

---

[466] Bartolomei, 5.

humans are notoriously poor at thinking of all the possibilities.[467] Each steps off from a different perspective. Pre-mortems look first at joint force COA and reasons for mission failure. Red teaming starts with the adversary and develops options based on its goals and character. Scenario analysis, also known as alternative futures, begins with the battlespace, identifying underlying forces that drive actors to certain outcomes.

Pre-mortems

The pre-mortem is the most elegant of the methods for its simplicity, but it can suffer from limited expert participation and a less rigorous process. Pre-mortems have gained traction among military planners as way to overcome placing too much confidence in their own plans.[468] The pre-mortem method seeks to shake us loose from pre-conceived notions, over-confidence, or personal attachment to a particular outcome by using mental simulation to find defects in a plan.[469] The planner is rewarded, not for defending a plan and arguing for its imperviousness, but for finding fatal flaws. In practice, pre-mortems involve three tasks: (1) assume the plan has failed at some future date; (2) actively seek out reasons for failure, probing for ill-advised assumptions, weaknesses, and complexity; and (3) develop strategies to account for possible causes of failure.[470] Well executed, it breaks down the emotional attachment to the plan's success, instead "showing creativity and competence by identifying likely sources of breakdown."[471]

Pre-mortems are useful for CT IPB if applied with some modifications. At a minimum, the pre-mortem should involve operations and intelligence personnel familiar with the joint force mission and proposed COA. Using the example of a mission to defeat an al-Qaida-affiliated cell in the tri-border region of South America (Argentina, Brazil, and Paraguay), a possible, and broadly stated COA is to use Special Forces to seize a high-ranking operative from his villa at night. Assuming the COA has failed, the first task is to identify all the possible reasons for its failure at any time prior to or during its execution. Likely results of this

---

[467] Heuer, 95.

[468] Gary Klein, *Sources of Power: How People Make Decisions* (Cambridge: MIT Press, 2000), 71.

[469] Klein, 71.

[470] Pre-mortems are also recommended for use by leaders and teams in high intensity, uncertain environments. See, Jim Stratton, Sam Grable, and Troy Thomas, "Expeditionary Air Force Leaders' Cognitive Skills for the Naturalistic Battlespace," *Air and Space Power Chronicles* (February 2001), URL: http://www.airpower.maxwell.af.mil/airchronicles/cc/stratton.html, accessed on 10 June 2004. Sam Grable and Troy Thomas, "Training the Mind to Deploy," *Air Force Comptroller Magazine* (July 2001, October 2001).

[471] Klein, 71.

"focused brainstorming" session will include logistical shortfalls, equipment breakdowns, compromise, relocation of target, strong resistance, and others. The second task is to select out all reasons for failure that can possibly be attributed to adversary and/or other stakeholder action, such as the last three examples. The third task is to subject each of these reasons to the tests of step two: perceptions, criteria, capabilities and effects. Keep in mind that several reasons may be related. For example, compromise by a Paraguayan official (COA: determine joint force plans and provide to cell leader) combines with the smuggling of the operative out of the area (COA: continually relocate leader to avoid capture) to undermine the joint force plan. From here, we simply continue with steps three (prioritize), four (detail) and five (collect). The key difference between pre-mortems and red teaming is that pre-mortems start by questioning the joint force COA while red teaming starts with the adversary COA. Ideally, time will allow us to run both and compare results.

Red Teaming

Red teaming has a distinguished record in the defense community as a way to challenge feasibility, vulnerability, risk, and operational value, particularly with regard to acquisition and concept development programs. It also has a strong history in military exercises, such as the Air Force's Red Flag or the Army's National Training Center, where an opposing force (OPFOR) serves as a red team, emulating adversary tactics and equipment to train the joint force. According to a recent report from the Defense Science Board (DSB), "red teaming deepens understanding of options available to adaptive adversaries and both complements and informs intelligence collection and analysis."[472] Red teams project themselves "imaginatively into the terrorists' minds to devise adversary strategies, operations and tactics."[473] It is a structured way of simulating the actions-reaction-counteraction of stakeholders in the wargaming phase of operational planning. For COA generation, it offers a methodology for producing "valid scenarios consisting of detailed action to complete a terrorist objective."[474] Successful red teaming depends on a (1) supported, qualified team; (2) accurate perspective; and (3) structured approach.

---

[472] Defense Science Board (DSB) Task Force, "The Role and Status of DOD Red Teaming Activities," Report to the Office of the Under Secretary of Defense for Acquisition, Technology, and Logistics (September 2003), 1.

[473] Joshua Sinai, "Red Teaming the Terrorist Threat to Preempt the Next Waves of Catastrophic Terrorism," briefing presented at the 14th Annual NDIA SO/LIC Symposium and Exhibition, 12 February 2003, slide 6.

[474] Judy Moore, John Whitley, and Rick Craft, "Red Gaming in Support of the War on Terrorism: Sandia Red Game Report," Summary of Red Game held 22-24 July 2003 (February 2004), 12.

Figure 95. Triborder Meeting

In December 2002, delegates from the U.S., Paraguay, Argentina, and Brazil meet for the first Three Plus One Triborder Area Counterterrorism Meeting.

Source: State, *Patterns 2002*, URL: http://www.state.gov/s/ct/rls/pgtrpt/2002/html/19987.htm, accessed 7 June 2004.

Implied in this methodology is the use of a team consisting of individuals selected for their subject-matter expertise, professional or cultural perspective, imagination, or even skill at critical analysis.[475] In the field, it is rarely possible to pull in experts from relevant groups, such as NGOs or community leaders; therefore, every effort must be made to bring in experts from the staff that may meet the above criteria, including talented individuals from the chaplaincy, security police, logistics, public affairs, operations, and intelligence. Also consider identifying participants who bring imagination or a critical eye even if they lack experience or expertise. Teams often fail due to a lack of institutional support, particularly because they can become time-intensive and through their introduction of uncertainty, they are perceived as disruptive to programs or COA to which the staff is already wedded.[476] But this disruption carries the value of mitigating surprise. Other typical causes of red team failure involve not taking the assignment seriously, being captured by bureaucratic interests, becoming too removed from the decisionmaking process, failing to deliver results in a timely manner, and leaking results prematurely.[477]

Getting an accurate perspective demands more than putting on terror's mask; it requires going deep into culture and drawing on all the well-grounded social and cultural intelligence recommendations available. It also requires attending to all the pitfalls of perception. In the words of red teaming expert Mark Mateski, "the view from a defense contractor's office or an academician's window is not the same as the view from the proverbial 'Arab street,' nor can a lifetime's worth of

---

[475] DSB, 3.

[476] John F. Sandoz, "Red Teaming: A Means to Military Transformation," Report for the Joint Advanced Warfighting Program, Institute for Defense Analysis (January 2001), 4.

[477] DSB, 5.

study ever replicate the texture of first-hand knowledge."[478] With this in mind, effort must be expended up front to ensure all prospective members and the team as a whole invest in analysis of the social and information dimensions of the battlespace as well as the worldview, desired end-state, narrative, operational code, and tactics of the terrorist group. This is equally valid for other stakeholders. What are the social norms of the Nigerian peacekeepers in Sierra Leone? How does NetAid initiate and develop relations with community leaders? What role will the International Committee of the Red Cross (ICRC) be playing in the operational area? Ideally, these stakeholders will be open about their perspective and operational codes; this is not always the case.

A qualified red team rooted in a well-developed social intelligence perspective can employ a variety of structured methods—brainstorming, alternative scenarios, and an evolving "attack tree" approach-to develop a full set of COA.[479] Regardless of the method, several ingredients should always be present. First, *clearly define the objective* of the red team. For example, the objective may be to identify the full set of actions by which terrorist cells in the triborder region can generate income, undermine governance, obtain sanctuary, or interfere with a joint force mission. Are we trying to predict the next big attack, or anticipate a shift in safe haven or training locations? Thinking in terms of options other than actions intended to interfere with the joint force is important since it is often likely that the terrorist group or other stakeholder is (1) not aware of our plans and (2) will execute COA that interfere by accident rather than conscious planning. For example, the relocation of an operative from a house in the triborder town of Ciudad Del Este may have less to do with the impending capture operation than it does with an invitation to dinner or a family emergency.

---

[478] Mark Mateski, "Red Teaming Terrorism, Part I," Method Paper 1.03, *Red Team Journal* (June 2003), URL: http://www.redteamjournal.com/methods/redTeamingTerrorismPt1.htm, accessed on 11 March 2004.

[479] The "attack tree" method is recommended by Mateski and developed by security expert Bruce Schneier. According to Schneier, "Attack trees provide a formal, methodical way of describing the security of systems, based on varying attacks. Basically, you represent attacks against a system in a tree structure, with the goal as the root node and different ways of achieving that goal as leaf nodes." For details and examples on the method, see "Attack Trees: Modeling security threats," *Dr. Dobb's Journal* (December 1999), URL: http://www.schneier.com/paper-attacktrees-ddj-ft.html#rf2, accessed 15 June 2004.

Second, once the objective is defined, *brainstorm on all the possible options for achieving the objective.* Do not rule anything out initially; save filtering for the third requirement—*test the options against pre-established constraints.* The constraints are most often going to be our familiar perceptions, five criteria, capabilities, and effects. Additional constraints can be added based on the red teaming objective, which reflects constraints of the CT mission. In the Sandia National Laboratories Red Gaming project, for example, realistic constraints were established for a terrorist event in the Washington DC subway system within a two year window:

Figure 96. ICRC

An Afghan woman waits for by her share of grain and oil from the ICRC.

Source: EUCOM, URL: http://www.eucom.mil/
Directorates/ECPA/index.htm?http://
www.eucom.mil/Directorates/ECPA/Operations/
oef/oef.htm&2,
accessed 7 June 2004.

People: Teams were allowed to recruit others in country and out of country—but if they were going to assume the presence of resources from out of country, they would have to plan for getting them into the country.

Risk: Their cell could be completely destroyed but leaving a trail to other al-Qaida leaders was not acceptable. They would want to get credit for al-Qaida for the event but they didn't want to be detected before completion.

Money: $100,000 was available from overseas to support the cell's effort, but they would need to communicate to get it. Making money was allowed. Charitable fund raising was also allowed.

Communications: Open source information was assumed, no special means of communication was assumed.

Skills: The team could assume that they had whatever knowledge or skills the real players had. At the end of the game the Game Masters would query the teams about how any specialized knowledge could have been gained—in particular what actions would be required.

Context for the Individuals: The team would assume that most of them had only been here for a few years and had tried to maintain a low profile. They were not citizens and were here on visas. All were extremely loyal and dedicated to the cause of al-Qaida.[480]

The fourth requirement is to *detail each option*, thinking three-to-five moves ahead within the context of a single COA. Importantly, many operational methods, such as wire transfers, entering a country, or detonating a bomb, are common across groups and scenarios. By developing a menu of "reusable" operational methods, team members can avoid reinventing the wheel for each option and focus instead on how operational methods link together in a unique manner to achieve the terrorist objective.[481]

The fifth and final requirement is to *develop a robust list of indicators and observables*. Returning to the Sandia project, several high-level principles emerged regarding their general nature that are consistent with CT IPB: (1) answer who, what, when and where for each; (2) link indicators to the phase, or life cycle of each COA; (3) attach additional qualities (visibility, link to another indicator); and (4) determine the likelihood that a particular indicator will be noticed.[482] This last one is particularly important, as we tend to see what we expect to see and gravitate toward familiar indicators—troop movement, activation of a communication network, recalls, and others. For CT, we must get more creative in our indicator lists—religious school enrollment, group membership, charity events, web postings, coded emails, sermons, and many, many more. The true value of red teaming is its emphasis on getting in the adversary's head and employing a rigorous method for generating COA and preparing them for evaluation as hypotheses.

---

[480] Moore, 14-15.
[481] Moore, 18.
[482] Moore, 18.

Alternative Futures

Also known as scenario analysis, the alternative futures methodology attempts to overcome two key shortcomings of traditional trend analysis: (1) forecasting of single outcomes with attached probabilities; and (2) failure to encourage the examination of basic assumptions.[483] These failures reflect our tendency to identify a specific organization or capability and then to extend it forward into time without fully accounting for the effects of the battlespace. Scenario analysis, however, draws on our CT IPB phase two work by starting with the battlespace to identify the underlying forces that are likely to shape outcomes. Rather than focusing on what is known with confidence, this method embraces uncertainty and makes no assumptions regarding historical continuity or change.[484] According to one of its expert practitioners, Alan Schwartz, the analytical goal is not to "forecast what a system will look like in the future. The goal is to estimate the range of behaviors the system can exhibit within a given time period."[485]

Like the other methods, scenario analysis is best performed by inter-disciplinary teams focused on a clear goal. What question(s) are we trying to answer? For example, will Islamist extremist groups increase their presence in the triborder region in the next two years? Or, will Hezbollah obtain weapons of mass destruction (WMD) by 2015? With the goal defined, the first task is to *identify the range of battlespace effects,* or driving forces that can influence the outcome. In the case of Hezbollah, what forces from across the battlespace dimensions will influence a decision to pursue a WMD capability? A *driving force* is any factor, condition, or effect that might serve as a catalyst for the outcome, including the core incentives for developing and acquiring weapons. In a study conducted for the DTRA, drivers for weapons proliferation in the Middle East by a range of actors, including Hezbollah, were identified as resource scarcity, socio-economic conditions, regime behavior, internal conflict, defense/deterrence incentives, offense/coercion incentives, and stakeholder relations.[486] The key is to consolidate the number of relevant drivers into the fewest categories possible while remembering that they are generally interrelated, thus reinforcing and modifying the others.

---

[483] Alan R. Schwartz, PolicyFutures, LLC, "Scenario Analysis for Understanding the Development of Terrorism in Central Asia," unpublished report of the first working group, 22 September 2002, 2-3.

[484] Schwartz, 3.

[485] Schwartz, 3.

[486] Brent Talbot, Troy Thomas, Tim Uecker, "All Our Tomorrows: Proliferation Drivers in The Middle East," unpublished research report conducted for the Defense Threat Reduction Agency, 23 April 2001.

The second task is to *sort the driving forces based on effects and uncertainty.* Forces have a direct or indirect effect on the outcome. The DTRA study noted that Hezbollah's incentives to acquire WMD, for example, are influenced directly by a defense motivation (against Israel and/or the U.S.), an offense motivation (against Israel), a stakeholder incentive (relationship with Iran), and regime factors (prestige).[487] Next, each is sorted into those "that can be forecast with certainty and those about which there is much uncertainty over the analytical time period."[488] In the DTRA analysis, all of these forces were assessed as likely to remain directly influential through 2015 with high certainty. Less certainty surrounded the possible influence of internal conflict within Hezbollah or Lebanon, or the impact of changing socio-economic conditions. These driving forces reflect effects on the strategic level; however, it is also appropriate to look at the forces behind the forces to deal with operational or tactical questions.

Our next task is to *combine the drivers to generate a set of scenarios, or alternative futures.* The best place to start is with the extremes of each driver.[489] For example, what if Iran dropped out of the WMD business and Israel signed peace treaties with all its neighbors? What if Hezbollah split into two or more factions and Israel formally announced a nuclear capability? Continue by combining the extremes of all the drivers, which will result in four scenarios for each pair, and in this case of 7 drivers, 84 different outcomes with varying degrees of certainty. The scenarios represent hypothetical future conditions that will suggest a positive or negative effect on the central question. Since there is rarely time to evaluate every possible scenario, the "art" of this approach is prioritizing based on effects and uncertainty, and then testing each scenario against our standard criteria. The set of alternative futures can also be reduced by bundling the drivers into a smaller set. Another benefit of this approach is that it provides insight into how changing conditions can influence outcomes, which provides guidance for CT missions focused on diminishing underlying conditions.

Next, *flesh out the scenarios by creating a plausible plot or sterling.*[490] Basically, we must be able to tell a credible story that links current conditions to the future outcome based on the influence of the drivers while accounting for the degree of uncertainty. Returning to our notional example, we might have a high degree of certainty that Hezbollah will continue to confront Israel, and Iran will remain a key sponsor, providing the incentive and means for WMD pursuit. Time is sufficient to acquire a modest chemical arsenal, but not to develop a biological

---

[487] Talbot, 4.
[488] Schwartz, 4.
[489] Schwartz, 4.
[490] Schwartz, 4.

capability. We are certain funding is available for both, but we are uncertain about the availability of key resources. Finally, we *identify leading indicators of each scenario.*[491] The indicators serve as the evidence against which we monitor and evaluate the alternative futures, or hypotheses.

Hypothesis Evaluation

Outfitted with our list of potential adversary COA, which has been filtered by a series of reality checks and prioritized based on potential mission impact, we are now positioned to compete them against each other. Evaluation is innate to hypothesis generation; however, we can guard against the natural bias toward a favored or consensus COA through the analysis of competing hypotheses (ACH) method. ACH protects us from the tendency to seek confirming evidence for one COA. It turns the tables on traditional analysis by seeking evidence to refute COA, thus embracing a more rigorous scientific method. When faithfully applied, it helps organized evidence and arguments around a core set of COA. It can be used to evaluate COA based on currently available evidence (intelligence reporting), and it can use future reporting to monitor several COA to determine which is being enacted. ACH consists of the following eight steps, expertly developed by Heuer in *Psychology of Intelligence Analysis:*

(1) Identify the possible hypotheses to be considered. Use a group of analysts with different perspectives to brainstorm the possibilities.[492]

---

[491] Schwartz, 4.

[492] Hypotheses or "claims" must be "testable." That is, they must be imagined and phrased (positively, not as a question) in such a way as to be "refutable." Further, to gain the most value from the process of comparing and refuting alternative, competing hypotheses, each must be as mutually independent or exclusive (not overlapping) as possible. The more exclusive each hypothesis from the others, the more authoritative will be its refutation, with a given weight of negative evidence. See Louise G. White, *Political Analysis: Technique and Practice*, 4th Ed. Ft Worth, TX: Harcourt Brace College Publishers, 1999), 40-41 and Gary King and others, *Designing Social Inquiry: Scientific Inference in Qualitative Research* (Princeton, NJ: Princeton University Press, 1994), chapters 3, 4, and 6.

(2) Make a list of significant evidence and arguments for and against each hypothesis.

(3) Prepare a matrix with hypotheses across the top and evidence down the side. Analyze the "diagnosticity" of the evidence and arguments--that is, identify which items are most helpful in judging the relative likelihood of the hypotheses.

(4) Refine the matrix. Reconsider the hypotheses and delete evidence and arguments that have no diagnostic value.

(5) Draw tentative conclusions about the relative likelihood of each hypothesis. Proceed by trying to refute the hypotheses rather than confirming them.

Question: Will Iraq Retaliate for US Bombing of Its Intelligence Headquarters?

Hypotheses:
H1 - Iraq will not retaliate.
H2 - It will sponsor some minor terrorist actions.
H3 - Iraq is planning a major terrorist attack, perhaps against one or more CIA installations.

	H1	H2	H3
E1. Saddam public statement of intent not to retaliate.	+	+	+
E2. Absence of terrorist offensive during the 1991 Gulf War.	+	+	−
E3. Assumption that Iraq would not want to provoke another US attack.	+	+	−
E4. Increase in frequency/length of monitored Iraqi agent radio broadcasts.	−	+	+
E5. Iraqi embassies instructed to take increased security precautions.	−	+	+
E6. Assumption that failure to retaliate would be unacceptable loss of face for Saddam.	− −	+	+

Figure 97. Competing Hypotheses

Source: Heuer, Chapter 8, URL: http://www.cia.gov/csi/books/19104/art11.html, accessed 10 June 2004.

(6) Analyze how sensitive your conclusion is to a few critical items of evidence. Consider the consequences for your analysis if that evidence were wrong, misleading, or subject to a different interpretation.

(7) Report conclusions. Discuss the relative likelihood of all the hypotheses, not just the most likely one.

(8) Identify milestones for future observation that may indicate events are taking a different course than expected.[493]

Each of the eight steps bears some relationships to previously introduced methods, and thus serves as a useful overall framework that can incorporate premortems, red teaming, scenario analysis, or any other hypothesis generation technique that proves useful.

The first step is improved by applying any of the generation methods to come up with a full set of options. Before starting to weed out COA, keep in mind the difference between an unconfirmed and a refuted hypothesis. An *unconfirmed* hypothesis should remain on the table until evidence emerges, or our criteria make clear, that it is not correct. When positive evidence does emerge to refute a hypothesis, it joins the trash bin of other *discarded* COA. Ideally, the number of hypotheses on which we settle will be between three and seven. Use the overall level of battlespace uncertainty as a guide—high uncertainty, more options. Drawing on the indicators and observables developed earlier, we compile a list of evidence that is applicable to all COA as well as evidence that is unique to each. Simply ask, if this COA were true, what would we expect to see or not see?[494] Unlike previous methods, step two requires us to identify factors that argue for and against the COA and consider the absence of evidence as evidence. Not merging terrorist organizations, or not activating a communications node, or not issuing a statement is often evidence of COA selection. As argued by Heuer, we tend to focus on what is reported rather than what is not.[495] Think creatively and figure out what is missing.

According to Heuer, step three is the most important in part because it is counterintuitive. Rather than evaluating one hypothesis at a time to see how well the evidence fits, we look at the evidence to see how consistent it is with each hypothesis. To avoid being overwhelmed by the data, a matrix is used to organize the hypotheses and evidence. Figure 97 is an example based on a historical case that

---

[493] Heuer, 97.
[494] Heuer, 98.
[495] Heuer, 99.

asks: will Iraq retaliate for the bombing of its Intelligence Headquarters? In 1993, the U.S. bombed the Iraqi Intelligence Services Headquarters in Baghdad in response to a failed attempt by Iraqi agents to assassinate former President George Bush while he was in Kuwait for a ceremony. Across the top, Heuer lists three hypotheses, and down the side there is a simplified list of evidence as well as key assumptions. For each item of evidence, work across the row to determine whether it is consistent, inconsistent, or irrelevant to each hypothesis; use any type of shorthand that fits.[496] While doing this, assess the evidence for *diagnosticity*. Does it tell us anything? The evidence is diagnostic when it influences our judgment on the relative likelihood of the various hypotheses.[497] Evidence deemed to have the same relationship to all hypotheses has little diagnosticity; it is like a high temperature, letting you know something is wrong, but being indicative of nothing specific. Rather, evidence that is unique and observable for a given hypothesis should weigh heaviest in our judgment. In Heuer's Iraq example, E1 is the same to all, whereas E4 argues for H2 or H3, and E6, which is an assumption instead of evidence, argues strongly against H1.[498] In step four, we pause to review and refine; weed out useless evidence and disproved hypotheses.

Step five takes the opposite tack from step three. Instead of working across the rows of evidence, the analyst works down the columns of hypotheses. Working one at a time, our goal is to identify evidence or arguments that suggest the COA is unlikely. Heuer suggests:

> A fundamental precept of the scientific method is to proceed by rejecting or eliminating hypotheses, while tentatively accepting only those hypotheses that cannot be refuted. The scientific method obviously cannot be applied into intuitive judgment, but the principle of seeking to disprove hypotheses, rather than confirm them, is useful.[499]

Since we can never "prove" a COA to be true, our goal is to find the one that has the fewest strikes against it. If the end result does not pass any of our other sanity checks (capabilities, effects, five criteria), it is probably because our matrix is overlooking important assumptions or evidence. In step six, we test the *sensitivity* of the evidence. That is, we must investigate the evidence or assumption on which our conclusion most heavily hangs. What is the reliability of the source? Is deception possible? Do alternative explanations exist? According to Heuer:

---

[496] Heuer, 100.
[497] Heuer, 101.
[498] Heuer, 102.
[499] Heuer, 103.

When analysis turns out to be wrong, it is often because of key assumptions that went unchallenged and proved invalid. It is a truism that analysts should identify and question assumptions, but this is much easier said than done. The problem is to determine which assumptions merit questioning. One advantage of the ACH procedure is that it tells you what needs to be rechecked.[500]

The final steps are familiar to us. Report the results with due consideration for standardized language for portraying probability, and continue to update and monitor to determine if events are unfolding in an unexpected manner.[501] When successfully performed as part of IPB, ACH avoids common analytical pitfalls, increases the odds of identifying the right COA, and leaves an "audit trail showing the evidence used" along the way.[502] It can stand on its own, or incorporate the results of other hypothesis generation methods.

PARTING SHOTS

Anticipating the future, particularly when it involves humans, is a risky business. But even when predictions misfire, the joint force is well-positioned to create its own future through the rigorous application of the IPB process. In phase four, our baseline goal is to identify all the options available to the adversary. Including in our initial list the one COA that is ultimately implemented is the only way to avoid surprise. Imagination backed by solid work in the first three IPB phases is at a premium. Thus, step two of phase four—identify the full set of COA available to the adversary—is the most important of the five-step process. It requires structured methods to generate a complete, creative set of hypotheses for filtering, testing, prioritizing, and in the end, operational planning.

To this end, brainstorming through pre-mortems, red teaming, and scenario analysis are suggested. Each steps off from a different perspective, reflective of our multi-level, systems-thinking approach. Pre-mortems cast us in the role of critics, seeking to identify reasons for mission failure that are attributable to the adversary. Red teaming make us the bad guy, thinking deviously about how we can disrupt the joint force's plans and what actions will achieve our objectives. Scenario analysis turns us into ecologists, looking for conditions in the battlespace that will shape future outcomes.

---

[500] Heuer, 106.
[501] Heuer, 107.
[502] Heuer, 109.

In accomplishing step two, each method is guided by step one—identify the adversary's likely objectives and end states. Building on our analysis of stakeholders, including webs of influence and the continuum of relative interests, and the insight gained from the network and systems models, FAST is debuted as an additional tool for penetrating the black box that is the terrorist adversary. Steps two and three—evaluate and prioritize each COA—introduce a series of tests, or reality checks, that are applied to the full set of COA. We can filter out, or at least move lower on the priority list, COA that (1) the stakeholder does not perceive as possible or likely to achieve its objectives (most difficult filter to apply); (2) do not meet the criteria of suitability, feasibility, acceptability, uniqueness, and consistency; (3) the stakeholder is not capable of implementing (limited by knowledge of capabilities and what the adversary perceives it can do); and (4) are not afforded by the battlespace.

The ACH methodology is capable of integrating and structuring these tests as well as other evidence in a manner that mitigates cognitive bias and challenges us to refute a hypothesis before it is trashed. Like the other methods, ACH requires completion of step four—develop each COA in the amount of detail time allows—to improve the results of evaluation and establish initial collection requirements (step four) for continual monitoring. When successfully performed, phase four enables us to answer with measured confidence, What will they do? The fourth and final phase does not close the door on the IPB process, but rather holds it open and invites us to return to previous phases, updating and refining analysis until the mission is accomplished.

CHAPTER 6

BEYOND TERRORISM

Terrorism is relentless. It is a scourge to history and a persistent aspect of the contemporary international landscape. Terrorism is more than a tactic: as a form of warfare, it is violence wielded against non-combatants to achieve psychological effects and influence target audiences. Its partisans are individuals, non-state actors, and states that embrace a broad spectrum of political goals, ranging from statehood for ethnic separatists to the establishment of a religious political order by extremists. Terrorist groups leverage the dark dynamics of globalization to move in the shadows of the nation-state, exploiting seams to transit the terrain of the physical, information and social dimensions. They embrace asymmetric values and methods to erode sovereignty, propagate an ideology, and in many cases, annihilate a perceived adversary. Countering the terrorist challenge demands all the instruments of national power, robust international collaboration, and an adroit intelligence capability. The joint military forces of the U.S. play an important supporting role in the global effort to diminish underlying causes, disrupt terrorist activities, and defeat terrorist organizations. Given the prevailing "hearts

Figure 98. CT Airlift

A pallet of food and blankets slips off the back of a C-130 Hercules as the crew performs a "combat offload" at Faya-Largeau Airport, Chad. The aid was delivered to Chadian forces after they engaged a group of transnational terrorists and sustained casualties.

Source: EUCOM, URL: http://www.eucom.mil/ Photo_Gallery/index.htm, accessed 18 June 2004.

and minds" setting of the struggle, joint force counterterrorism (CT) missions extend beyond the application of physical force to shaping environmental conditions, participating in the narrative of public diplomacy, and strengthening the CT capabilities of allies. Mission accomplishment is enabled by an asymmetric knowledge and decision advantage derived from the skilled performance of intelligence preparation of the battlespace (IPB). IPB builds situational awareness and delivers a deep evaluation of stakeholder capabilities and courses of action (COA). IPB is operational, geared to command decisionmaking and the execution of CT missions as in this recent example out of the Pan-Sahel Initiative (PSI):

> A terrorist leader, Ammari Saifi [Salafist Group for Preaching and Combat], took 32 European tourists hostage near the Libyan border and transported some of them to northern Mali [2003]. To free the hostages, U.S. military officials say, Germany paid him a ransom of nearly $6 million...making him instantly one of the most powerful Islamic militants in North Africa....Earlier this year, Saifi went on a shopping spree in northern Mali, gathering weapons, vehicles and recruits, while American and Algerian intelligence monitored his activities with growing alarm. In February [2004], Algerian forces intercepted a convoy carrying weapons north from Mali. Algerian officials say the cargo contained mortar launchers, rocket-propelled grenade launchers and surface-to-air missiles. The U.S. European Command sent a Navy P-3 Orion surveillance aircraft to sweep the area, relaying Saifi's position to forces in the region. Mali pushed him out of the country to Niger, which in turn chased him into Chad, where, with U.S. Special Forces support of an airlift of fuel and other supplies, 43 of his men were killed or captured. Saifi himself got away...[503]

The objective of the present study is to improve the intelligence contribution of IPB to the CT operations highlighted in this example and the countless others on our horizon. Going beneath the surface of conventional wisdom and traditional approaches, it has explored and clarified the CT challenge and its intelligence demands, worked to advance IPB tradecraft to meet these requirements, and applied new learning to the terrorist problem. In this final chapter, the core elements of CT IPB are reviewed in consolidated form and core propositions are outlined.

---

[503] Craig Smith, "U.S. looks to Sahara as front in terror war," *International Herald Tribune*, 12 May 2004, 4.

PASS AND REVIEW

What are we trying to achieve? The answer is derived from mission analysis, which clarifies the desired end state, supporting objectives, and joint force involvement. It frames the problem, focusing our efforts on the appropriate level—strategic, operational, and tactical—and structures the impending asymmetric contest. While working through each IPB phase in collaboration with the commander and staff, we continually return to mission analysis to increase fidelity on timing, phasing, force dispositions, operational constraints, risk and other factors. Whereas mission analysis keeps us on target, systems thinking underlies our entire approach. IPB reflects the tenets of systems theory, directing our attention to multiple levels of analysis, dynamic relationships, and recurring feedback. Rather than centering our efforts on the adversary's organization, the systems-guided approach of IPB has us examine the relationships between the environment and the organization as a whole and within the organization among its functions. Moreover, our analysis moves vertically through levels to assess nested and cascading effects as well as horizontally across dimensions to determine relationships among stakeholders, information, and resources. IPB as modified and improved in this work provides the manual, scaffolding, and tools to organize and work through the high degrees of uncertainty inherent to CT missions. Figure 99 breaks out the steps for each of its four objectives and phases.

Define the Battlespace

1. Analyze the mission
2. Determine detail required and feasible
3. Limit the battlespace
4. Identify mission-relevant characteristics
5. Determine knowledge gaps
6. Act on collection requirements

Describe Battlespace Effects

1. Analyze mission-relevant effects
2. Describe the effects on capabilities and COA

Evaluate Stakeholder Capabilities

1. Perform COG analysis
2. Update or build multi-level models
3. Test model against current situation
4. Evaluate actual capabilities

Determine Course of Action

1. Identify desired end-state and likely objectives
2. Generate the full set of available COA
3. Evaluate and prioritize each COA
4. Detail each COA to extent feasible
5. Refine collection requirements

Figure 99. Phase Breakout

Source: Adapted from JIPB by author.

IPB is performed by teams spanning staff functions and directorates. Orchestrating the process, clarifying the mission, and establishing commander requirements demands strong leadership. At a premium are leaders with the wisdom and vision to integrate the IPB process with the joint force effort to obtain a knowledge and decision advantage over the adversary. IPB leaders and teams are expected to size up what must and can be accomplished given the time and resources available and act decisively and deliberately to deliver decision-quality results. We must recognize that it is only through capable leadership of skilled teams that IPB can provide the edge expected in our ability to observe, orient, decide, and act (OODA Loop).

Define the Battlespace

In phase one, the battlespace is recast in non-linear terms. The objective is to define the battlespace in a manner that answers the question, What out there matters most? A six-step process guides us toward the phase's deliverable—an inventory of factors or features that can influence the mission. The steps are modified to account for the wider range of CT missions, stakeholders, and adversary capabilities. Rather than dealing with an overwhelming global operating environment, the battlespace is limited by several enduring concepts: area of operations (AO), operational area (OA), and area of interest (AOI) are modified to account for the relative positioning of stakeholders across multiple dimensions. The battlespace serves as an over-arching mental construct that encompasses the geographically based and assigned AO, the arena where operational effects are achieved (OA), and the arena of indirect influence (AOI). The multiple stakeholders, including the joint force, terrorist group(s), and other state and non-state actors, each have an AO, OA, and AOI for which we must account. Where they overlap, engagement and possibly conflict occur, and in many cases, the joint force will reposition itself to bring it in line with other stakeholders in order to maximize the "points of contact."

Whereas the physical dimension has been the traditional focus of IPB, the character of the threat and spectrum of CT missions necessitates giving more attention to social intelligence and information dimensions. The dimensions not only aid intelligence work, but provide a conceptual basis for operational planning. Specifically, the physical dimension consists of geography (land, air, sea, and space), weather, and artifacts (man-made structures). The social dimension relates culture to political and economic factors. The information dimensions bring together the information itself, enabling technology, and the all-important cognitive or human piece. For each sector, our task is to identify the characteristics, activities, or factors that might have an impact on the mission.

Dimensions and sectors organize our effort, balance analysis, and present a landscape on which to position stakeholders either graphically using simplistic "blobology," or more dynamically through the use of information technology (IT). To this static picture of what factors are likely to affect the mission, we add time horizons and nested levels. For the former, it is important to consider the expected duration of the mission and its internal phasing to further refine the applicability of the inventoried battlespace characteristics. In terms of nested levels, strategic-level features, such as trends in urbanization, shape operational and tactical-level developments, and tactical-level events have strategic consequences. The rapidity and impact of developments across levels is accentuated in an era of globalization. For a short-term, operational-level mission, for example, sitting religious officials in key churches, temples or mosques are more likely to be relevant than religious students expected to complete their studies in a few years. Phase one builds situational awareness and picks out for further analysis those features of the battlespace with the potential to influence mission accomplishment.

Determine Effects

In phase two, effects-based thinking guides us to an understanding of the relationship between the environment and stakeholder objectives and capabilities. The objective is to describe the effects of the battlespace in a manner that answers the question, How does it impact us? Phase two orients us to the battlespace and delivers both a holistic and specific understanding of what the battlespace affords all stakeholders. Even though the process involves only two steps, the demands of each are substantial. The first step is the toughest, requiring innovative, detailed analysis clearly presented using graphics and precise descriptions.

The concept of effects is fundamental to IPB, and it is elaborated in phase two to distinguish between direct, indirect, cascading and cumulative effects. Direct effects have a nearly immediate impact on the mission. If delayed in time and space at all, it is only briefly. Therefore, all factors with the potential to have a direct effect are part of the OA and must be analyzed up front in phase two. Indirect effects are also important, particularly given their subtle, time-delayed and spatially-removed influence. They are part of the AOI and are evaluated as time and resources allow. Both have cascading influence across the levels as well as a cumulative impact on capabilities and COA. The cumulative impact of indirect effects is often overlooked, resulting in a surprisingly direct influence while the mission is underway.

Phase two involves sorting out and explaining how the mission-relevant characteristics identified in phase one impact mission accomplishment. In terms of methodology, the time-tested OCOKA (Observation and Fields of Fire, Cover and Concealment, Obstacles, Key Terrain, Avenues of Approach) is salvaged by modifying each of its elements to account for diverse CT missions and players. On the other hand, the present study offers a significant improvement over the information and social dimensions of existing doctrine. Organizational, media, cyberterrorism, and cognitive effects originate from the information dimension, generating constraints and opportunities related to the availability and quality of information, the sophistication and reliability of technology, and the limitations of human cognition. If the information dimension is the oxygen of modern terrorism, the social dimension is its food. Effects from the social dimension capture cultural influences such as religion, the politics of power, and socio-economic conditions of communities. Demographic analysis provides a picture of how communities look on paper that becomes dynamic when integrated with an analysis of cultural and perception effects.

Complementing the dimension-specific methods are methods for determining overall, or net effects. The CT battlespace is turbulent, reflecting varying degrees of uncertainty related to change and complexity. Net levels of uncertainty drive information requirements, decisionmaking, organizational structures, and COA planning. A return to the concept of nested effects stresses the vertical and horizontal axes of influence. When stakeholders are mapped in relationship to each other, the result is a web of influence that the joint force must manipulate and negotiate to be successful. The relationship between stakeholders and the battlespace is also co-dependent. As open systems, all organizations depend on resources and information to enable capabilities. These dependencies represent vulnerabilities when the resource or information is critical and scarce. The concept of affordance reminds us of the importance of perception—action is predicated on what we perceive the battlespace affords regardless of whether our

Phase		Question	Outcome
Define Battlespace	M I S S I O N	What out there matters most?	Inventory of mission -relevant battlespace conditions
Describe Battlespace Effects		How does it impact us?	Understanding of what battlespace conditions allow
Evaluate the Adversary	A N A L Y S I S	What can they do to us?	Assessment of sources of strength, capabilities and vulnerabilities
Determine Adversary COA		What will they do?	Full set of prioritized and evaluated plans

Figure 100. IPB Core Elements

Source: Author.

perceptions reflect ground truth. Thus, a terrorist group may take unexpected actions because it perceives advantages and disadvantages we do not. When integrated, net and dimensional effects offer a first look at what the battlespace allows. By comparing opportunities and constraints across dimensions and for each stakeholder, a picture emerges of comparative advantages.

Evaluate Capabilities

In phase three, we evaluate stakeholder capabilities to determine sources of strength, the array of capabilities, and potential vulnerabilities. The objective is to determine capabilities in relation to the joint force mission and in light of what the battlespace affords to answer the question, What can they do to us? The continuum of relevant interests offers a sliding scale to gauge the orientation of each stakeholder in relation to the joint force's mission. In addition to sizing up CT players as ally, accomplice, neutral, hindrance, adversary, or unknown, their relations are further qualified by a set of hard and soft linkages. Starting with adversary stakeholders, the four steps of this phase involve COG (Centers of Gravity) analysis, modeling, reality testing, and capabilities specification.

Centers of gravity and their associated critical capabilities, requirements, and vulnerabilities are the marrow of phase three. Capabilities enable COG, but they are dependent on resources for their execution. For example, training terrorists requires recruits, secure space, and equipment. The most important of these resources are critical requirements, and if any of these requirements are vulnerable, they represent potential high-value targets. These "critical factors" are the guideposts of operational planning, and all subsequent work in phase three is intended to figure them out with as high a degree of confidence and precision as our knowledge and skills allow. Importantly, all stakeholders have critical factors, varying to include the social contract or professional reputation of an NGO, the business model or branding (product image) of a multinational corporation, the ideology or network structure of a terrorist group, and the skilled professionals or IT infrastructure of the joint force. In step one, we make an initial, informed assessment of COG, but allow our work in subsequent steps to challenge, refine and ultimately identify the rungs on the COG ladder—COG-CC-CR-CV (Critical Capabilities, Critical Requirements, Critical Vulnerabilities).

Step two entails building models that accurately portray the organization, capabilities, and characteristics of stakeholders. Where traditional models fall short, network and system models take over. Both look at the organization as a whole, standing in dynamic relation to its environment, and break the organization down into core functions, or capabilities. The network model is built around the idea of key nodes linked together to form a network of social relations. Five "fields of analysis" are useful for determining critical factors: organization, narrative, doctrine, technology, and social ties. The first sees the organizational structure, and in particular the network structure, mixed with the more traditional hierarchy, as a capability itself. Narrative refers to the story linking the organization and its members to a world view and historical thread, which give meaning and purpose. Doctrine gets at the principles and practices, or operational code, while technology deals with the range of IT and weapon systems available. The last, social ties, looks at the linkages among people; their organizational value derives more from social capital (interpersonal or relational skills) than personal characteristics.

The systems model sees organizations as constantly exchanging resources and information with the battlespace through a core set of boundary-spanning capabilities. Support capabilities recruit people, collect intelligence, acquire resources, transfer money and otherwise attend to the dependencies discussed earlier. Maintenance capabilities wed people to the group through socialization and a schedule of rewards and sanctions to ensure role compliance. Cognitive capabilities determine the innovation, adaptability, and strategic direction of the organization through learning, strategy development, decisionmaking, and command and control. Finally, conversion capabilities craft people and resources into something more valuable than the sum of their parts. The production capability creates cocaine for trafficking, the service delivery capability maintains a clinic to foster community support, and the operations capability conducts the terrorist attack. Among others, one important contribution of the systems model is its emphasis on capabilities other than the act of collective violence. These other capabilities may actually contribute more to the organization's ability to survive crisis (negative entropy), hold together in the face of turbulence (congruence), and prosper over the course of its life cycle.

All models paint stakeholders under ideal conditions, which is why we perform a sanity check. We adjust the models for the real world, or what the battlespace affords. Under ideal conditions, al Qaeda would train, hypothetically, a thousand recruits every three months in basic techniques; however, the destruction of training camps disrupts training, resulting in a throughput of only two hundred every six months. The reality-tested models are restated as capabilities with a time dimension. The Provisional IRA, for example, is capable of one radio-detonated bombing every six months, based on their operational code and limited by robust security. Working up the ladder, this analysis refines proposed COG or reveals new ones, and working down the ladder, it uncovers critical requirements. If vulnerabilities can be identified, the joint force can exploit these to indirectly affect the COG. At a minimum, COG analysis is done for the terrorist and reversed for the joint force. Failing to understand our own vulnerabilities is a formula for mission failure.

Anticipate Actions

In phase four, we anticipate future actions by the terrorist group and other stakeholders. The objective is to identify, evaluate, prioritize, and monitor all the available COA to answer the question, What will they do? Sometimes referred to as preditive analysis, we forecast COA without a crystal ball, fully aware of the intrinsic difficulties and the likelihood we will not get it quite right. Nonetheless, phase four is necessary to avoid surprise and make sure the right mix of joint force capabilities is part of operational planning. The balance between intentions and capabilities is weighed toward intentions at the strategic level and capabilities at the tactical.

Stakeholder analysis is the core method used in this phase, building a three-dimensional picture of CT players using the web of influence, continuum of relative interests, functional analysis systems technique, and the network and systems models. At a minimum, we must successfully accomplish the second step—generate all the options for future action open to the terrorist and as appropriate, other stakeholders. The best way to avoid surprise is to make sure that an approximation of the adversary's ultimate COA is included in our intial list. Even if we do not give it the right priority, or detail its branches and sequels precisely, we can avoid surprise. Coming up with a good list demands structured methods that overcome cognitive bias and champion creativity. Pre-mortems, red teaming, and scenario analysis each contributes a different perspective for hypothesis generation.

We evaluate and prioritize each COA through a series of tests in step three. COA are filtered using five criteria: suitability, feasibility, acceptability, uniqueness, and consistency. If the COA passes through these filters, we assess whether the stakeholder is capable of implementing the plan. Recognizing that our knowledge of capabilities may be flawed, we should retain COA that are on the margins of assessed ability. The third test leverages the work of phase two and asks, does the battlespace allow it? Is the technology there? Can these skills be learned? Is it culturally acceptable? Essentially, the five criteria are being applied across the dimensions of the battlespace. Analysis of competing hypotheses (ACH) offers the optimal methodology for organizing and evaluating COA using these tests and any other evidence that might have diagnostic value. ACH drives counterintuitive thinking, asking us to discount potential COA in a manner consistent with the scientific method. Each of the methods involves detailing the COA to the extent time, resources, and information allow, which will improve our ability to evaluate, prioritize, and monitor its implementation. Upon completing phase four, we revisit previous phases to refine and improve our analysis. We do not stop until the mission is achieved, and even then, we are encouraged to debrief our work to improve for the next go.

CORE PROPOSITIONS

Counterterrorism IPB owes much to the practiced methods of intelligence support to conventional military operations and the rich corpus of tactics, techniques, and procedures embodied in joint and service doctrine. In this work, we have embraced the four objectives and phases of traditional IPB because of their practical utility, backed by a potent theory about the relationships between organizations and their environment. By harvesting enduring concepts and methods and adapting existing IPB steps to the CT mission, we also speed its transfer to the field. That is, we can stick with the overall process and leverage many of the standardized terms and techniques for CT. The IPB punch can be substantially strengthened for CT only if many of these concepts are modified, new ones are adopted, and our toolbox of analytical methods is expanded to tackle the spectrum of missions, stakeholders, and asymmetric capabilities of the threat. Ten core propositions result that shape and underlie all phases of CT IPB:

1) Systems thinking offers a powerful approach to solving complex problems. Countering terrorists requires an approach that can effectively deal with high levels of uncertainty (rapidly changing environment and complex array of ever-changing factors). Systems thinking provides the intellectual scaffolding and tools for evaluating and acting on two sets of linkages: (1) relations between the organization as a whole and the battlespace; and (2) relations among the internal workings, or functions, of the organization. As an approach, it captures the adaptive, evolving character of all social organizations, providing insight to the exchange of information and resources with the battlespace, the feedback loops that enable learning, and the leverage points that allow us to achieve lasting effects.

2) Effects-based analysis and operations sharpen focus on outcomes. IPB is an operational process focused on achieving specific mission outcomes, or effects. An effects-based approach views the adversary as a complex system and time an as essential ingredient to analysis and operations. Direct and indirect effects cascade and accumulate to impact organizational capabilities and courses of action. Thinking in terms of effects ensures we remain centered on our goals while considering changing circumstances and actions can ripple through the battlespace and organizations to alter conditions, constrain options, and shape capabilities. As opposed to a target or capabilities-based approach, which measure success in terms of destroying things or denying actions, effects-based operations incorporate them both as intermediary stops on the path to achieving a desired end-state.

3) Levels, dimensions, and time provide a three-dimensional skeleton for performing IPB and executing CT missions. Effects are achieved within levels and dimensions over time (Figure 101). The three levels of analysis and action—strategic, operational, and tactical—are nested; effects, characteristics, and actions have a cascading impact on the adjoining level(s). Although IPB is primarily an operational-level process, it is shaped by strategic-level guidance and trends. Tactical-level actions are molded by operational constraints, but often have strategic consequences. Effects are also achieved and experienced across the physical, information, and social dimensions of the battlespace. Dimensions carve up the battlespace into mutually reinforcing, interrelated arenas, which are reassembled to build

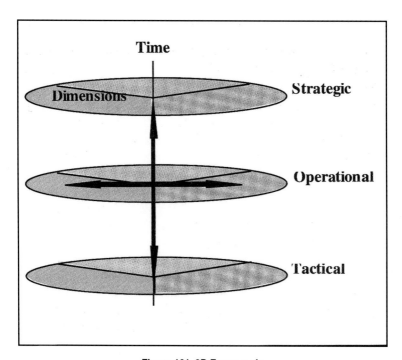

Figure 101. 3D Framework

Source: Author.

holistic battlespace awareness. By adding the time component we turn a static snap-shot into a dynamic motion picture. Mission analysis directs work to the appropriate level, dimension, and time horizon.

4) Counterterrorism missions are wide-ranging and multi-faceted. The joint force has an important role to play in the four pillars of the national strategy for combating terrorism: diminish, disrupt, defeat, and defend. The joint force is part of a coordinated interagency process that emphasizes public diplomacy, conflict resolution, and good governance. It provides lethal and non-lethal options for shaping battlespace conditions, strengthening allied CT capabilities, disrupting militarily accessible terrorist activities, and defeating organizations when and where they can be directly engaged. The great diversity of missions, which span the spectrum of conflict from combat to humanitarian operations, requires intelligence to address a wider array of conditions, threats, and stakeholders.

5) Counterterrorism involves non-traditional stakeholders with asymmetric capabilities and intentions. CT operations involve a host of players. Religious leaders, local politicians, non-governmental organizations, international organizations, multi-national corporations, allied forces, and John Q. Public are often part of the mix. Getting a fix on who matters and why demands persistent stakeholder analysis, resulting in a crowded web of influence that can be leveraged, manipulated, isolated, and strengthened. IPB must account for all the stakeholders with potential influence and evaluate their capabilities and intentions as time and resources allow. In many cases, such as foreign internal defense or civil affairs, other stakeholders may be more important to mission success than the terrorist group itself. Moreover, contemporary terrorist organizations employ asymmetric tools and tactics and in some cases, values, to obtain surprise or exploit perceived weaknesses in the joint force.

6) Social intelligence is vital to a decision-quality understanding of the battlespace and adversary. Terrorism is generally rooted in an ideology that reflects the human perceptions, socio-economic and political conditions, and culture of at least the group's members if not the community from which it is spawned. Therefore, there is a pressing need to build the concepts and competencies that allow us to analyze social dynamics in a manner that gets beyond folklore. To that end, cultural intelligence as operationalized here provides for dealing with our own mirror-imaging and perceptual biases as well as for integrating consideration of perception and demographic effects, affordance theory (perception drives action), and the worldview of adversaries as reflected in their prevailing narratives.

7) Stories open the book on terrorist group identity and strategy. Stakeholder narratives are echoed in rhetoric, publications, recruiting and socialization processes, and operational actions. Analyzing narratives answers key IPB questions, including issues of identity, cultural roots, ideological influences, sense of history, and the meaning of existence. The stories we tell connect our actions to a symbolic framework and a narrative thread that arcs through history. The more compelling narrative often wins, particularly when the struggle is between competing interpretations of contemporary events. By analyzing the stories told and enacted by our adversaries we answer key questions and gain insight into how it shapes the battlespace, other stakeholders, and the terrorist group itself. The narrative and the ability to propagate it are usually critical factors.

8) Centers of gravity and the other critical factors are the guideposts for operational planning. All stakeholders have one or more centers of gravity, which are nested at each level and serve as a source of strength to the organization. Strategic centers of gravity allow the adversary to resist, while operational ones enable the accomplishment of tasks under tough conditions. When dealing with allies, centers of gravity are protected and reinforced. For terrorists, the joint force seeks to achieve direct effects on the COG, undermining the group's ability to operate and possibly rendering a crushing blow. More often, the COG is in doubt or inaccessible by direct means, requiring us to analyze the critical capabilities that permit it to function. The most lucrative way to disrupt a critical capability is to determine the resources on which it depends to operate, such as weapons, conditions, or even an idea, and look for deficiencies that may be vulnerable to joint-force targeting. The evaluation of capabilities in phase three of IPB is a means to an all-important end—pinpointing centers of gravity.

Figure 102. Afghan Child

A young girl from the village of Tora Ray peeks at soldiers from her house doorway in Afghanistan, 6 April 2004.

Source: DOD, URL: http://www.defendamerica.mil/ photoessays/apr2004/p041504a9.html, accessed on 18 June 2004.

9) The dynamic character of CT requires regular net assessments. Conflict is relational. The contest between the joint force and terrorist group is a series of actions, reactions, and counter-reactions that change the participants over time. Therefore, our analysis of the adversary can never be conducted in splendid isolation, but must always take into account the disposition and capabilities of the joint force as well as other stakeholders. In essence, IPB is comparative analysis, and the overall appraisal of how everything stands in relation to everything is net assessment. In phase one, mission-relevant factors are compared. Effects are contrasted in phase two through the relative positioning of stakeholders in the battlespace and an assessment of comparative advantages across sectors. In phase three, capabilities are compared and perception analysis is brought to bear to get a sense of how each player might view the strengths and weaknesses of the other. Finally, COA are wargamed in phase four to anticipate how the action sequence might play out.

10) Recurring, critical self-evaluation, if ignored, risks mission accomplishment. It is a mistake to think of IPB as something we only do to understand the adversary. Understanding the decisionmaking process of the enemy is an enduring, yet highly elusive intelligence requirement. It is never possible when we fail to think through our own strengths and weaknesses; failing to do so ignores an essential aspect of the adversary's OODA Loop. Even when we are not concerned with the perception of other stakeholders, our operational planning, force protection, and other joint force activities are improved by an understanding of our own critical factors and what the battlespace affords. Therefore, reverse IPB is an element of every phase. In phase two, for example, we reverse it to assess the effects of the battelespace on the mission, while in phase three we objectively seek out our COG and associated vulnerabilities. In phase four, we reverse it to assess likely adversary COA, which are based on their perception of what we can and might do.

PARTING SHOTS

Like terrorists themselves, the counterterrorism effort must also be relentless in diminishing conditions, disrupting activities, and defeating terrorist organizations. Intelligence is at the nexus of the soft and hard instruments of power that are integral to moving beyond terrorism, or at least relegating it to an unacceptable practice constrained in effect. Our drive for decision-quality intelligence has as its destination a battlespace awareness and knowledge advantage over the adversary. Intelligence preparation of the battlespace offers the optimal set of procedures, concepts, and methods for achieving this goal Our confidence in its value, however, is tempered by recognition that beneath the surface lie dangerous unknowns, pushing us harder to penetrate the murky waters of modern terrorism. Our toughest terrorist adversaries work in the shadows of nation-states and embrace an all-consuming ideology that allows no quarter. Prevailing against such foes requires integrating intelligence with long-term strategies for mitigating conditions and countering their extremist, exclusionary narrative with a more persuasive vision of human security through tolerance. In modest fashion, this work seeks to improve prospects for the joint force to enable this vision.

SELECTED BIBLIOGRAPHY

Air Force Doctrine Document 2. *Organization and Employment of Aerospace Power.* Maxwell AFB, AL: Air Force Doctrine Center, 17 February 2000.

Air Force Pamphlet 14-118. *Intelligence.* "Aerospace Intelligence Preparation of the Battlespace." 5 June 2001.

Akbar, M. J. *The Shade of Swords: Jihad and the Conflict Between Islam and Christianity.* New York: Routledge, 2002.

Ali, Abdullah Yusuf, trans. *The Meaning of the Glorious Qur'an.* London, UK: Nadim and CO, 1976.

Alexander, Yonah. *Combating Terrorism: Strategies of Ten Countries.* Ann Arbor, MI: University of Michigan Press, 2002.

Arquilla, John and David Rondfedt, ed. *In Athena's Camp: Preparing for Conflict in the Information Age.* Santa Monica, CA: RAND, 1997.

Arquilla, John and David Ronfeldt. *Networks and Netwars.* Santa Monica, CA: RAND Corporation, 2001.

Argyris, Chris and Donald Schon. *Organizational Learning II: Theory, Method and Practice.* Reading, MA: Addison Wesley Publishing Company, 1996.

Asprey, Robert B. *War in the Shadows: The Guerrilla in History.* New York: William Morrow and Company, 1994.

Bazerman, Max H. *Judgment in Managerial Decision Making.* New York: John Wiley and Sons, Inc., 1994.

Bartolomei, Jason and William Casebeer. "Using Systems Engineering Tools to Rethink US Policy on North Korea." Unpublished report to the Defense Threat Reduction Agency, March 2004.

Benjamin, Daniel and Steve Simon. *The Age of Sacred Terror.* New York: Random House, 2003.

Bergen, Peter L. *Holy War, Inc.: Inside the Secret World of Osama bin Laden.* New York, NY: The Free Press, 2001.

Berkowitz, Bruce. *The New Face of War: How War will be Fought in the 21st Century.* New York: The Free Press, 2003.

Bertalanffy, Ludwig von. *General Systems Theory.* New York: George Braziller, 1968.

Billington, James H. *Fire in the Minds of Men: Origins of the Revolutionary Faith.* New York: Basic Books, Inc., 1980.

Bodnar, John W. *Warning Analysis for the Information Age: Rethinking the Intelligence Process.* Washington, DC: Center for Strategic Intelligence Research, Joint Military Intelligence College, December 2003.

Boot, Max. *The Savage Wars of Peace: Small Wars and the Rise of American Power.* New York, NY: Basic Books, 2002.

Brown, Lawrence. ""The Enemy we were Fighting was not what we had Predicted." What is Wrong with IPB at the Dawn of the 21st Century."" School of Advanced Military Studies. Fort Leavenworth, KS: US Army Command and General Staff College, 2004.

Bunker, Robert J. *Non-State Threats and Future Wars.* Portland, OR: Frank Cass, 2003.

Byman, Daniel L., Peter Chalk, Bruce Hoffman, William Rosenau and David Brannan. *Trends in Outside Support for Insurgent Movements.* Santa Monica, CA: RAND, 2001.

Clausewitz, Carl von. *On War.* Edited and translated by Michael Howard and Peter Paret. Princeton, NJ: Princeton University Press, 1984.

Clausewitz, Carl von. *On War: General Carl Von Clausewitz.* Volume 1. Translated by Colonel J. J. Graham. London, UK: Routledge and Kegan Paul, 1966.

Crenshaw, Martha. "Theories of Terrorism: Instrumental and Organizational Approaches." In *Inside Terrorist Organization.* Edited by David Rapoport. Portland, OR: Frank Cass Publishers, January 2001.

Crenshaw, Martha, ed. *Terrorism in Context.* University Park, PA: Pennsylvania State University Press, 1995.

Cummings, Thomas G. *Systems Theory for Organization Development.* New York, NY: John Wiley and Sons, 1980.

Cummings, Thomas G. and Christopher G. Worley. *Organization Development and Change.* Cincinnati, OH: South Western College Publishing, 1997.

Daft, Richard L. *Organization Theory and Design.* Mason, OH: Thomson South-western, 2004.

Defense Science Board Task Force. "The Role and Status of DOD Red Teaming Activities." Report to the Office of the Under Secretary of Defense
for Acquisition, Technology, and Logistics. September 2003.

Department of State. *Patterns in Global Terrorism 2003.* Washington, DC:
U.S. Department of State, 2003.

_____. *Patterns in Global Terrorism 2002.* Washington, DC: U.S. Depart-
ment of State, 2002.

_____. *Patterns in Global Terrorism 2001.* Washington, DC: U.S. Depart-
ment of State, 2001.

Dyson, Stephen Benedict. "Drawing policy implications from the 'Operational Code' of a 'new' political actor: Russian President Vladimir
Putin." *Policy Sciences,* December 2001.

Eshel, David. "The Rise and Fall of the Al Aqsa Martyrs Brigades." *Jane's
Intelligence Review,* June 2002, Vol. 14, No. 6.

Fassihi, Farnaz. "Two Novice Gumshoes Charted the Capture of Saddam."
Wall Street Journal, 18 December 2003.

Field Manual 34-130. *Intelligence Preparation of the Battlefield.* Fort
Huachuca, AZ: U.S. Army Intelligence Center, 8 July 1994.

Field Manual 101-5-1/MCRP 5-2A. *Operational Terms and Graphics.*
Washington, DC: Department of the Army and U.S. Marine Corps,
30 September 1997.

Glenn, Russell W. ed. *The City's Many Faces.* Santa Monica, CA: RAND
Corporation, 2000.

Grabo, Cynthia. *Anticipating Surprise: Analysis for Strategic Warning.* Washington, DC: Government Printing Office, December 2002.

Grable, Sam and Troy Thomas. "Training the Mind to Deploy." *Air Force
Comptroller Magazine.* Series in July 2001 and October 2001.

Griffin, Nicholas. *Caucasus: Mountain Men and Holy Wars.* New York, NY:
St Martin's Press, 2001.

Gunaratna, Rohan. *Inside Al Qaeda: Global Network of Terror.* New York:
Columbia University Press, 2002.

Hanle, Donald Hanle. *Terrorism: The Newest Face of Warfare.* Washington,
DC: Pergamon-Brassey's, 1989.

Hanzhang, General Tao. *Sun Tzu's Art of War: The Modern Chinese Interpretation. trans.* Yuan Shibing. New York: Sterling Publishing Co., Inc., 1987.

Harrison, Michael I. and Arie Shirom. *Organizational Diagnosis and Assessment: Bridging Theory and Practice.* Thousand Oaks, Ca: Sage Publications, 1999.

Hart, B.H. Liddell. *Strategy.* New York, NY: Signet, 1967.

Hatch, Mary Jo. *Organization Theory: Modern, Symbolic, and Postmodern Perspectives.* Oxford, UK: Oxford University Press, 1997.

Heuer, Richards J. *The Psychology of Intelligence Analysis.* Center for the Study of Intelligence. Washington, DC: Government Printing Office, 1999.

Hoffman, Bruce. *Inside Terrorism.* New York, NY: Columbia University Press, 1998.

_____. "Plan of Attack." *The Atlantic Monthly,* July/August 2004.

Howard, Russell D. and Reid L. Sawyer eds. *Terrorism and Counterterrorism.* Guilford, CT: McGraw-Hill, 2003.

Hudson, Rex A. "The Sociology and Psychology of Terrorism: Who Becomes a Terrorist and Why?" Washington, DC: Federal Research Division, Library of Congress, September 1999.

Ignatieff, Michael. "It's War- But it Doesn't Have to be Dirty." *The Guardian,* 1 October 2001.

Jawahar, I.M. and Gary L. McLaughlin. "Toward a Descriptive Stakeholder Theory: An Organizational Life Cycle Approach." *The Academy of Management Review.* July 2001, Vol 26. Issue 3.

Jenkins, Brian. "International Terrorism: A New Mode of Conflict." *International Terrorism and World Security.* eds. David Carlton and Carlo Schaerf. London, UK: Croom Helm, 1975.

_____. *International Terrorism: A New Mode of Conflict.* Los Angeles, CA: Crescent Publications, 1975.

Joint Chiefs of Staff, Joint Publication 1. *Joint Warfare of the Armed Forces of the United States.* Washington, DC: Government Printing Office, 14 November 2000.

_____. Joint Publication 1-02. *Department of Defense Dictionary of Military and Associated Terms.* Washington, DC: Government Printing Office, 12 April 2001. As Amended Through 17 December 2003

_____. Joint Publication 2-01.3. *Joint Tactics, Techniques, and Procedures for Joint IPB* Washington, DC: Government Printing Office, 24 May 2000.

_____. Joint Publication 3-06. *Doctrine for Joint Urban Operations.* Washington DC: Government Printing Office, 16 September 2002.

_____. Joint Publication 3-07.2. *Joint Tactics, Techniques, and Procedures for Antiterrorism.* Washington, DC: Government Printing Office, 17 March 1998.

_____. Joint Publication 3-13. *Joint Doctrine for Information Operations.* Washington, DC: Government Printing Office, 9 October 1998.

_____. Joint Publication 3-61. Doctrine for Public Affairs in Joint Operations. Washington, DC: Government Printing Office, 14 May 1997.

_____. *National Military Strategy of the United States of America 2004.* May 2004.

Jones, Morgan D. *The Thinker's Toolkit: Fourteen Skills for Making Smarter Decisions in Business and in Life.* New York: Random House, 1995.

Kahneman, D., P. Slovic, P. and A. Tversky, ed. *Judgment under Uncertainty: Heuristics and Biases.* New York, NY: Cambridge University Press, 1982.

Katz, Daniel and Robert L. Kahn. *The Social Psychology of Organizations.* New York, NY: John Wiley & Sons, 1978.

Kauppi, Mark V. "Counterterrorism Analysis 101." *Defense Intelligence Journal.* Winter 2002.

Keegan, John. *A History of Warfare.* New York, NY: Vintage Books, 1993.

_____. *Intelligence in War: Knowledge of the Enemy from Napoleon to Al-Qaeda.* New York: Alfred P. Knopf, 2003.

Klein, Gary. *Sources of Power: How People Make Decisions.* Cambridge: MIT Press, 2000.

Kurlansky, Mark. *The Basque History of the World.* New York: Penguin Books, 1999.

Laqueur, Walter. *Guerrilla Warfare: A Historical & Critical Study.* New Brunswick, N.J.: Transaction Publishers, 1998.

_____. *The New Terrorism: Fanaticism and the Arms of Mass Destruction.* New York: Oxford University Press, 1999.

Lesser, Ian O., Bruce Hoffman, John Arquilla, David Ronfeldt, and Michele Zanini, eds. *Countering the New Terrorism.* Santa Monica, CA: RAND Corporation, 1999.

Lewis, Bernard. *The Crisis of Islam: Holy War and Unholy Terror.* New York, NY: Modern Library, 2003.

Marine Corps Doctrinal Publication 1-1. *Strategy.* Washington, DC: Department of the Navy, 1997.

Mateski, Mark. "Red Teaming Terrorism, Part I." *.Red Team Journal,* June 2003.

Medby, Jamison Jo and Russell W. Glenn. *Street Smarts: Intelligence Preparation of the Battlespace for Urban Operations.* Santa Monica, CA: The RAND Corporation, 2002.

Meigs, Montgomery C. "Unorthodox Thoughts about Asymmetric Warfare." *Parameters.* Summer 2003, Vol. 33, No. 2.

Metz, Steven. *Armed Conflict in the 21st Century: The Information Revolution and Post-Modern Warfare.* Carlisle, PA: Strategic Studies Institute, April 2000.

Metz, Steven and Douglas V. Johnson II. *Asymmetry and US Military Strategy: Definition, Background, and Strategic Concepts.* US Army War College, Carlisle, PA: Strategic Studies Institute, January 2001.

Mintzberg, Henry. *The Design School: Reconsidering the Basic Premises of Strategic Management.* New York, NY: John Wiley and Sons, 1990.

Naval Doctrine Publication 2. *Intelligence.* Washington, DC: Naval Doctrine Command, no date.

Norton, Augustus Richar. *Amal and the Shi'a: Struggle for the Soul of Lebanon.* Austin, TX: University of Texas Press, 1987.

Nutt, Paul C. *Making Tough Decisions: Tactics for Improving Managerial Decision Making.* San Francisco: Josey-Bass Publishers, 1989.

O'Neill, Bard E. *Insurgency in the Modern World.* Boulder, CO: Westview Press, 1980.

_____. *Insurgency and Terrorism: Inside Modern Revolutionary Warfare.* Washington, DC: Brassey's, Inc., 1990.

Peters, Ralph. "The Human Terrain of Urban Operations." *Parameters,* Spring 2000.

Pillar, Paul R. *Terrorism and U.S. Foreign Policy.* Washington, DC: Brookings Institution Press, 2001.

Rabasa, Angel and Peter Chalk. *Colombian Labyrinth: The Synergy of Drugs and Insurgency and its Implications for Regional Stability.* Santa Monica, CA: RAND, 2001.

Rapoport, David, ed. *Inside Terrorist Organizations.* London, UK: Frank Cass Publishers, 2001.

Rattray, Gregory J. *Strategic Warfare in Cyberspace.* Cambridge, MA: MIT Press, 2001.

Reisman, W. Michael and Chris T. Antoniou, ed. *The Laws of War: A Comprehensive Collection of Primary Documents on International Laws Governing Armed Conflict.* New York, NY: Vintage Books, 1994.

Renfro, Robert. "Modeling and Analysis of Social Networks." Ph.D. Dissertation. Graduate School of Engineering and Management, Air Force Institute of Technology, Air University, Air Education and Training Command, December 2001.

Rosenau, James N. *Turbulence in World Politics: A Theory of Change and Continuity.* Princeton, NJ: Princeton University Press, 1990.

Sandoz, John F. "Red Teaming: A Means to Military Transformation." Report for the Joint Advanced Warfighting Program, Institute for Defense Analysis. January 2001.

Scarantino, Andrea. "Affordances Explained." *Philosophy of Science,* December 2003.

Schneier, Bruce. *Beyond Fear: Thinking Sensibly About Security in an Uncertain World.* New York, NY: Copernicus Books, 2003.

Schmind, Alex P. *Political Terrorism: A Research Guide to Concepts, Theories, Data Bases and Literature.* New Brunswick, NJ: Transaction Books, 1983.

Scott, John. *Social Network Analysis: A Handbook.* London: Sage Publications, 2000.

Selznick, Philip Selznick. "Foundations of the Theory of Organization." *American Sociological Review* 13, 1948.

Shafritz, Jay M. and J. Steven Ott, ed. *Classics of Organization Theory.* Fort Worth, TX: Harcourt College Publishers, 2001.

Shultz, Richard H. "Showstoppers: Nine reasons why we never sent our Special Operations Forces after al Qaeda before 9/11." *The Weekly Standard.* 26 January 2004.

Sinai, Joshua. "Red Teaming the Terrorist Threat to Preempt the Next Waves of Catastrophic Terrorism." Briefing presented at the 14th Annual NDIA SO/LIC Symposium and Exhibition, 12 February 2003.

Smith, James and William Thomas. *The Terrorism Threat and U.S. Government's Response: Operational and Organizational Factors.* US Air Force Academy, CO: USAF Institute for National Security Studies, March 2001.

Snow, Donald. *Uncivil Wars: International Security and the New Internal Conflicts.* Boulder, CO: Lynne Rienner Publishers, 1996.

Stern, Jessica. *Terror in the Name of God: Why Religious Militants Kill.* New York: Ecco Publishers, 2003.

Strange, Joe. *Centers of Gravity and Critical Vulnerabilities: Building on the Clausewitzian Foundation so that we can all Speak the Same Language.* Perspectives on Warfighting. Quantico, VA: Defense Automated Printing Service Center, 1996.

Stratton, Jim, Sam Grable, and Troy Thomas. "Expeditionary Air Force Leaders Cognitive Skills for the Naturalistic Battlespace." *Air and Space Power Chronicles.* February 2001.

Thomas, Troy S. "Prisoner's of War in Islam: A Legal Inquiry." *The Muslim World.* January 1997, Vol. LXXXVII, No. 1.

————. "Slumlords Aerospace Power in Urban Fights." *Aerospace Power Journal.* Spring 2002.

Thomas, Troy S. and Stephen D. Kiser. *Lords of the Silk Route: Violent Non-State Actors in Central Asia.* Occasional Paper 43. USAF Academy, CO: Institute for National Security Studies, May 2002.

Thomas, Troy S. and William D. Casebeer. *Violent Systems: Defeating Terrorists, Insurgents and Other Non-State Adversaries.* Occasional Paper 52. USAF Academy, CO: Institute for National Security Studies, March 2004.

United States. *National Strategy for Combating Terrorism.* February 2003

United States Army Intelligence Center. *MOOTW Instructional Materials for the Military Officer Transition Course.* Fort Huachuca, AZ: United States Army Intelligence Center and Fort Huachuca, 1999.

Vick, Alan, John Stillion, David R. Frelinger, Joel Kvitky, Benjamin S. Lambeth, Jefferson P. Marquis, and Matthew C. Waxman. *Aerospace Operations in Urban Environments: Exploring New Concepts.* Arlington, VA: RAND Corporation, 2000.

Vlahos, Michael. "Terror's Mask: Insurgency within Islam." Occasional Paper. Laurel, MD: Joint Warfare Analysis Department of the Applied Physics Laboratory, Johns Hopkins University, May 2002.

Waltz, Edward. *Knowledge Management in the Intelligence Enterprise.* Boston: Artech House, 2003.

Warden III, John A. "The Enemy as a System." *Airpower Journal.* Spring 1995.

Wasserman, Stanley and Katherine Faust. *Social Network Analysis: Methods and Applications.* Cambridge: Cambridge University Press, 1996.

White, Jeffrey B. "A Different Threat: Some Thoughts on Irregular Warfare." *Studies in Intelligence.* Washington, DC: Center for the Study of Intelligence, 1996.

INDEX

9/11 74

A

Actionable Intelligence 2
Adversary 1, 2, 3, 5, 8
Afghanistan 18, 22, 51, 71, 87, 126, 129, 135, 244
Air space 90
Ally 5
Al-Qaida 2, 74, 126
Arquilla, John 94, 112, 158-159, 252
Asymmetric 1, 3, 5, 12, 17, 18, 21, 27, 31-33, 54, 73, 102, 127, 135, 167, 201, 231-233, 240, 242
Attrition 33
Aum Shinrikyo 15, 125, 199, 200
Avenues of Approach 84, 86, 88, 235

B

Basque Fatherland and Liberty Party 8
Battlespace 3, 5
Benjamin, Daniel 11, 71
Bergen, Peter L. 91
Bosnia Herzegovina 43, 74
Boyd, John 34
Brainstorming 75, 201, 215, 217, 219, 228

C

Capability 20, 22, 27, 31, 73, 126, 129, 131, 133, 145-14, 148, 150, 155, 159, 164, 167-168, 174-180, 196, 199, 206, 208-209, 211, 222-224, 231, 238, 243
Cascading Effects 105, 233
Casebeer, William 131, 162, 213, 247
Center of Gravity 126, 130, 134, 167, 184
Central Command 30, 165
Central Intelligence Agency 3, 7, 75, 199
Chad 29, 231-232
Chechnya 17, 19, 196, 207
Chemical, Biological, Radiological, and Nuclear

Disrupt 23, 27-29, 74, 80, 83-84, 86, 108, 127, 145, 155, 158, 160, 183, 191, 200, 208, 215, 228, 231, 242, 243

Doctrine 3-5, 24, v31, 37, 42-43, 43, 45, 47-49, 54-55, 60, 69, 72-73, 76, 81, 83, 87, 90, 92-99, 110, 114, 121, 123, 126-127, 129, 130-131, 133, 136-137, 139, 141, 133, 147, 159, 166, 168, 184-185, 191, 193, 196, 198-199, 201-202, 208, 236, 238, 240, 251

Driving Force 222

Drug Trafficking 29, 71, 82, 145

E

Effects 3, 25, 28, 31,34-36, 48, 61, 69-79, 81-86, 89-90, 92-95, 97-99, 101, 104-120, 122-124, 127, 129, 138, 143, 145, 152, 154-155, 161, 167, 189, 191-194, 196, 198-200, 205, 208, 217, 220, 222-223, 227, 231, 233-237, 240-241, 244-245

Effects-based Operations 35, 76, 241

End State 24, 196, 233

Enduring Freedom 100, 149, 160, 268

Environment 1, 3, 26-27, 33, 35-43, 45-46, 53, 55, 60, 63, 71-74, 77, 80, 94, 99, 101-103, 108, 110, 122, 125, 129, 132-133, 136, 138, 14-145, 154-159, 171-173, 181, 184, 202, 209, 233-235, 237, 240

Ethnic Separatist 8, 15-16, 21, 43, 57, 197

European Command 30, 232

F

Fatwa 8, 13

Federal Bureau of Investigations

Ferghana Valley 104, 108

Field Manual 35, 39, 43, 46, 146, 206, 249

Field of Analysis 167

Fields of Fire 84, 85, 88, 235

Force Protection 21, 54, 245

Foreign Internal Defense 30, 42, 81, 152, 242

Function 11, 35, 38, 47, 49, 59, 65, 108, 118, 131, 133, 137, 140, 143, 161, 174, 181, 185, 194, 201, 214-215, 243

Functional Analysis Systems Technique 198, 211, 213, 239

Fundamental Attribution Error 75-76

G

Geography 234, 205, 118, 84-83, 81, 71, 66, 60, 59, 55-54, 49
Georgia 107, 196-197
Global War on Terrorism 2
Globalization 14, 16, 40-41, 69, 106, 151, 154, 163, 231, 235
Governance 15, 27, 41-42, 56, 59, 66-67, 106, 118, 129, 154, 220, 242
Gunaratna, Rohan 74, 160

H

Hamas 1, 11, 49, 51, 102, 108, 112-113, 115, 174, 199
Harakat ul-Jihadi-Islami 75-76
Harakat ul-Jihad-i-Islami/ Bangladesh
Harakat ul-Mujahidin 153
Hatch, Mary Jo 52, 103
Heuer, Richards J. Jr., 75
Heuristics 75-76, 251
Hezbollah 9, 14-15, 17, 4, 52, 58, 82, 125, 176, 181, 186, 222-224
Hindrance 150, 237
Hizb ul-Mujahidin 191
Hoffman, Bruce 6
Hypothesis 45, 192, 202, 210, 212, 215, 224-229, 239

I

Ideology 37, 57, 133, 143-144, 147-149, 154, 175, 177-178, 181, 184-186, 189, 231, 237, 242, 245
India 115
Indirect Effects 48, 78-79, 85, 105, 122-123, 194, 235, 240
Indonesia 40, 192
Information 2, 80, 129
Information Dimension 49, 55, 59, 64, 67, 72, 88, 92, 94, 106, 110-112, 154, 236
Information Technology 2, 41, 56, 60, 71, 94, 166, 235
Insurgency 17, 33-32, 49, 133, 146, 148, 157, 161-162, 209-210, 255
Intelligence 5, 129, 268
Intention 2
International Humanitarian Law 12
Iran 14, 52, 176, 223-224
Iraq 32
Iraqi Freedom 268

Irish Republican Army 9, 64, 94, 151
Islamic International Peacekeeping Brigade 196
Islamic Movement of Uzbekistan 100

J

Japan 100, 214
Jenkins, Brian 6
Jemaah Islamiya 1
Jihad 8
Joint Chiefs of Staff 3, 7

K

Kahn, Robert L. 57, 173, 251
Kashmir Liberation Front 191
Katz, Daniel 57, 173
Key Terrain 84, 87-88, 90, 235
Kiser, Stephen 154
Klein, Gary 216

L

Laden, Osama bin 8, 13, 18, 33, 71, 115, 129, 161-162, 164, 247
Land Domain 55, 89
Laqueur, Walter 20, 113
Lebanon 52, 118, 189, 223, 252
Liberation Tigers of Tamil Eelam 18,52
Life Cycle 108, 178, 181-184, 209-210, 221, 238, 250
Limited War 33
Link Diagrams 155, 168

M

Mali 29
Mauritania 29
Mechanistic Organization 102
Media Effects 113-114
Military Combined Obstacle Overlay 97
Military Operations other than War 40, 196
Mirror-imaging 75, 110, 163, 201
Moro Islamic Liberation Front 79
Morocco 109, 135

N

Narrative 95, 116, 129, 133, 159, 161-162, 164-165, 177, 186
National Strategy 2, 16-17, 23, 25-27, 29, 151, 156
Negative Entropy 181-184, 238
Nested Levels 61, 235
Network 2
Neutral 53, 61, 100, 150-153, 235, 237
Niger 29 232
Noble Eagle 9-90, 267
Noncombatant 6-7, 12-13
Northern Command 30, 153

O

Objective 32-33, 42, 87-88, 129, 131, 173, 194, 196-197, 199, 205, 208, 217, 219-221, 232, 234-235, 237, 239
Open Systems 154, 170-171, 174, 184-185, 236
Operational 2, 3, 5, 28, 37, 88
Operational Code 165-166, 249
Opposing Force 217
Organizational Effects 112

P

Pacific Command 30
Pakistan 67-68, 74, 82, 86, 115, 125, 149, 153, 178, 189, 191
Palestinian Liberation Organization 90
Pan Sahel Initiative 29
Pattani United Liberation Organization 82
Pattern Analysis 98, 155, 168, 170, 178, 180, 198
Perception 92, 95, 110, 116, 120-123, 139, 161, 165, 198, 201, 213, 219, 236, 243-245
Peru 81, 186
Philippines 2, 16, 28, 74-75, 79, 114, 175, 191
Physical Dimension 49, 55, 60-61, 64-65, 72, 80, 83, 87-88, 99, 110, 117, 123, 234
Pillar, Paul 14
Political Motivation 7, 9, 21
Popular Front for the Liberation of Palestine 90
Pre-mortem 216
Priority Intelligence Requirements 38
Provisional Irish Republican Army 94

Psychological Operations 30-31, 44, 78, 95, 114
Public Affairs 114, 218, 251

R

Recruiting 28, 41, 89, 93, 112, 132, 175, 198, 243
Red Teaming 75, 135, 165, 192, 198, 212, 215-220, 222, 226, 228, 239, 249, 252, 253, 254
Relational Ties 157-158, 167
Resource Acquisition 176, 186, 198
Resource Dependency 108, 176
Reverse IPB 36-37, 127, 134, 151, 167, 193, 198, 245
Rewards and Sanctions 177, 238
Ronfeldt, David 112, 158-159, 247, 252
Russia 130, 189-190, 199, 214

S

Salafist Group for Call and Combat 16, 191
Satellites 53, 86, 91
Scenario Analysis 192, 212, 215-216, 222, 226, 228, 239
Sector 56, 58-60, 66, 74-75, 86, 95, 97-98, 105, 109, 110-111, 122, 234
Sensitivity 227
Simon, Steve 11, 71, 247
Single-loop Learning 160, 179
Situation Template 205, 208-209
Social Dimension 42, 49, 53, 56, 59, 72, 86, 88, 95, 105, 110, 116, 120, 123, 143, 183, 234, 236
Social Intelligence 219, 234, 242
Social Network Analysis 2, 52-53, 158, 167, 179, 253, 255
Socialization 129, 177, 182, 186, 206, 238, 243
Somalia 47, 67, 83, 90, 127, 192, 212
Southern Command 30
Space 18-19, 28, 30, 37, 40-42, 46-50, 55, 58, 61, 64-65, 78, 83-84, 86-92, 95, 113, 138, 155, 159, 170, 186, 199, 208, 216, 234, 235, 237, 254
Spain 13, 16, 131-132, 158
Special Operations Command 29
Special Operations Forces 23, 47, 254
Sri Lanka 18, 21, 41, 52, 108, 176
Stakeholder 38, 49, 52-53, 56, 72, 84, 89, 95, 106-108, 119, 122-123, 126-127, 136-137, 146, 148-149, 151-153, 158, 160-161, 167, 175-177, 181,

185-187, 189-193, 198-201, 203, 205, 211-212, 214, 220, 223, 229, 232-233, 235, 237, 239, 242-243, 250

State-sponsorship 14, 16, 27

Story 41, 44, 114, 157, 161-164, 224, 238

Strategic 1, 5, 17, 24-31, 35, 37-38, 40, 42-44, 46, 49-50, 54, 60-63, 74, 76, 78, 87, 105-106, 112-113, 123, 130, 133, 142-143, 154, 158-161, 167, 175, 185, 189, 192, 194-196, 206, 208, 223, 233, 235, 238-239, 241, 243, 248-249, 252-253, 268

System 8, 16, 21, 30, 37, 56-57, 60, 68, 74-75, 77, 80, 84, 94, 99, 101, 105-106, 108, 112, 116, 141-143, 153-154, 159, 171-174, 176-181, 183-186, 203, 213, 219-220, 222, 237, 240, 255

Systems Theory 77, 142, 172, 213, 233, 248

Systems Thinking 60, 82, 101, 142, 233, 240

T

Tactical 2, 5, 25, 28-31, 37-38, 40, 42, 44, 46, 49-50, 54, 60-61, 65, 76, 78, 84, 87-88, 97, 99, 102, 105-106, 113, 123, 133, 158-160, 180, 186, 189, 192, 194-195, 196, 201, 206, 208, 223, 233, 235, 239, 241

Terrain Zones 65-66

Terrorism 1-7, 9-12, 14-17, 19-21, 23-26, 28-30, 32-33, 40, 43-44, 48-49, 74-76, 88, 90, 94-95, 111-113, 116, 125, 128, 132-133, 137, 148-149, 151, 153-155, 160, 180-181, 185, 189, 190-191, 217, 219, 222, 231, 236, 242, 245, 247-250, 252-255

Thailand 82

Thomas, Troy 61, 65, 105, 154, 216, 223, 249, 254

Time Lines 168

Total War 33

Transactional 57, 158, 175, 182, 197

Transcendental 11, 57, 175, 182, 197

Tzu, Sun 20, 34, 250

U

Uncertainty 99-104

Unconfirmed Hypothesis 226

Unified Command Plan 46

United Nations 7, 189

United Self-Defense Forces 129

United States 3, 6, 26, 129, 250-251, 255

United States Air Force 112, 254

United States Army 169, 255

United States Marine Corps 45, 249
United States Navy 13, 129
Urbanization 62-64, 66, 105, 235
Uzbekistan 100, 104, 108, 123, 149

V

Values 9-10, 31, 57-58, 95-97, 116, 119, 152, 159, 177, 179-180, 231, 242

W

Wargaming 40, 140, 208-209, 217
Weapons of Mass Destruction 27, 30, 125, 199, 222
Weather 20, 36, 38, 42, 49, 54-55, 59, 71, 83-84, 90, 92, 100, 139, 234

Y

Yemen 47, 66, 89, 179, 189